The Out-of-Body Experience

OOBEX

OOBEX

OOBEX PUBLISHING

This book is dedicated to Linda,

my partner and friend.

The

Out-of-Body

Experience

by

Graham Dack

OOBEX PUBLISHING

First published in Great Britain (1999) by
Oobex Publishing
114 High Street
Braunston
Northamptonshire NN11 7HS

Telephone 01788 891514

ISBN 0 9534458 0 1

NOTICE

Designed by Ivydene Studio.

Produced by Dick Richardson, Country Books, Little Longstone DE45 1NN

Printed and bound by MFP Design & Print. Manchester M32 0JT

Contents

List of illustrations

Chapter One
By way of an introduction

It is 5am and once again I find myself deep in meditation, relaxed to such an extent that I cannot, any longer, feel sensation in my physical body. It feels like an empty shell resting below my consciousness. My remaining senses have turned inwards to catch the slightest sounds, the merest movements, and the caressing waves that blow gently over the surface of my skin.

Through my closed eyes I see the staring faces of the people that watch me. I remember that once upon a time, a long time ago, these faces would strike a fear in me but thankfully not for many years now. I regard these watcher's as malevolent, perhaps friendly, perhaps in need, I am not sure. The one thing that I am sure of is the fact that they are usually the first thing I 'see' when closing my eyes at night. They disappear and reappear as do the monsters that used to trample their way through my nightmares, hideous in the extreme, but powerless against understanding and a brave heart.

I decrease my pulse rate slightly, gently exhale, and with a final sigh, those gentle vibrations that innocently played over the surface of my body, suddenly explode into a blasting electrical rush that blanks all my thoughts and feelings and ends any control I have over my body. I feel as though my very 'self', my very 'soul', is being ripped out of my insides with the tearing of a thousand stitches that holds me together. It pulls at the inside of my ears and at the back of my nose in a frantic haste to escape my physical shell, I wish that it was over quick and clean, and *most* times it is.

As quickly as this internal volcano erupts, it also subsides and with it goes all my earthly aches, pains and problems, and once again I find myself free, perfectly free, to dwell in a place that could easily be mistaken for 'paradise'. My conscious mind is as clear and as 'normal' as yours is at the very moment you are reading this. My mental clarity is such that I am perfectly aware that my physical body resides at home in bed, I have the use of all my usual memory facilities, all my normal reasoning ability, in fact I retain all that I regard as the essential 'me' but minus that dragging, anchoring material body.

This must surely be the greatest, the most ultimate, experience that can possibly be achieved whilst still being alive on this earth of ours. My conscious mind has the ability to truly exist outside of my physical body and travel this earth, and other planes, in a way that has been rarely understood. I intend to be totally open in explaining, step by step, how this phenomenon works and how it can be achieved. Also how *you* can progress and be able to do the same. Be aware that these experience's dig deep into the very foundation of how we understand life and will bring a new realisation of how, where and why, humankind exists in the universe.

This is not a book that deals *solely* with out-of-body experience, it is an investigation into a side of life that has come to light because of this revelation of spirit behaviour that we knew so little about. We know even less about how it affects our cognitive world. Now that the light of understanding has dispelled the shadows of mystery we can all recognise it for what it truly is.

However, it has further reaching implications into the fields of personal welfare, health and religion, and when

I talk about religion in this book I am talking about how we fit our own *individual* spiritual beliefs with our own individual world. I am *not* discussing the merits, or otherwise, of any established religious doctrine. Indeed, I would hope that my teaching will enhance whatever beliefs you already hold.

Whatever religious house we may gather in and whoever else may be there is not as important as our own personal beliefs, and I am of the strong opinion that there are more God respecting people that *do not* attend any kind of group prayer, than *do* attend group prayer. This book may alter your perceptions, irrelevant of your current beliefs, but it is not my intention to do anything other than bring awareness and the light of realisation into the gloomy room where science and religion stare stolidly at each other.

There is also a huge medical potential that remains untapped and misunderstood. Later, I will try to tempt the taste-buds of the medical people with my own health observances, in the hope that they can take up the reins and organise sensibly controlled trials. It will be up to them, as experts in their field, to recognise any potential within these pages.

We have the opportunity to look at the real quality of life, and what that means, but just as importantly, we look at the quality of death in exactly the same way. For the first time we can appreciate the whole picture and look at the relevant implications from an all encompassing viewpoint.

Possessing a practical knowledge of oobex (out-of-body-experience's) will give you a different way of looking at many of the important issues that affect our human life, like how we view abortion, euthanasia and death in general. Other health issues are looked at along with different lifestyle's and the way we relate to those around us. A section is also given over to the issue of non-human animals and a perspective of their status in this universal life.

It is very easy to become bogged down with extolling the tangible advantages of spirit projection to humankind, and forget about simple recreation. It is *fun*, more fun than it is possible to attain from our earthly pursuits and, like it or not, it is educational, mind broadening, stress relieving, and teaches control. As with every good thing, it can be used in a bad way, and these issues will also be dealt with in a thorough manner.

It is my sincere intention to explain my experience's in an honest way so that the reader can understand the process in a simple and straightforward fashion. I have written this book as the ordinary man I am, with the layman and laywoman in mind. It has not been coloured to appeal to occultists, or spiritualists, and there is no pretence to be scientific, or academic.

I have consciously *not* read the classic works of religion, and philosophy, until *after* the main bulk of this text had been written, for the good and simple reason that I did not want my research to be trapped between the rails of preconception. As far as possible, my mind has been free, and uncluttered, to produce, and reproduce, my results as honestly as possible.

I give little time to those that dismiss out-of-body-experience's as mere hallucination, this is *not* the case. I give you here the opportunity to prove to yourself otherwise. Even Jung was of the opinion that hallucination was not a specific symptom of mental disorder, but could be purely human in origin. Obviously, there will be poor people that suffer mental disorder, or drug users that suffer mental delusion because of their condition. This distinction must be accepted once and for all, and put to bed forever! Before we condemn something as vast and as intricate as the

10

unconscious mind we must have knowledge of the beast. I have experience's out of my body, *not* out of my mind!

My wish is that everybody will be able to find his, or her, particular bone to gnaw on, and to eventually expand in their own specialist field. This book should appeal equally to the truth seeking scientist as it does anyone else.

It was necessary for me to have achieved a certain enlightenment in my own personal development before I could pass this knowledge forward. It would have been impossible for this book to have been written any earlier than it was, but once I *had* achieved the knowledge and expertise necessary, this book developed like unstoppable lava flowing from a volcano. It *had* to come out, I felt as though I had no personal choice in the matter.

And so, what I *have* is what I *give*, and it is up to the individual to take up the challenge to prove to themselves the merit of this book of realisation. For my part, I promise to give you all the knowledge that I possess to enable you to achieve an out-of-body experience plus many detailed accounts of a variety of actual projection's to help familiarise yourself with the phenomena. For your part, I require you to keep your mind open throughout these pages, whether you agree or not, and let the experiment be your guide. Please read my book completely, from cover to cover, *at least once*, before you try to project.

If you should take up the oobex challenge, it will affect all parts of your life, and in a positive manner. Simply because it does affect all parts of your life, it is *important* to get the whole picture first, for understanding is the key to the mystery. Suppose a man, or woman, was somehow kept in a box until adulthood and it became time for this person to be released into the world. Now pretend it was *your* job to explain to them how to behave, and what to expect. Take crossing a road as one example, you would have to explain what a road was, what traffic was and why it was there, the concept of speed, material make-up, what danger was, what rules are, etc., etc., etc. Not only would the task be enormous but however thorough you were, this person would still have to go out and learn for themselves.

This is a little like out-of-body projection, it is real, it does exist and it is important to know as much about it as possible before you take those first steps. This is what I hope to achieve with my book, a good and safe foundation for an incredible journey of self-fulfilment and knowledge.

I have included two extensive chapters that contain, and outline, some of the more relevant practical experience's from my personal records. These records were recorded within hours of each experience and, as such, are a true indication of the procedures that led up to each projection. I discuss the salient points that arise in a manner so that you will be able to recognise the same effects in your own experiments. I believe that these two chapters probably hold the most substance pertaining to the 'nuts and bolts' of spirit projection, and are therefore invaluable.

Every word that you read is important, each phrase has a meaning that you may not initially appreciate. This book is written for both your conscious, and subconscious, minds to digest. You may think that you understand only to find later the real truth, for this book is coupled with important practical experience. We are all different and therefore you will all project at *different* stages of development. I have no way of knowing at what level, during the book, subconscious acceptance will bring success. Don't worry if you start projecting and there is more to learn, better that than the other. Similarly, if you are like me it will take several readings and *much* practise before it happens. I think it makes success all the sweeter!

I would like you to write to me with your oobex experience's, or any problems that you may have encountered, so that we can begin to build up a proper body of knowledge that can be accessed by everybody for the benefit of all. In return we can let you know about developments with our research, the experience's of others, and any other matters pertaining.

It is my real belief that anybody can project if they are truly committed to doing so. If I take a very pessimistic view and say that even if, in the fullness of time, it transpired that only *one* other person has managed to experience the ultimate experience, as I have, then all my work will have been more than amply rewarded.

Oobex not only penetrates and embraces the finer emotions of humankind but encompasses the fundamental law of universal decency. *Not* the ill-conceived pseudo-correctness of our growing artificial existence. In your hands you hold the balance of future human development.

Finally, the conscious mind that you are using to read these words is located in your spirit-body, not your physical head..... *that* has no mind at all. When projected, we are so much *more* ourselves having lost the physical material weight, and this is the first mind blowing realisation. You will not become anything other than you really are, but up until now you have had no way of *knowing exactly* what that is. By the end of this book you will prove to yourself the truth of my words.

Graham Dack
Ist February 1999

Chapter Two
Background and discovery

This book has given me the chance to write down some of my experience's, and to put my thoughts into some kind of order. By personal research and experimentation I have discovered that even if we don't all project on a regular basis, we possess within us the *ability* of doing so. The fact that we choose not to take advantage of these opportunities is the reason the whole business is still shrouded in mystery. Because this choice involves fear we repel the option. This fear has been compounded by occult stories, religious dogma, and old wives' tales so the whole subject has to be seen from new, unpolluted, eyes. Eyes that are open to experimentation and reason.

I have tried to convey this vast, and intricate, subject in a way that can be understood by just about everybody. Being a normal chap of average intelligence, I have taken pains to cover as many eventualities as I can and, therefore, I apologise if my capabilities fall short of tempting the eye of the academic. But I haven't written this book for you. I have written this book for everybody that has ever wondered about the great mystery of life. Please read the whole book and gain the whole picture, before you make any judgement, a little like those paintings where the further you stand back, the better it appears. Take one tiny part, in isolation, and it makes little sense.

I will begin my conversation by giving you a quick insight into my background, and how I came to be in this position in the first place.

I spent my early childhood living in the beautiful, and unspoiled, seaside resort on the south-east coast called Broadstairs. Even to this day, I think of my time there with nothing but pleasant memories, and I have to say that, irrelevant of where I have lived since, my real home is still Broadstairs, that is where my heart remains.

I was a dreamer, my nose being always in a book, or up in the clouds, and life was full of promise and excitement. I remember staring at a particularly weather-beaten old piece of chalk face near my home and conjuring up some magic words in the complete expectation that a secret door would swing open to reveal an old passage, perhaps used by smugglers. It never happened of course but I was happy to return from time to time and have another go. I have always been patient in a determined sort of way.

Because of my habit of daydreaming, I used to not pay as much attention to what people said to me as I should, I found that my own thoughts were far more absorbing. This was reflected, painfully, in my school work. I do remember my father plucking me out of the school dining room just as I was waiting for my dinner because I was supposed to be eating at home. I was very unreliable with dates and times, often missing events that I should have attended. But I was a willing boy and would happily run errands to the shops even if I did come back with ten pounds of carrots and a potato, instead of eight pounds of potatoes and a cucumber!

My grandparents, whom I loved dearly, lived over the other side of town so I could call in there whenever I wished. I don't think that I took anything for granted, I was simply a very happy youth and contented with my lot.

The sea in its raw magnificence and its scent and colours, fascinates me still. It could easily fix my gaze for hours on end, while I floated off into some altered state of consciousness, an early dip into the realms of self-hypnosis.

The sheer volume, and power, of that water, scared me, and I loved it doing so. But I couldn't say the same thing about heights though! From the shoreline those majestic cliff faces rising high into the air were defiant in their battle to keep the sea at bay, and getting a real beating for the trouble. Looking out from the top however, these cliffs played a starring role in many of my nightmares. It wasn't really looking out that was the problem so much as looking down, over the edge to the beach far, far below that scared me, and I didn't like it. Even if I squirmed on my stomach so that just my eyes looked over, I still held the belief that I would fall over the edge.

One reason to remember my infant school was because I had to use an old iron footbridge to cross a main railway line to get there. With all the sensibility that I still possess, my friends and I used to empty the contents of fireworks along the top of the bridge, set light to one end and watch it fizzle along creating the patterns that we had drawn. All good school boy stuff in those days. Of course the real fascination of this bridge were the steam engines that puffed underneath on their way to and from London, they were big, black, and beautiful. I can still remember the smell of the warm sooty scent of their smoke and being boys we had to stay on that bridge and watch each other disappear in clouds of smutty steam as the train passed underneath.

I managed to complete the first year of my junior school in Broadstairs. It was a single sex church school, close to the water, and it was the church where my parents were married. It had four classes, one for each year, and the headmaster was a fanatic about music. It was known within the family as the singing academy, and boy! was he serious about it. This man was a real Dickensian character, I remember him glowering down at us from a very high

16

wooden desk that had a curly cane lying along the front. In fairness, I never saw him use it, and I liked, and respected him for his convictions, even though he was so strict. But then, I could sing, and so could my older brother, who was lucky enough to experience the four full years at the 'singing academy'. So I think we may have been secretly in his good books.

My perfect world came to an end when I was eight years old. My father, for all the right reasons, landed himself a good job with a considerable increase in salary in Luton, Bedfordshire. An industrial town set in the heart of the country where lots, and lots, of people live.

I suffered a large culture shock. Just about everything here was as different as it possibly could have been from my previous idyll. Everything was bigger, more sprawling, more abrasive. My school, to my mind, was huge, it had four classes for each year, and horror of horrors, I had to sit next to a girl! I didn't like it, she didn't like it! I knew that this was now my new life and I just had to get on with it but I was not happy. You see, I knew what happiness was because I had lived there. A certain brightness had been dulled in me and I didn't feel special anymore. I wasn't special anymore. I became very reliant on my books and my daydreams for these were my constant companions and my sanctuary. I did adjust to this lifestyle and of course I made friends, I had to, I had no other choice.

It was a couple of years after the move and I was around ten years old when I had my first strange experience. Funnily enough I don't remember thinking that it was strange at the time. In those days I used to sleep on the top bed of a bunk with my younger brother in the bed below. The bedroom door was always left open at night with the landing light left on because my brother had problems with the dark. In fact, at one stage the bedroom light was left on for several night's in an effort to help him. This was great for me because I would read and read long into the small hours, slowly and surely straining my eyesight!

On the occasions that my books were confiscated, or the light was eventually turned off, I would play a little game before going to sleep. I would quietly concentrate and imagine that I was slowly becoming upright, that my whole bed was turning 90% into the standing position. It took time to achieve and if I lost my concentration I would drop back, and if I regained my concentration I would recover and continue. By proper perseverance I would eventually achieve the upright position, I really felt that I was standing upright, even though I could clearly feel the mattress behind my back and had full knowledge that I was, in reality, horizontal. The exciting part came when I decided to see what would happen if I let the process continue so that I tipped forward......

Each time I 'fell' with all the reality of gravity. My whole bodily senses were telling me that I was really falling and needed to save myself! My hands desperately grasped the mattress, I clawed at the sheets and my eyes were wide open in an effort to reorient myself with a landmark from the darkness of my bedroom. Each time I saved myself from falling, I would lie there with my heart pounding, savouring the afterglow that the excitement brings. I knew it was a real experience and I knew it was very powerful, powerful enough to frighten me, but I also knew that as long as I was quick enough I could maintain the control to end it.

I had dreams, also, where I would be falling over the edge of the cliffs or over the edge of the station platform into the path of an oncoming train. Again, I would awaken with my little finger nails dug deeply into the mattress and my knuckles white with fright having just escaped another 'tragic' end to my life. On many occasions I was too scared to go back to sleep because of the reality of the experience.

These things seemed to come in patches, I could go ages without anything untoward happening and then all of a sudden I would be deep in the mire again. Of course, I had brought it all on myself by playing that silly game, but I wonder which came first? Was it one of these dreams that gave me the idea to 'tip' up my bed, or was it the tipping up of the bed, that instigated these dreams?

Anyway the two did not cross my mind as having any *similarity*, one was real, the other a bad dream, simple as that. So, yes, I continued to play my game. In fact I played it so often that it didn't frighten me anymore as I knew that I had control. On one momentous night, forever etched into my memory, I managed to screw up all the courage that I could muster and let myself go. I released myself into oblivion. I 'tipped' forward without stopping to see just what would happen. My hands were outstretched to save myself as I made contact with my bedroom ceiling! I bounced against it ever so slightly, as a balloon would, and came back to the bed. It is difficult to believe now but at the time I thought that it was my physical body that had levitated to the ceiling, in fact, I continued to think that for many years. I also believed that this was the extent of the 'game', and it never crossed my mind that I should develop it past this point.

As I grew up and had other subjects to hold my interest, my little game became forgotten like a toy that I had grown out of. It was to be another ten years, or so, before I read something that gave me the belief that out-of-body experience's were possible. With the benefit of maturity I recalled my game as possibly being something to do with it and I decided to investigate. I searched for that toy everywhere, but alas it had gone. Now I could only get that bed to tip up to about 60%, even on one occasion managing to get upright, but never any further. It had abandoned me, as I had abandoned it, and I thought that I had lost something precious, forever.

Idle curiosity seems to set up the subconscious mind more efficiently than heavy conscious concentration, and I certainly wondered about out-of-body experience's, wishing that I had the knowledge that would allow me to enter this secret world. I was in my early twenties when a single act cemented my interest forever. I went to bed and lying on my left side facing out I waited for sleep to throw her blanket over me. All of a sudden, and without any particular preparation at all, I 'fell' out of myself onto the floor. But that didn't stop me, I carried on falling through to the cellar below where I stood wondering in total amazement at what had just happened. There was an upright wooden post that was attached to the bottom of the stairs, and I tried to grasp hold of it because my body felt very unstable, like a balloon on the end of a piece of string. My left arm was trying to wrap itself around this post as I surveyed the contents of the cellar. I felt like a diver holding his breath underwater for I instinctively knew that I had limited time before returning to the surface.

A force, with all the strength of buoyancy, shot me back to my prostrate body, and there I lay in awe at what had just happened. My body was tingling all over and for a little while I didn't move at all, I think I could have but I wanted to savour the moment to its fullest extent. So it *was* possible! And more importantly, it was possible for me!

It was to be many years before I had another out-of-body experience, and it wasn't for the sake of trying either. I needed those years to unravel the complicated jumble of dreams and experience's that emanated from my mind at night, just as it does for us all. Like a beam of light in the darkness, I came across a book 'The Projection of the Astral Body' by Sylvan Muldoon, written with the help of

Hereward Carrington. This, more than anything else, gave me the confidence to keep trying. I still read it now, from time to time, especially when I am trying a certain type of projection, and I will be referring back to it, and others, as I go through this book. Good books written by experienced projector's on this subject are very rare.

Something else that may be of interest to you is my visualisation ability, or lack of it, depending on which way you view it. Everybody, in thought, can remember what things look, and feel like, and can use their imagination to put these things together in forming a fantasy, or daydream.

Some people are very adept at being able to visualise, in their minds eye, specific objects or how a room would look if decorated in a certain way. All of this is imagination but some of it is actually 'seeing' a projected vision of the end product, inside the head. Being able to think of an object and then see it mentally, is controlled visualisation. This is a great thing to be able to do if you are this type of person, sadly, I am not one of them. Certainly in meditation or straightforward relaxation this ability is a great asset. It allows you to concentrate on one particular thing at a time, and saturate your thoughts with it. This will be a necessity, as you will find out later, in being able to relax correctly for achieving an out-of-body experience.

Many books on this subject are written by people who project naturally, they almost can't stop themselves, so they try and find out how it happens, and write it down. Many books are written by researchers who have never had a 'proper' out-of-body experience in their lives, which is painfully obvious to any experienced projector. This particular book has been written to incorporate much more than oobex's, and has been written by a projector that has had to learn the hard way from scratch. And from scratch I will teach you all you need to know to experience your first projection.

I mentioned my inability to visualise, that isn't quite true. All my life I have had a 24 hour a day television running inside my head. At anytime at all I can close my eyes and 'watch' what is going on! The problem is that I can't control it. If I try to visualise, for example, a horse, I try with all the concentration I have at my disposal to bring it to mind. I use my memories of riding to help me, and the fact that I see horses every day on my walks makes them a good and easy subject. In my head, reluctantly, very reluctantly, I will be given a picture of 'something'. It won't resemble a horse in any way, it will be more like a lizard. It will be the minimum likeness necessary to appease my desires.

I was at a meditation class once, my one and only time, and I was asked to imagine a big oak tree. I tried so hard, in my mind I wanted a majestic oak, standing proudly in the middle of a magnificent park. What I eventually got was a small wizened old piece of hedge and as I watched it, it fell over!

I have done a certain amount of personal research into this, but not with great success. I know that I don't have to close my eyes to 'see' these visions, it simply makes watching easier. Standing in front of a plain coloured wall works just as well as is looking into darkness, with closed eyes being the best of all. These visions are usually in colour, often in black and white (grey tones), and sometimes both together. On occasions I have even seen one sequence overlaid on top of another sequence so that I can watch both at the same time.

I have also found out that if I casually think of a general topic, I can influence these visions. If I were to 'idly' contemplate the countryside, I would get a true and perfect

22

moving picture that would include my horse, and my tree, as they should be seen in reality. These places are not recreated from my conscious memory, anymore than the content of dreams. I cannot go out for the day, come home, close my eyes and 'see' where I have been. The phenomenon is far too remote for that kind of mental familiarity. It works as though it is being operated by somebody else, an intelligent subconscious controller, but why do I have it and what is it for? I firmly believe that everything we have, we have or had, for a purpose. So I came to the conclusion that I possess a natural kind of clairvoyant ability, but why?

This ability appears to be remarkably similar to an activity called scrying, crystal gazing, or remote viewing. I have recently read an absorbing book called 'Life before Life' written by Raymond Moody and Paul Perry, that outlines, also in a practical and understanding way, not only the value and truth of crystal gazing, but more importantly, a study of regression into past lives. However, the section relating to scrying seems to hit familiar ground to me, it is almost as though I can 'see' naturally within my head, what other's need the aid of a crystal ball to see.

On my journey of self-understanding, I have stumbled across hidden paths that I did not know existed, and I have had to make choices in an effort to follow the most beneficial way. Often I have come to a dead end and have had to backtrack. Often I have gone that way again and chosen the other path, if I am lucky. I am also fairly sure that I have missed opportunities, to my chagrin. You will undoubtedly find the same on your explorations.

I have a problem proving to myself that what I 'see' has any relevance to anything in reality, and this is partly because of its independent nature. I have an old pocket-watch, and whenever I hold it in my hand, and close my eyes, I 'see' that I am looking at a music-hall stage with dancing girls and plenty of action, colourful dresses, etc. I also see the rest of the audience around me watching the show. It feels as if I am looking through somebody else's eyes, and the watch somehow links my consciousness to theirs, and transcends time. But where is the proof?

Having said that, I have had one or two incidences that have been verified by other people, and one that could have been a lucky coincidence. You can make up your own mind.

I was given an old shotgun, by some friends, to see what I could 'see'. I had never seen this gun before and I knew nothing of its history, etc. When I held the gun and closed my eyes I saw moonlight and the dark shadows of bushes and trees. Again, as though I was actually looking through somebody else's eyes, I saw myself going in and out of these bushes in a slow and furtive manner. Whilst I was seeing this, I was talking to my friends at the same time. I told them that I felt as if I was a soldier creeping through the scrub on some kind of mission. All of a sudden I saw something that I couldn't make head nor tail of. I said to my friends that I was seeing something strange, and that all I could do was to tell them what it was, and risk the ridicule.

I saw four big jet-black squares, apparently suspended in mid-air, a little way into the murky distance. To me this seemed utterly absurd, so I opened my eyes and began to apologise but had to stop when I saw their faces. They told me that they had just purchased this gun from a man they suspected of being a poacher. What really confirmed it for them was when I mentioned these four jet-black squares. They said that in the locality was a large country house estate, privately owned which had no access to the public. However, in the grounds of this house was a large formal garden that boasted an uncommon arrangement of four large square pools, as an ornamental water feature.

At night the water would appear much darker than anything else around it, giving it this intensely black character. Needless to say this gun, and its owner, should not have been there.

On another occasion, I was with a couple of friends that had come up from London, and we happened to get into a deep conversation about a fourth friend to whom we were all acquainted. He had been acting oddly of late and we were very concerned about his welfare. After much deep discussion I closed my eyes on the off-chance of seeing something. We knew that he had been on holiday in Wales so it wasn't surprising for me to see rolling hills and footpaths cutting their way through the bracken. What did surprise me was that every so often my vision clouded and cleared again. It dawned on me that I was looking through this person's eyes, and he was smoking a cigarette!

While I am looking, I am talking, so that my friends could have the benefit of my experience. I found that I could open my eyes and close them again without losing the plot. To be honest, giving a running commentary on a walk through the countryside gets to be boring and doesn't prove anything so I was more than pleased when the scenery changed to a townscape. Still smoking away, 'I' was, apparently walking through a town on the outskirts of south-east London, in the county of Kent, where my friends had come up from and where our other friend lived. I didn't know where I was but as I described buildings, and any features that appeared to me, my friends would confirm the location. The sceptics would say that I could have been anywhere, one town is very similar to another, and I agree. But each description I gave was excitedly confirmed as true by my friends, and then once more I saw an out of the ordinary sight. I was describing the houses that overlooked a river, when I saw an old weatherboarded cottage painted bright blue. With absolute sincerity, both my friends confirmed its existence! It is possible that I was picking up some kind of telepathic transference from one, or both, of these girls but I really don't think so.

Before I give you the next example of this clairvoyance, I must emphasise how normal it feels to 'see' these things. The only prerequisite is to lock-on to the subject first so that my subconscious mind could show me the right programme. With the gun, and my pocket watch, I was able to hold them and feel the effects that a previous owner had instilled into the object. If that object has had an interesting, or varied life, then it does make it easier. Had they been shut away in a cupboard for years on end then I would not be able to see very much! 'Seeing' people is slightly different, the way my subconscious mind was directed to lock-on to our friend in Kent was to discuss him first so he was prominent in all our minds. Once this has been achieved, I simply close my eyes and tell it as I see it. There is no nonsense about trances, or evoking spirits or any other malarkey!

This following example happened some years ago in the village where my parents still live. It was early evening and I was in my local 'pub having a drink, and waiting for some friends to turn up. A gentleman that I knew came in and asked me if I had seen his daughter, she was supposed to have come home hours ago and he was seriously concerned for her welfare. I was very fond of this girl and I knew her, and her boyfriend, very well so I also became concerned for her safety. So do I try to mentally find her or not? Obviously there is a privacy issue here and one that became very apparent to me later.

To this day I admire this gentleman's faith in me. I told him that I might be able to 'see' where his daughter was if I went into a corner and concentrated on her for a minute or so. He didn't throw his hands up in desperation at this idiot, instead he looked at me hard and said, 'If you can do it, then do it, this is my daughter and I am worried.' I went and sat down by myself and thought about this girl. I imagined that she was talking to me and that I could hear her voice, I imagined that I could see her pretty face before me. What follows is an example of remote viewing.

On closing my eyes I had a scene, as usual, unfold before me. It took a couple of seconds to recognise the content but it was clear to me what was happening. I was looking down a country lane and parked up, but facing away from me, in a little lay-by was the boyfriend's car. Through the rear window I could see an intense row was raging, arms were being thrown around and it all looked a little nasty. I was already aware that these two were having severe problems with their relationship and that the girl had been trying to find a way to break up. My concern was that the car was in an isolated place and that the row appeared to be becoming increasingly violent.

Having gained all this information I returned to the father, told him all that I had seen, and gave him the option of being involved or not. There was no decision to make, he asked me to jump in his car with him and guide him to where I 'thought' they were.

This was a weird experience for me as I had never actually had the opportunity to prove to myself, with witnesses, that what I 'saw' mentally was really tangible. What worried me about this example was that I had not looked through any 'eyes' to see the action, as in previous occasions, so where *was* I looking from? Also, I was watching in real-time, not historically, again something that I hadn't attempted before. As we got nearer to the scene, you can imagine what was going through my mind. If I was wrong, I would look and feel a total fool, and if I was right,

I could be betraying a friendship. I mean, who does want their father turning up during a domestic argument? Anyway it was too late now!

We turned the last corner, and about two hundred yards up the lane we saw the car, exactly as I had 'seen' it, so we pulled in behind. The gentleman got out and went up to their car, whereupon the couple got out and I have to say they were not best pleased to see us. I was told, in no uncertain terms, that we were not the cavalry turning up at the last moment to rescue the girl, and in future I should mind my own business!

Well I have put it down to research. Part of me didn't want to become involved, part of me was worried about the daughters' safety, but a big part of me was very happy that it worked and I had proved it to myself. The privacy issue is important and one that I allow my conscience to police. I must also add that I was pretty quickly forgiven and we all laughed about it later, but nevertheless the lesson had been learned.

Finally, on the subject of remote viewing, I happened to be watching one of those television programmes that purport to investigate unusual psychic powers. In this particular episode they were exploring remote viewing and so they had a researcher, in a secret location, looking at a vista known only to himself. Back in the studio they had, as a guest, a remote viewer to recreate the scene on paper, just as it was being seen by the viewer. Out of interest I closed my eyes to 'see' what I could see. My immediate vision showed the inside of a huge building. In the foreground were several massive turbine generators, the scale was made apparent by a man, in an overall, dwarfed by the machinery. The remote viewer, back in the studio however, was completely accurate by rendering a drawing of the Battersea Power Station, in the distance, with the river in front. This was exactly the scene that was being looked at by the researcher.

This is an example of my superconscious mind showing me, not what I want to see, but what it wants me to see. For some inexplicable reason it revealed to me the inside view of a power station, rather than the outside view. It often appears to me that I am being respectfully toyed with!

Now you have a rough idea of my background, apart from what I have told you I enjoy a near normal existence, and life has dealt me a fair balance of good and bad luck over the years much the same as anybody else. I would like to understand more about my visualisation and put my ability to a good use in helping people, if possible. You may think that this ability is a benefit to aid out-of-body projection, but I disagree. To be able to hold a strong mental image and to focus your concentration solely on it, without any other distractions having the opportunity to encroach, is a positive asset. To try and concentrate on a constantly moving and changing image is difficult indeed. So much so that I don't even try anymore, my relaxation coming from the tranquillity of watching the changes happen.

Between my first adult projection and the time that I began keeping records, I experienced many hundreds of out-of-body experience's and I truly regret not having the foresight to write them down. However, once I did start I began to realise how other facets of life began to make sense. These were things that I didn't initially take much notice of, or necessarily attributed any direct connection with spirit projection.

I have endeavoured to make full reference to the peripheral issues in this book, and by peripheral I do not mean unimportant, for many of these realisations are very important indeed. Some may say more important than the out-of-body experience's themselves. The content of this book will give you all the necessary information needed for you to experience regular out-of-body separation as often as I do now!

Chapter Three
What is spirit projection?

It is important to understand that once you have embarked on this journey, and you have experienced any kind of success, there will be no turning back. Once the prospects of that 'secret' land have been glimpsed, once you have flown like superman, with all your earthly senses intact, you *will* be hooked.

As a process, spirit projection has been known about and practised for thousands of years, it is not some new airy fairy idea that hasn't any foundation. Existing at our very centre is our soul. Our soul is clothed in a number of bodies, similar in construction to a set of Russian dolls, the final outer sheath being the physical body. We die and lose that physical, followed by the etheric, followed by the astral, and so on. It may also regain these bodies, in the case of reincarnation, only to lose them yet again, in the cycle of death and rebirth.

The 'silver cord' is mentioned in the Old Testament of the Bible in Ecclesiastes, chapt.12 verse 6. In the First Epistle of Paul the Apostle to the Corinthians, chapt.15 verse 44, it reads: 'There is a natural body, and there is a spiritual body. And so it is written, The first man Adam was made a living soul; the last man Adam was made a quickening spirit.' This passage is well worth reading as it goes on to explain that as we are of earth, so we are of heaven and flesh and blood cannot inherit the kingdom of God. There is much more there to take in, so please take a moment to read it, if you can. While you are there, it is also worth reading the Second Epistle of Paul the Apostle to the Corinthians, chapt.12 verse 2. Amongst other things it mentions: 'I knew such a man, (whether in the body, or out of the body, I cannot tell: God knoweth) how that he was caught up into paradise, and heard unspeakable words, which it is not lawful for a man to utter.' Many ancient writings and drawings, from a variety of cultures, tell of a spirit in varying guises leaving the physical body at the time of death.

It has been told to us that Jesus raised people from the dead. But He himself said that these people are not dead but sleeping. We are all capable of achieving this hibernation state, every time we project. I wonder if he brought these people back to life by saying 'abra-cadaver'!

Although out-of-body travel has been known about since humankind has existed, it has been practised by few and researched by less. It has in the past been linked with black arts, and indeed I am sure the process has been used for nefarious activities by misguided people, and will always be so. But isn't that the case with all things in life? Many terrible things have been done under the Good and Holy Banner of Religion, also.

Throughout time many kind and honest folk have been persecuted as witches, or sorcerers and the like, for spiritual practice. Stories of evil monsters, goblins of every kind, are told as though they really exist and can cause harm to you if you ever dare to explore the process. Nothing could be further from the truth, and all I can say is that the originators of these stories were motivated by their ignorance of fear. I will speak a lot about fear, in this book, but with understanding and control of the beast.

As you practise this art, your subconscious mind will become adjusted to the idea that it is quite normal for the spirit-body to exist outside the physical body. Usually when you specifically wish it to *and* when you make use of the particular relaxation procedures that I will be explaining to you in due course. When it does, it is also quite common to find yourself, consciously, having an out-of-body experience without *any* knowledge of *any* lead up practice or sensations. When this happens, it appears to be a spontaneous projection, but believe me all the work has been done subconsciously, because you have instilled the 'will to project' into your subconscious mind. If you can project like this, then you are very lucky and you will wonder why all this work is necessary.

Everybody unconsciously projects their spirit-body at some time, and to a greater or lesser extent, depending upon their makeup, it is a natural and common act. As you read on you may begin to recognise certain sleep sensations that you have already felt yourself, perhaps hearing your name being called, or violent jumps, or your head being thumped. You may have flying dreams, or nightmares, or even wake up feeling numb. It is my wish to teach you how this happens so that you can become consciously aware, and used to them, whilst you are experimenting. Spirit-body projection is simply a normal occurrence but cloaked in the guise of dreams.

Throughout the ages this spirit detachment has been known by many different names. It has been called, amongst others, the fluidic body, the luminous body, the phantom, the subtle body, the sidereal body, the resurrection, the etheric body, the spirit-body, the astral body, the double, the Holy Spirit, the Ka, etc. Some of these names will mean different things to different people so it is important to standardise the terminology before we get too involved. Also it is important to realise as early as you can, that the soul, and the conscious mind, both use the *spirit-body* as a vehicle, they are *not fixed in the physical*.

33

I am going to tell you about two specific types of oobex. The first one is etheric projection, and the second is the now famous *astral*. It can be argued that *all* spirit projection is astral, but for the sake of clarity, I am applying this term solely to one specific type of projection.

The majority of people by far, when projected, dwell within the astral environment, and will enjoy complete success without *ever* having to know anything about the etheric. However, those that do project etherically will wonder in disbelief at what is said about the astral and will be very confused that their experience's are not shared. This has been the main area of confusion for many years, as the differences between the two types of projection have never been adequately explained.

To put it simply, if you travel on a train it is not necessary for you to know anything about the rail network, where the points are, how far apart the rails are, who controls what, and so on. You just involve yourself in the business of travelling on the train and your destination, etc. If the rails were not there, you would not be able to make that journey. The etheric plane is your rail system, and the astral plane is your train. For our purposes it is necessary to understand the etheric plane, for it is *vitally* important to us, specially whilst we are alive. Once you understand how that system works, I can go on to explain the more user friendly, astral plane.

We have a conscious mind, a subconscious mind and a *superconscious* mind. There may be others, and there will be a myriad of subdivisions, but I am a simple man, and I must stick to my own experience and my own understanding. I also know that I may use a different terminology to others when describing certain processes, but I am essentially a practical projector, and I try to express myself in that way. If you like, promoting a common-sense approach to the subject.

There are very few readable books on the market that purport to be guides on out-of-body experience's that I have not given the old heave-ho to! The ones that are good, however, are worth their weight in gold to a serious student, and I will mention which ones they are as I go.

We will learn to use our conscious imagination, to set up the 'will' of the subconscious mind that enables us to project through the use of relaxation, dream awareness, and desire. It is now necessary to understand a little about how the superconscious mind works during a projection.

When we have a conscious out-of-body experience we do so with all mental clarity. We think as we do on the physical plane, but with more options open to us. We are certainly quicker and livelier without the pull of the, seemingly, lumbering physical body. So, when projected, we do so with the conscious, subconscious and superconscious minds' working very much as they would when we are in our physical bodies. Not much difference at all. Our subconscious and superconscious minds are there, like a mountain of reserve backing up the conscious mind, *irrelevant* of where we 'exist'. It is our superconscious mind that makes calculated decisions for our personal protection in life, in *all* we do.

Sleep is a natural restorative, we use it to relax our muscles, to repair our physical bodies, and to relieve the usage of our organs. Man is a hunting animal and to be able to, originally, survive we needed to sleep so that we were always ready to escape danger, enhance our chances of self-protection, and capture food. We would have had to have slept in shorter bursts than we do now, so that we were always ready for any eventuality. This is why we still have sleepy periods during the day. The usual story of the survival of the fittest.

But man was also a thinking animal and needed more than food for his energy intake. He needed sleep to recharge his mental batteries. This energy source is known as *neural* energy, and it powers our mental processes. After a good nights' sleep we are more capable of solving problems and using our grey cells in general. Last thing at night, or after a hard day, we sometimes can't work out the simplest of problems, whereas in the morning the solution is clear.

Dreaming enables us to work off the stresses and strains of the day and helps us pass the eight hours, or so, by being a sort of internal entertainment or mental cleansing system. However, in reality, the act of dreaming has a much greater role to play for it is the 'cover all' that many important processes hide beneath. It is the sugar, that makes the unpleasant pill acceptable.

The dream process works like a filter, whatever influences the 'whole you' whilst asleep, is converted into dream content. This applies equally to your physical body lying in bed, or to your unconscious spirit-body when projected.

One of the processes that dreaming allows us to undertake without bothering us unduly, is the subconscious projection of the etheric body. Again I must emphasise that we are all individuals and as such we experience variations on a theme, just as *some* people dream regularly, *some* think that they never do, *some* suffer nightmare's, etc. All these things are in the same bag but affect us in *slightly* different ways.

Let us understand that we, in the western world, no longer live as natural animals, we have influences on our lives that are definitely unnatural. Our conscious minds are

36

cluttered with television fantasy, computer wizardry, employment issues, mortgages, bills to pay, and so on. We go to bed with stress and often wake up with stress, because we are not *designed* to live in this way. Over the years we have adapted, and adapted very well, but there is no getting away from it, we are still basically animals, so let us bear that in mind as we look at ourselves during this re-education.

A normal sleep pattern should be likened to the shape of a spoon. We go to bed healthily tired and, metaphorically, drop into the deep bowl of the spoon. Here we experience the essential sleep, the part of sleep that we cannot do without, whatever else our lifestyle entails. This is the *recharge* time when little dreaming is done, or I should say, rarely remembered. Our spirit-body, *every single night*, discoincides very slightly from the physical to access the universal energy. The more tired we are, the greater is the required separation to recoup the lost energy, the energy we call neural (nerve) energy. Should this process be delayed or disturbed in any way we would spend the rest of the next day feeling dreadful. I needn't ask any of you that have had the pleasure of attending a new-born baby, whether or not you know *exactly* what I am talking about!

Once we have spent enough time in the bowl of the spoon to recharge ourselves with neural energy, we gradually work our way up the handle to full wakefulness. It is the 'up the handle' area that we need to become more familiar with, and spend more time enjoying. It is here that the greater part of 'you' can be accessed *and* appreciated. This is the workshop area that we will be working in throughout the duration of this book.

One of the factors that affects the length of time spent on recharging our energy level, is *routine*. If we regularly go to bed at a certain time, and regularly have eight hours sleep, then our body will automatically have a regular period for recharging. If, for any reason this is seriously upset, then it takes us a day or two to get back to feeling normal. Having this type of routine is good for our personal health and welfare. A quality sleep is *still* the best tonic for keeping young, fit, healthy and mentally alert.

When we awaken early in the morning and attempt an out-of-body projection, we do so in the knowledge that we have already taken the essential part of sleep. This gives us the peace of mind to try and consciously experience what most of us do *unconsciously* every night. But routine works *against* projection because the body becomes used to matching the required recharge depth with the time available. If we break this routine by waking early, our subconscious mind will have to alter its recharge pattern. It will move the spirit-body further out, to deepen the intensity of the recharge and, in so doing, lessen the time needed. This is how some people thrive on less sleep while others need considerably more.

After the spirit-body has satisfactorily completed its recharge, it *can* remain exactly where it is, and you can dream as usual, or it *can* project further and leave your physical body behind. Although you can still dream your normal type dreams you now have the *added* option of consciously becoming aware of the journey that your spirit-body is making. When this phenomena happens, it is called *etheric* projection, and you are *projecting* your etheric body, whether you are conscious of it or not. This type of projection is very common and is the one that is nearest to our earthly existence. It is, nevertheless, very rare that we ever know anything about it, as it usually happens without any conscious intervention whatsoever. When consciousness intervenes during a projection, the neural energy recharge ceases and you begin to *use up* neural energy again, the

38

same as you do in the waking state. Recharge *only* happens when consciousness is absent.

So let us look at what is endemic to the etheric environment or, if you like, etheric plane. This is very straightforward to explain, because the etheric environment is earth. What we see is exactly the same as we see when physically awake, because we are seeing our own earth, our own homes, etc. When consciously projected, we can wander around our own homes, visit the neighbours, nothing will be altered, apart from ourselves. The very important distinction to remember, is to note if there are *any* changes from the physical reality, for if even *one stick* of furniture has been moved, or has disappeared, then you are *not* consciously existing on the etheric plane.

The preparation procedures, contained later in this book, are specifically designed to instil into the subconscious mind the *will* to project your spirit-body. For the instigation, of that movement, must come from there.

When the subconscious 'will' decides to move the etheric body away from the physical, it does so in a set manner. After, or during, your initial recharge period of deep sleep, your spirit-body develops a condition known as catalepsy. This is where the spirit-body becomes completely rigid, a complete cessation of sensation and movement and, indeed, if you should become conscious at this stage, it can be very scary and difficult to break free from the condition, until you know how, that is. Catalepsy can also be induced by hypnosis, to directly influence the *physical* body, and has been done so by stage hypnotists for many years.

What has been perceived as a 'trick' and nothing more, *actually* has an extremely important function to perform. If you have ever tried to move an unconscious body, you will know how difficult it is. They appear to be a dead weight, and they flop everywhere making it virtually impossible to move. But, if that same body weight was presented to you in a rigid form you *would* be able to move, or lift it, more easily. The reason that this peculiar condition of catalepsy exists is so the etheric body *can* be moved easily, as one solid mass, away from the physical body so that each part of the phantom leaves its physical counterpart at *exactly* the same time. And, more *importantly*, so that the phantom body can be controlled, pushed, pulled, whatever, all from one point. In my case this point has always been at the back of my head, just above where my backbone enters my skull. I understand that this is also the case common to *most* people, but apparently not all. It is here that the incredible spirit cable can be found linking the spirit-body to the physical body. See Figure 4, page 135. I will speak a lot more about the cable later, but basically it is a multi-stranded cable that links the physical brain sensory areas to the corresponding spirit-body areas.

Have you ever seen these little toy cars that are battery powered and have a lead protruding from the back with the other end attached to a control unit? The child then operates the controls to make the car perform. This is similar to etheric projection in that the child is the controlling subconscious will and the lead is the spirit cable, with the car being the projected body, moving as a solid mass, at the whim of the child.

In the cataleptic condition the phantom body rises horizontally upwards keeping parallel to the physical body, for a variable distance. The projected etheric body will usually work within the confines of the sleeping area although, of course, it doesn't have to. The spirit form then moves steadily towards the foot of your bed or over to one side, keeping parallel to your physical body before turning, still on the horizontal plane, 90% to the physical and lowering itself to a comfortable height above the floor. The

40

final resting place can be just about anywhere, but usually near to the physical in the room where you normally sleep. It is just as likely to turn a complete 180%, and lower itself down to one side of the bed, or go down to the foot, so that it settles in an *opposite* direction to your physical body, i.e. top to tail. In this position it can pass the hours away until it has a need to return for any reason whatsoever, or to wake up. See Figure 1, page 42.

This kind of projection is normal, and common, to us all. It happens to us all on a regular basis, it is just that we are not aware of it. So when we all think of this out-of-body stuff as being weird, and perhaps only available to one or two odd-bods, we are wrong because it is, in fact, as common as cheese. You, the reader, are *already* a spirit-body projector, *and* experienced at it! This unconscious process is controlled by the superconscious mind. It is our 'mother hen' who decides with reason, where we go and what we do, how long we are away and when we must come home. This works independently of the conscious mind and always puts our safety first.

There are some interesting variations to the route that the phantom body will take when projecting. It is essentially a routine procedure but, for a change, the spirit form can settle itself in another room in the house, other than in your sleeping quarters. If, for example, you happen to be staying in an unfamiliar bedroom, for whatever reason, the phantom may well decide to spend the night, in its usual position, beside your *own* bed at home. Distance holds no barriers, so even if you were 12,000 miles from home, your projected body, still attached by the cable, could still be fast asleep at home.

Have you ever awoken at night and, before you have gained all your senses, stared at your surroundings and thought that you were looking at another room, other than

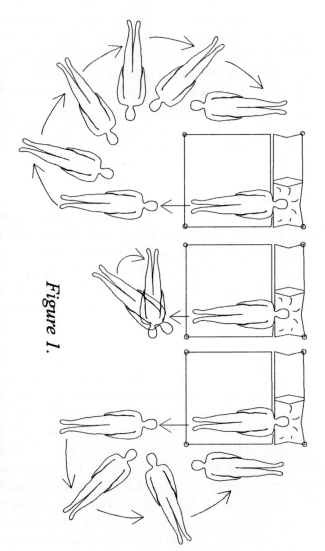

Figure 1.

Three common routes the unconscious spirit may take in nightly repose.

42

your bedroom? Have you ever got up in the middle of the night to go to the bathroom, and found that the bedroom door has mysteriously moved to the opposite corner to where you supposed it to be? So convinced are you, that you will try to open the wardrobe door, or search along a wall amazed that the door has magically disappeared? These are all indications of etheric projection. Your spirit-body has just spent several hours in another room, or in an opposite direction to your physical body, so when you become partially awake, you still feel as though you are still existing at the place where the spirit-body has been reclining.

So this is the route that an etheric body takes during an unconscious projection, the only variation to this is the final destination of the resting phantom. Even if you *were* able to be consciously aware of the etheric body leaving the spirit-body, you would not be able to affect the progress made, due to the cataleptic condition. It is not until the spirit has progressed away from the immediate range of the physical, will the catalepsy discontinue and release its hold. Now, it is *important* to become familiar with the *route* the etheric body takes, as it is also necessary to understand what sensations will be experienced during the process. I am firmly convinced that we are *not* naturally supposed to consciously experience the full etheric projection process from the beginning because of these strange sensations, and the processes, that are entailed because they can be unpleasant.

There are also some unhealthy temptations that will be discussed later. But, as the system *does* exist, and *can* be accessed, then we must understand the implications as fully as possible for it is necessary to know what our body gets up to, even if we are not consciously aware of it. It is likely, indeed preferable, that this conscious awareness, if it comes at all, should sally forth at the point where catalepsy ceases, and that *really* is the best way to enjoy etheric projection. The options that are open to you, once you are released from the cataleptic condition, will be dealt with later.

Etheric projection is tied to this earth, so the practical implications are vast. These, to name but a few, range from spying and espionage, to being nosy and looking around your neighbours house. Existing in the etheric body allows you to be the ultimate voyeur or simply to check on what your employees are getting up to whilst you are away on holiday. Yes, you can see that we have a privacy problem, and can our consciences allow us to indulge in these practices?

Firstly, you can meet other etherically projected people on the etheric plane who can also watch what you get up to, so no secrets are possible, and secondly, you have to 'suffer' the peculiarities of ingressing and egressing the physical body. Also there is the little matter of your own conscience and emotions to deal with.

All in all, the etheric body and, by association, etheric projection, does not exist as a system for us to experience at a conscious level. The fact that a few of us *can*, does not alter that fact. We would be in a fine mess if etheric projection was easy, and a normal thing to do. No, etheric projection is designed to be beyond our normal reach, and really it should remain so.

We will look at the major differences between the two main types of projection, plus the relationship with the dream world, for this is what the book is all about. Understand that the jumbled dream content is created from *all* our planes of existence, whether we have conscious knowledge of it or not, and usually we don't.

The vast astral plane, like the majority of the earth plane, is foreign to us apart from our personal locale, and places we like to visit, etc. The astral environment is solid to the touch, and as *real* as the earthly plane, but only once you are there. It contains many influences gathered from our everyday lives, how we live, what we eat, how we treat people and so on. It is the quality of this earth life that affects the quality of the astral life, when the time comes. It also contains much that we *do not* recognise, and would not be able to consciously recreate.

The astral plane is also solid and stable, as earth, and not changeable, like dreams. What we get up to on the astral plane will only affect mental conditions, and development, without having the important temptation of impacting onto other physical beings, unlike the earthly etheric. The astral body also has the advantage of separating from the physical body more easily, and in a quicker, more manageable, fashion.

The two main types of projection also have many things in common, well they *are* related, but only through you. I have mentioned that our dreams can disguise the movements of the etheric body. Well, astral projection can also mask those etheric manoeuvres. Dreams can also mask the movements of the astral body. At night we can be existing at different levels of consciousness, enjoying different environments, *all at the same time.* Yes, we can be in two places at once!

The best time to become consciously aware of projection, via any spirit-body, is *after* the initial stages are over, and you are a nice distance away from the physical body. It is like a lot of things, if your initial experience turns out to be an unpleasant one then you may not continue, but if fate initially deals you a kinder hand you will probably go on to blossom.

Uncontrolled fear is mainly due to a lack of experience and generally due to a lack of knowledge. I think that my personal experience's may help for a greater understanding although, unfortunately, the majority of my projections were never recorded up until the end of 1994, for I was happy enough, on my own, enjoying the secret world and the pleasures that I discovered.

At some stage it dawned on me that I might die without passing on my knowledge and findings. To avoid t his being lost forever, I began my recordings. Also, I found that I had an overwhelming wish to help others, and give something back in return for this life I have led. If this book can help other lives, and bring a brighter light of kindness, I will have succeeded in my wish.

You will be pleased to know that, since then, I have recorded each and every excursion, in the spirit of research and understanding, but I admit, not always with great success. I am human, and as such, I have my failings, as we all do. The main advice is perseverance, I remember one time my projections coming to a full stop and it was only after trying to project every night for three months did they finally return! That might be the level of commitment that you will also need, at times. The advantage of sharing personal experience's is that there are *so many variations* on a rule and it will highlight the differences more effectively. We can also analyse each projection, or failed projection, to see the why's and wherefore's with the added benefit of hindsight.

There are many ways to project yourself onto the astral plane, each of you will find an individual preference, and what this really means is that you will find a way that works for *you* naturally. Once you have found that way, and become accustomed to it, you can expand into the other possibilities.

Sometimes you can project and not even realise it. This is especially so when awareness comes to you whilst you are still lying in bed. It feels as if you have simply woken up as normal, and you will believe that your attempt at out-of-body projection has not been successful. The usual thing to do is to go back to sleep *totally* unaware of your spirit detachment and how *close* you became to a full projection.

The sensations can be as subtle as a feather balanced on the end of a hair or as dramatic as poking your fingers into a live electrical socket. Somewhere in-between is preferable.

This really is a vast subject to get the hang of. I must also say that the rewards are *so* great that it makes this effort seem insignificant.

Chapter Four
Etheric and astral projection

It is an unlikely, and very rare, event but for the sake of education we are going to *pretend* that you are about to experience a *fully conscious etheric projection* from *start* to *finish*. In the next few chapters I will go on to teach you all the preparation and relaxation you will need, but for now we will *assume* that you have successfully completed all your relaxation procedures and every necessary condition has been met.

The first tangible realisation that you are beginning a projection is the feeling of being 'glued' down to the bed and unable to move a muscle, all is silent and a feeling of isolation is with you. At all times you must try to remain calm and relaxed, confident in the knowledge that this has happened to you many, many times before, without causing you any harm. It is imperative that you don't let your conscious mind get too involved with what is going on. Think of it as though you are an observer instead of the participant.

Simply relax and go along with the sensations. If you need something to occupy your conscious thoughts, then *lightly* think of rising up into the air and floating. *Really* think of what it must be like to *actually* do this. After a while the heaviness fades away completely, and you are left feeling weightless. At this stage the vibrations begin, strong and pulsating, through the entire length of your body. These vibrations manifest themselves as feeling like an electric current flowing through you. We will deal in detail with this fascinating sensation later.

The next thing you realise is that you are actually floating, rising up in the air, being pushed and pulled, up and down, side to side, but nevertheless progressing upwards. This upwards movement can either be a slow steady vibrating rise, a side to side drunken type vibrating rise, or a push out pull back vibrating rise, a corkscrew rise, or any combination of all four, if factors intervene. The slow and steady rise is exceedingly preferable as it doesn't make you feel as queasy as the others, not that you get a choice. See Figure 2, page 50.

The first time you ever experience this rise you will swear that it is your physical body that is levitating towards the ceiling. From the inside, it is difficult to know where the rise stops and the floating horizontal movement starts as it all moulds into one movement. Now here is another strange development - should you be unconscious, at this point, the etheric body will simply continue to place the sleeping spirit somewhere, to rest the night away. But, if we assume you are *conscious* at this point then, by now, it is likely that your sense of sight will have returned, along with your hearing. In this condition the controlling force, otherwise known as the superconscious mind, will upright the phantom to a standing position and release you from the catalepsy. See Figure 3, page 51.

On one occasion I regained consciousness after this process had all finished and found my spirit-body in the resting position. As I became aware of my surroundings, I realised that I was suspended approximately eight inches above the floor of my bedroom, close to the side of the bed, but with my feet up at the head end, and my head down where my physical feet were! When this was realised, my spirit-body moved feet first, as if on wheels, through the

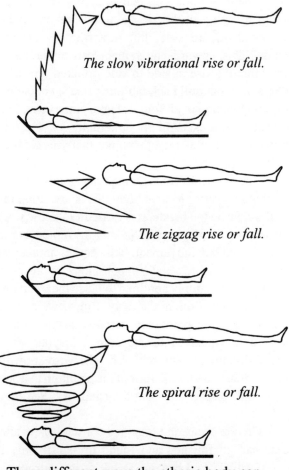

The slow vibrational rise or fall.

The zigzag rise or fall.

The spiral rise or fall.

Three different ways the etheric body can
leave, or return to, the physical body.

Figure 2.

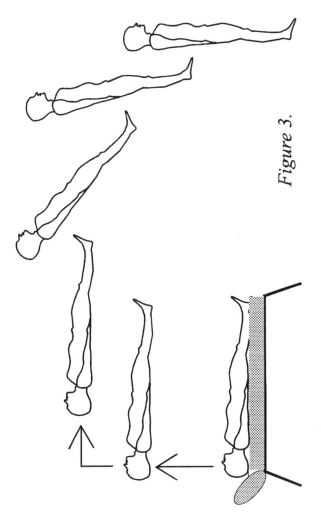

Figure 3.

The direction the unconscious spirit-body takes as it leaves the physical.

open bedroom doorway, across the passage, and straight through a very solid two foot thick stone wall, into the rear garden. There I landed on my own two feet and I was free to wander around the garden, getting myself accustomed to the special experience of etheric separation before levitating to the roof of the house to sit and watch the early traffic on the High Street, outside my home. The sense of peace and contentment is indescribable, and must be personally felt to be fully appreciated.

Once you have been uprighted and the catalepsy has disappeared, you are free to explore the world in your etheric body. If you turn towards the bed, you will see the heart stopping sight of your own physical body lying there asleep. The first time that this amazing thing happened to me, I felt truly scared that I wasn't in that body anymore but, quite unexpectedly, I also felt affection, the kind of love that you would have for a faithful dog, or a very true friend. I then learned my next lesson, which is if you allow *any* emotion to become slightly more prominent, so that the delicate balance of your senses becomes unbalanced, then you will be pulled back into that physical body in the time it takes to blink an eye. Such a return will likely cause a repercussion.

When you initially go to sleep, you know that you are heading, quite quickly, for the deep part of your sleep pattern. Your spirit-body needs to disassociate from the physical body and naturally tries to do so at the earliest possible moment. However, for this to happen, it is necessary for you to have lost consciousness, and consciousness has a habit of popping in and out as it leaves. Several things can cause this, such as idle thoughts that pass through your mind, a memory kicking in, noises in the vicinity of your bedroom, your partner moving, etc.

When one is in the process of losing consciousness and something causes it to return, it will do so *immediately*. So fast that it actually causes your physical body to jump, sometimes quite violently. This can happen *many* times as you drift off to sleep and I am sure that you have experienced this 'jumping' either personally, or with your partner or child. This strange jumping, sometimes accompanied by a grunt or gasp, is known as repercussion. If you find it annoying then think again, because this is the tangible evidence of the safety procedure at work protecting you from any possible danger. If you are projected from your physical body and something threatens you, or you become scared (or both!), or an emotion becomes too strong, or in fact *anything* that upsets the delicate balance of the experience, you will be catapulted back into the physical body with *lightning* speed. A violent repercussion *can* result in a subsequent headache and disorientation.

Very often it is something quite mundane that will bring you back, like finding yourself in a strange place, or the worry of being in someone else's house without their permission. I must say that in all of my projections I have not been threatened by anything more severe than my own ignorance. All my devils and demons are dealt with in the relaxation and dream stages, never at a personal level in the projection itself. That isn't to say that they are not there, but I have *never* seen anything untoward whilst projected in the etheric body, only whilst in the astral body. Even then it is very rare, and not personally threatening. So you can see that at the merest hint of trouble you are brought home safe and sound, and there is nothing that you can do about it except to try and project again. That essentially explains repercussion, but more will be said as we go through.

When our etheric body returns to the physical body following a normal unconscious projection it does so very much as it left, only in reverse. Just as with the exit, the re-entry is best done in the unconscious state as the sensations are just as severe or, at least, they can be. Also, if left to its own devices, the superconscious mind will make a far better job of it, without the complication of having the conscious mind intervening. Even if the sensations are a trifle weird, a natural re-entry is far preferable to a severe repercussion.

I have told you about the route that the etheric body takes and what happens to it in a normal *unconscious* projection. I have also told you what to expect should you manage to gain consciousness during any part of that process. I have explained that the phenomena is controlled by the superconscious mind that decides where the etheric body goes and what it does, etc. Should the superconscious mind suddenly decide to send the etheric body to the other side of the world, it could do, just as easily as sending it to another room. Your etheric body could easily have spent the night lounging on a tropical beach and you would have no conscious knowledge of it! So you can see it is all there, the knack is to gain conscious awareness to enjoy some of it, and when that happens the control moves to your conscious mind so that you can make conscious choices for your own personal benefit.

Remember, the superconscious mind can override the conscious mind at anytime it thinks fit *and* for any reason, as in deciding to bring you home. Also, when you get near to your physical body it becomes *increasing* difficult to stay out as a phantom. Apart from these exceptions it is very much your choice to do as you wish whilst projected.

Although the etheric world is the same as the one we live on, we do have access to a wider range of in-built travel options. We can have our own normal walking pace, we can *fly* and we can instantly arrive at the required destination.

Walking is very much the same as with the physical body, but the beauty of etheric walking is that it allows you time to think, and experiment. Should you come across a building and wish to see inside, all you have to do is gently press yourself up against any part of the structure and you will be able to pass through it. Lets say for arguments sake that you choose to enter the building via the wall, you would notice a slight resistance as you press yourself through the fabric that makes up the composition of the wall. A little like a barrier made of foam rubber that disintegrates as you touch it. For me this is a *most* pleasurable exercise and I sometimes do it *purely* for the hell of it! To be able to pass through an apparently solid object is a precious experience to have had.

Should you wish, it is possible to stand in the wall almost as though you had become a part of it, but only allowing the front of your face to push through to observe the contents of the space on the other side. These things are done in the name of idle research as you are pretty much invisible anyway, except to those that have clairvoyant vision and can see 'ghosts'. It is interesting to note that another etherically projected person will feel absolutely solid to you should you meet them while you are in your etheric body. It is the people here, in their physical bodies, that you can pass through as though *they* are the ones that have little substance.

I have just mentioned the word 'ghost' and it is a bad word because all of us, as etheric bodies, can be observed as 'ghosts' and yet it is the *real person* that projects. The dictionary states that a ghost is the disembodied spirit of a deceased person. Not true! In the accepted meaning of the word, it should say that a ghost is the disembodied spirit of *any* person, *alive* or *dead*. Many of the so called 'ghosts' are, in reality, projected spirit-bodies belonging to healthy living people. In actual fact the word is still misused because it is the real thinking *you* as a spirit-body that is erroneously called a 'ghost'. The meat and bone physical body, left behind in bed, is the real ghost, for it is *this* that is the empty shell!

We will assume that you have been walking around, in your projected body and you wish to experiment with flying. You have the option of vertical take-off, horizontal take-off, or anything in-between. The simple answer is to think it and do it. If you want to levitate, think of levitating and, as you do, stretch yourself upwards as though it is the most normal and natural thing in the world to do. You will rise into the air with amazing grace and ease. There are no muscles to become involved, purely thought processes, so if you wish it to happen, it will, especially if it ties in with something that the etheric body is used to doing anyway, like flying.

Levitating vertically is fine up to a point. It doesn't take very long to lose sight of the place from where you began, and it doesn't take very long to wonder what on earth you are doing getting further and further away from terra firma. Excessive height is a very lonely and isolated environment and, although the view is great, eventually it can become quite boring. Now if only I could take a video camera with me......

Horizontal flying is a completely different kettle of fish. It is more fun than you can ever imagine! If you launch your spirit-body forward and lean over, you will fall to the ground with a gentle bouncing motion as an ordinary balloon would once you have let go of it. You have to *think* flying, have the confidence to fly, and you surely will. If you like, you can lie down on the ground and give yourself a good push off with your feet or hands, just like pushing a boat off across the water. To think it, is enough, but we 'earth beings' have habits that enhance our confidence, and there is nothing wrong with that. In fact you can forget all about 'earth' rules made by man. Once projected it is the universal law that counts and *that* is tailored by your own conscience. Flying allows you to travel to a destination, or simply to move away from your location to somewhere that you would rather be, even for idle recreation.

This spirit projection is not necessarily a serious business unless you make it so, just the same as in your physical life. The nearer you fly to the ground, the faster it feels, and if you pick a busy city, like London, allow yourself about eight inches clearance and go for it, the excitement is unparalleled. By the way, you don't have to keep thinking about how far you are above the ground, it will remain constant until you think otherwise. It follows that if this speed is *too* fast for your comfort, then increase the distance between you and the ground so that the perception of speed is decreased. There is no need to dodge and swerve to avoid obstructions, *but you will*, and that is half the fun of it.

Another phenomenal way to travel is the instantaneous method. You think of a destination and in a flash, you have arrived. Simple as that, although I have never found this to be 100% effective. The method certainly works but the destinations aren't always the ones that you wished for!

So, etheric projection is tied to the earth plane and is usually an unconscious course of action. The projected body usually reposes near to the physical body location with occasional outings as the 'will' determines. The unconscious spirit-body dreams the dreams that you are so familiar with unless the conscious mind intervenes. I will forgive you for thinking, why then has he told me all this if I am unlikely to ever experience it? The answer is, you may be one of the lucky few that, after training, will naturally and consciously project to the etheric plane.

But, of course, there is another reason. A far, far more important reason why it is necessary for you to know about etheric projection, and this is one of greatest realisations about understanding how we operate in our universal lives.

Do you recall me saying earlier, how external stimuli influences your dream content? Well, by external I mean anything that is external to the dream, but not necessarily external to you. In other words, you can cause your own external influences that will affect your own dreams. Suppose for example you found yourself creeping through the jungle in your dream, and in the background you can hear the growl of a nearby lion. The chances are that you will try to keep as quiet as possible so as not to bring attention to yourself and, every so often, the growling stops only to come back very close to scare you. This whole dream was probably created in your mind to make sleeping sense of the fact that you were snoring. When you become scared, you hold your breath and the growling stops. When you think that the lion has gone, you relax and begin snoring again.

Often when sufferers of enuresis wet the bed, they have dreamt of swimming, or being attacked with a knife and they are lying there bleeding. These are examples of how our subconscious mind will alter, and usually greatly enhance, the character of the stimulus to incorporate it into the fabric of the dream. Why does it do this? As projectors, we welcome this type of interference as it brings our consciousness to the fore in our dreams.

Everything has a *reason*, and little by little I am giving you the answers. If our subconscious mind did not alter and enhance the stimuli, we could not be able to sleep with any quality at all. And if we do not have quality sleep then we cannot live healthy lives. It is the movement, coupled with the sensations involved with etheric projection, and the neural energy recharge, that has to be disguised and made palatable to enable us to sleep. Otherwise these sensations would certainly wake us up before we could ever refresh our minds.

The all essential recharge that happens in deep sleep would be very haphazard because it needs you to be *unconscious* before it can ever work, and without the *disguise* of dreams you would be too aware of your circumstances to remain unconscious.

Yet another reason, is that an interesting dream will concentrate your interest away from your true condition, to protect you from the vast spirit world and all that that entails. Lets face it, if you could dwell in 'paradise', instead of in your present location, most people would pick 'paradise', therefore it *has* to be made difficult. The astral environment is often erroneously called 'paradise' and is the nearest we can get to the real paradise whilst still living on earth. People can enjoy the fruits of the spirit world, but not to the detriment of the physical earth, or our individual physical bodies.

We exist on this earth primarily for two reasons. One is to produce more physical bodies, so that more spirit-bodies can have a home, which is especially important following world epidemics and disasters, wars, plagues, etc. This was very important at certain times in the past, but not now. By far the main reason we exist, is to enable us to have the chance of advancing the quality of each spirit, so it becomes balanced, understanding, caring and worldly. For this beautiful earth is our training ground, it is here that we learn to mature before we eventually becoming eternal entities.

Most of us go through low points in our lives where it becomes difficult to see the way ahead. Times when we think, is it all really worth it? But these are the times when we learn, when our character gains the benefit of being strengthened, and in the fullness of time we are able to look back and understand how we got ourselves into that kind of situation. Misguided affection, immaturity, innocence, ignorance, weakness and sheer bad luck, can all contribute to personal crises.

This kind of life experience allows us to understand others when *we* see *them* going through a similar situation. The real danger is that if we all could easily project our spirit-bodies to another plane, the temptation would be to attempt to go there permanently! The suicide rate would rocket and this of course would be counterproductive to the universal law and cannot be allowed. It would also mean that we would have to learn the lesson again, from the start, and have to live with the weight of the emotional damage caused to your loved ones. Also, the damage done to the people that you were destined to meet, love, or create, and also to *their* children, etc. We are not in the position to understand the full picture of what destiny is, nor should we be. It is not our decision to take our own lives, or anybody else's, we do not have that right. It is not the loss of the physical body that is important, it is the termination of the spiritual development *in this life* that is wrong.

So let us look at how the unconscious etheric projection affects our dream content. Parts of this will be recognisable to just about all of us. You will now understand how previously unrecognised phenomena is actually part of a natural process. I cannot emphasise the importance of understanding how this works.

I am going to ask you to think back over your history of dream experience's and I want you to see which of the following examples relates to a dream memory that you have had. Irrelevant of the story line, which is not important, have you ever tried to run away from something but have been *unable* to get away. However hard you try, you cannot affect your speed, your feet are like lead and you are getting increasingly worried that you are going to be caught? Whatever it is that is chasing you is getting nearer and nearer, but you cannot go any faster and panic sets in.

In my dream, just the other night, I was driving my car along a dual carriageway when I came up to a set of lights. At these lights the carriageway branched into three lanes of traffic that were all full. As the lights changed we all accelerated away to try to get across the junction first because the carriageway decreased in width to only two lanes, so it was imperative to get there first to avoid the merging traffic. But no matter how hard I pressed the accelerator my car refused to go any faster. I somehow merged with the other traffic thinking to myself that something is wrong with my car, just when I need the extra speed it lets me down, and so on.....

Another example would be where you are being pulled *towards* 'something' and no matter what you do, you cannot stop yourself from being drawn in to it. The 'something' could be purely the thought that, whatever it is, it is *scary* and you are being forced to meet this unknown adversary. Or perhaps the 'something' could actually be seen as a terrifying monster, or demon, that you are being sucked into. What about the sheer terror of knowing that something 'evil' is behind your own front door forcing it at the hinges and the locks, to come in to get you? All you can do is sit there terrified and unable to move.

All these examples are classic dream occurrences and if used as part of a juicy story-line can easily escalate into the stuff of humdinger nightmares! But what have we actually got here, and what do all these examples have in common with each other? Well, the lack of movement is one. It is not the fact that you cannot go any faster because you also would not be able to go any slower either. The truth is that you are being kept at a constant speed. The feelings involved here range from concern to sheer terror. And *what* is this 'something' that is out to get you.

Your etheric body is projecting but you are not conscious of that fact for you, in that etheric body, are dreaming. Your dream is necessarily disguising the movements of the etheric body by creating the dream content around the etheric activity. When, in your dream, you are trying to move faster but can't, it is because your, cataleptic, etheric body is in the process of leaving your physical body and is being held at a determined pace by the spirit cable. Your manoeuvres are actually under the strict control of the superconscious mind whilst you are in such close proximity to your physical body. Once your spirit-body has been put far enough away and released from the cataleptic condition you will once again be able to control your speed in a dream, because the tension of the cable will be reduced to nothing, until it is time to return.

Similarly, when you are being drawn towards something horrible, you may have feet of lead, you may struggle, sweat and panic, but all to no avail. This is because your etheric body is coming back to your *own* physical body, again under the control of your superconscious mind via the cable. The fear actually helps the process as another safeguard. Should conscious awareness intervene while you were panicking then you would immediately experience a repercussion and the whole job gets done a little quicker.

Generally speaking it is only a small percentage of these projection's that cause any sort of nightmarish

62

problems, many more are just pleasantly normal with the *vast* majority being totally unconscious and, literally, the stuff of dreams.

I have an example that I would like to relate to you. Just to set the scene, my bathroom at Ivydene is located in the same end of the house as my bedroom, and one night, during a dream, I became aware that I was in my bathroom. The strange thing was that I couldn't stand up, or if I did, I immediately fell over. I didn't feel drunk but that was the closest I could get to explaining these movements. I would go from lying on the floor, to being on my right side, to trying to stand up and succeeding in falling down in the opposite direction and back over onto my left side. I remember beginning to giggle as my dream made sense of this as drunken behaviour. Little by little I made my tipsy way to the bedroom, as by now the whole thing had become hilarious to me! All of a sudden it stopped and I lay in bed wide awake reviewing this experience.

Looking back, it is easy to see that it was the excessive swaying motions of my etheric body that caused me to dream that I was drunk, along with the accompanying happy feelings thrown in for authenticity. The swaying was so excessive that I am sure that I was very near to becoming dream aware. I was annoyed that I hadn't realised that I was dreaming and taken the opportunity of controlling the situation and extending the projection into a conscious oobex. It is very frustrating to know that you were so close to a fabulous experience and not taken advantage of a situation that had presented itself.

The swaying motion happens because the etheric body is being drawn back into the physical following a projection. So I had unconsciously been out and about without any knowledge of it. A piece of my life has happened, once again, that I have no memory of. But I *know* it happened.

When water is forced through a hose at high pressure, it snakes. The force of the water is too great for the hose to remain stable. When a spirit-body is extensively projected, the cable that joins the two bodies has diminished in thickness to nothing more than a thread. On returning to the physical this cable becomes thicker the nearer it gets. I think that with the above example I had, indeed, been out on an extensive projection, for the *thickened* cable was pulling me in from a far greater distance than it normal would. Instead of pulling me in from a couple of feet above my physical body it was reeling me in, at that stage, from around twenty feet.

It was this distance that caused the swaying motion to be so excessive. The cable is very powerful, very strong, and over this kind of distance, very unwieldy. A little like the high pressure water hose.

And so we have the normal unconscious return, the easy dream return, and the nightmare return. The nightmare return is truly awful as all who recognise this will concur.

Seemingly, against your will, you are drawn towards something extremely unpleasant, even horrific, and the fear can be buttock clenching. Sometimes you can see the 'thing' that is reeling you in. I have to tell you now that in reality the 'thing' seen or unseen is in fact *your own* physical body awaiting your return, and is *definitely not* a monster from the edge, or the very devil himself, absolutely not at all. The intense fear is again the natural built in precaution against you taking conscious control of a situation that you are not ready for, as fear, now said many times, is the key to instantaneous return and rendering you safe and sound.

Once you fully understand the process these fears will gradually disappear as you become used to these feelings. An excellent exercise is to embrace anything that scares you whilst dreaming. Give out loving signs, smile, pretend to not notice them too much and talk to them in a matter-of-fact sort of way. Whenever I have done this the entity 'morphs' into a happy, pleasant character, and another gateway has been recognised, but not entered!

Immediately prior to a conscious projection it is often the case that we experience a thump, bang, or a noise like a jet fighter flying through the brain. This feels as though it is right *inside* your brain and on occasions can be very frightening in itself. I will always remember the first time I felt a *severe* head thump. I could hear a faint buzzing noise in the distance, but within a split second and with the speed of a missile the buzz had turned into an explosion *inside* my head. I felt serious fear, the noise was brain-mashing and to compound the unpleasantness, it happened again in quick succession. I was afraid for my life and my panic was such that I had to remain awake for the rest of the night in case it happened again. I must add that that this was the one and only time that this particular sensation has ever caused me a problem as severe as this.

Now, I actually *invite* the sensation as it is a strong indication that a projection is nigh. This peculiar phenomenon is caused by a drop in blood pressure to the brain. If your etheric body is away, on an outing, and the physical blood pressure causes this sensation to happen to the physical body, the dream will interpret this as danger, and rightly so. Depending on the sort of lives you have led, this could mean being bombed during a war situation, or someone beating down your front door, to get you!

I recall a perfectly normal dream where I was walking through my parlour in the general direction of my back door. The door was locked and barred and provides a very secure barrier to anyone trying to get in. My back

65

garden is also secure, in that it doesn't provide access to callers. This can only be done via the front door and that is where I would expect any trouble, should there ever be any.

So there I am, casually walking past my own back door when the whole door with the framework suddenly rocked from the impact of three massive impacts originating from the other side. The noise alone was deafening, the suddenness scared me rigid, and the fear was substantial. In the dream, I thought my end had finally come. Whatever was outside that back door felt like evil incarnate. Needless to say, I woke up scared, but relieved. Safely back under conscious control, I recognised the fact that I had been out in my etheric body, my blood pressure had dropped too low and my superconscious control, via my dream, had very efficiently brought me home.

Now that I have spoken about the etheric body, I hope you have a good idea of the life it leads. Try to relate all you have learned to your own sleeping experience's. By recognising the etheric body action we can make sense of many hitherto misunderstood problems. Conscious awareness can try to flash in at any time during an unconscious projection, as it gets stronger the dream content deals with it by giving you a livelier story-line and by sending you off on a wild goose chase.

I will mention again the best book ever written, in my opinion, that explains the intricacies of etheric projection. That book is 'The Art of Astral Projection' by Sylvan Muldoon, and Hereward Carrington. I strongly urge anybody interested in this subject to get a copy, if you can. In this book I find very little to disagree with, but with one major exception, and that is the title. This amazing book, and I have bought several copies over the years as presents for friends, is all about *etheric* projection, not *astral* projection.

Sylvan Muldoon had the rare ability of maintaining consciousness whilst projecting etherically. He did not project astrally, and openly admits to having no knowledge of other sphere's of life. However, his experience's have given us invaluable information about the bedrock projection and all of its accompanying appurtenances. This book has been one of the causes of many disagreements regarding out-of-body experience's, for the majority of projector's do not share the same findings as Muldoon. I find this completely understandable because, as I have said, Muldoon was fundamentally an etheric projector, not astral. The two must not be confused with each other.

I am assuming that you are having a conscious *etheric* projection and that you are satisfied that all is well and you are enjoying yourself. It is normal, and preferable, for conscious awareness to remain with you until you are returned to the physical body. I say preferable for a reason. At any time during the projection consciousness can be lost, it doesn't make the preceding projection any the less real, but it means that there will be a period of sleep between the projection and the waking state. However *real* the memory is, a seed of doubt will have been sown because you have been asleep. You cannot be absolutely sure if you have had a lucid dream, an astral projection, or an etheric one. Whereas, if consciousness remains unbroken, lasting through to full waking, then you will be able to know clearly. And remember, this knowledge is needed for your own personal research, not to impress other people, so you must, and can, be honest with yourself.

It is quite common, during an unconscious etheric projection, for consciousness to pop in and out and so create some 'real' elements into a dream sequence. Somehow, the subconscious mind can cope with all that is thrown at it. It can merrily produce a dream sequence that masks the unconscious meandering of the spirit-body, even when the conscious mind suddenly flashes in and records the *true* environment. There can be a whole series of these 'mental' snapshots happening during one projection. This has the effect of radically altering the dream sequence every time as the subconscious mind juggles with the dilemma. But this is not all that it has to deal with.

An etheric projection, in full flow, can become astral. Just because it started out as etheric doesn't mean that it will stay that way, and vice versa. And consciousness can be lost just as easily from an astral projection, as it can be from an etheric one. So do you begin to see all the permutations that are possible here.

- Dreams can mask an astral projection, or an etheric projection.
- An astral projection can mask an etheric projection.
- An etheric projection can be a conscious, or unconscious, experience.
- An astral projection can be a conscious, or unconscious, experience.
- Dreams can be non-memorable, memorable, vivid or lucid.

All the above can happen in any combination to cause confusion and doubt, with one exception; an etheric projection is on the base-line, just one level above the physical existence, so it does *not* mask anything else.

I will now go on to explain astral projection and how different it is to etheric projection and the dream experience. The etheric body and the astral body behave very similarly *once* separation has been effected. Not only do the two bodies leave, and return to, the physical body in different ways, but they also exist in *very* different environments. Apart from this, the movements and abilities that you have during a projection are very similar.

When the astral body leaves the physical, it does so without the formality of the etheric body, and has a variety of options to use. Although the actual separation is out of your conscious control it is effected very much quicker than an etheric detachment. When the physical body is so calm that it is virtually incapacitated (I call this hibernation mode) and the subconscious mind has the 'will' to project, a *massive* energy rush will be felt as the spirit-body becomes a separate entity. The spirit-body, astral or etheric, is now *vibrating at a higher rate* than the physical body.

It is often the case that the astral body will leave the physical body during this 'rush'. It is also common to find yourself still reposing within the physical shell after the 'rush' has diminished, completely unaware that you are, indeed, actually detached! It is not until you decide to move do you discover the truth of it. In this position it is possible to twist yourself within the physical shell to face the opposite way, or to sit up and walk away leaving the shell behind.

On many occasions, as I have said, the astral body will exit on the 'rush' and become upright a few feet from the prostrate physical, where you will *immediately* be in full control. On other occasions you will be elevated, turned to one side and then placed upright on the floor, again with full control. Even though you may recognise the immediate environment as being your earthly bedroom, with careful attention to detail it may actually be found to be astral in nature. Remember, if any detail has changed from the normal, then it is not etheric, but *probably* astral, and this will be very apparent when you begin to move away. Upon feeling the 'rush', it is also common to found oneself on part of the astral plane that is foreign to our conscious mind, and you will be free to explore to your hearts' content.

Thankfully, there are *many* ways of separating that are to be experienced, including all the infuriating times when you do everything right, and still full separation is *not* achieved.

An even more fascinating and pleasurable astral separation can happen when you are already part-way through an *unconscious* astral projection. This is where you become conscious that you are dreaming, and your dreams are masking the true astral projection. Upon realisation you can induce the 'rush' quite easily to find yourself conscious in the astral body 'somewhere'. Wherever your astral body was and whatever it was doing is no longer an unconscious act because your consciousness now exists within that body. The 'rush' directly relates to the conscious mind being present. This will all become clearer once we get onto the practical subject, helped by the examples of my own meandering later.

I would like to mention the phenomenon of 'near death experiences'. This is a subject that exists a little like a relative never seen, but known to be near. Obviously data can only be extracted from those that *experience* near death. In this respect I would recommend the books by Raymond Moody, written with the help of Paul Perry. Similarly the works of D.Scott Rogo, will also prove invaluable to the serious student.

One such publication, 'Life After Death' outlines the raft of related experience's in a clear and introductory manner and includes one section that is of particular interest to oobex. It details the findings of Dr.Michael Sabom, a cardiologist at Atlanta Medical Centre, Georgia. He compiled the results of many patients that claimed to have had 'near death experiences'.

In one such test, the general conclusions showed that, of the 67 patients interviewed, 'at the time of unconsciousness, 29 patients experienced amnesia, while 38 encountered a near death experience, of which, 18 patients experienced the passage of consciousness into a foreign region or dimension (transcendence), 11 viewed their body and physical surroundings from a *detached* position of height (autoscopy) and 9 experienced both transcendence *and* autoscopy.

So let us look at what we have here using our oobex eyes. Firstly we can discount the 29 that remember nothing, this could be due to many things including the very deep sleep we all have where nothing is remembered. What *is* interesting to us, is that 18 patients experienced 'transcendence', *we* know this as *astral*, 11 experienced 'autoscopy', *we* call this etheric, and the remaining 9 experienced both. We also now know that the astral can *appear* to be etheric, *especially* if you are in a foreign environment, and *especially* if this is a 'one off' projection where you are *inexperienced* in recognising exactly where you are in the spirit world. So you can see that many people who have an out-of-body-experience will immediately *assume* they were *near* to death, when in fact they may not have been.

Often, many of these 'one off' experience's contain sequences that incorporate a common theme, for example, such things as travelling through a 'tunnel', being met by a celestial being, and having an assessment of the life that they have led to date, etc.

These accounts give me the belief that oobex is *not* a near death experience, simply a *part* of that process, even though we try to replicate that exact situation prior to projection. I have *never* travelled down a tunnel *or* been met by *anybody* celestial.

Why near death experience's are different, in certain respects, to oobex is a bit of a mystery, but the 'near death'

71

report's indicate that the tunnel effect happens *after* spirit separation has been effected. Maybe, the physical body *does* have to be nearer to an actual death situation to cause this phenomenon. But just as easily, if any conscious realisation *suddenly* appears in the *lucid dream state*, and if one *expects* to see a religious figure waiting to greet them, then they will. See my section on lucid dreaming. There are *many* report's of this nature.

Unfortunately these trials tend to be a one-off, but extensive reading of these report's show a great many experience's that are recognisable as oobex phenomena, and the *real* test would be for an experienced oobex projector to have a 'near death experience'.

These people often talk about the loss of physical feelings, a sudden clarity of mind, an understanding of events, peacefulness from the turmoil of pain, and a real reluctance to return to the stress and strain of earth. They also speak of being somewhere so beautiful, and express a common certainty that there *is* a place that you go to when you die, it *is* beautiful, and it *does* exist. Nothing will shake their conviction in this, and they live the rest of their lives in quiet contentment with an air of confidence regarding death. These are all classic oobex perceptions.

One worry that must be dispelled is the reliability of the spirit-body returning to the physical body following an out-of-body experience, be assured that it happens only too easily. The hard part is staying out! At the first sign of any danger, any emotional change, or if the projected body gets too close to the physical, the return is instant. Just like the exit, the return, if absolutely vital, will be out of your control. Your superconscious mind will take these decisions for you, and it will err on the side of safety. Remember, it has done this on countless occasions without you ever even knowing. Real understanding can only come with practical experience, and that is what I would like to acquaint you with here.

You must get it into your understanding that 'you' and your physical body, are two separate entities that have come together for a length of time that is governed by however long it takes for the physical body to wear out, and/or die.

Oliver Fox has written a very lovely and worthwhile book that celebrates astral projection, entitled 'Astral Projection, a Record of Out-Of-The-Body Experiences'. A very honest and unassuming record of one mans' experience's into the worlds that I am describing. In his book Oliver Fox wonders why he cannot see his own physical body when projected, and yet Sylvan Muldoon can. The simple answer is that Oliver Fox projects, predominantly, astrally - so he can only see his astral world, with his astral eyes, from his astral body. He cannot see the physical world where his physical body lies. Sylvan Muldoon projects, predominantly, etherically - and so he sees the physical world as it is, which *does* include his physical body.

I think these two books show very clearly the difference between the two types of projection and for that fact alone are worth reading. These are two of the books that would accompany me if I had to spend the rest of my life on a desert island, purely to keep me focused!

Chapter Five
The effect of dreams

If you follow the all important relaxation procedures correctly, one of several things will happen to you. I have already said that I believe it is necessary to lose consciousness before it is possible to experience an oobex. So it is preferable to either, lose consciousness for a split second and remain in the correct state of mind, or simply go to sleep and hope that the need for a degree of dream awareness will remain long enough for it to reappear. The third option is to awaken in what is called the hypnopompic state, or near to it, and to *recognise* it as such, so that you can project from this position.

We will begin by looking at what will probably be the most likely outcome that a projector, new to the task, can initially expect, which is the gaining of *awareness* during a dream. But we are not interested in the ordinary regenerative dream state. By following the relaxation procedures, yet to be outlined, you will find that you will be able to alter your dream level so that you will no longer be dreaming in *quite* the same way as you used to. These dreams will now be occurring in a different depth of sleep, one that is nearer to the conscious surface of sleep.

Prior to learning this, it is most probable that should anyone remember their dreams, it will usually be the last one, or two, that they experience just before waking up during the night, or in the morning. We are actually extending that *same* period to allow you to enjoy those, more memorable, dreams for an increased length of time.

74

There are two general categories of memorable dream, and they are, 'vivid' dreams, and 'lucid' dreams. As you read about these different types of dreams, you will begin to notice certain factors already existing in your own dreams that you had not previously recognised. This is something that you can begin to do *immediately*.

It is quite usual, and a good sign, for a projector to experience vivid dreams when in the act of trying to create an oobex, even if the projection fails. If it was our sole intention to create vivid dreams, then we would be very successful! Any 'failure' usually comes about because all the necessary conditions have *not* been correctly attained to promote a successful projection. There is more to this than simple relaxation, *much* more. We will be looking at these conditions as we go through the various procedures.

The most important thing to do is to recognise the content of these dreams. Not what they were actually about, but the *effect* of the content. There are hundreds of books, been written, purporting to reveal the hidden meanings of dreams, and to my mind the majority of them are a waste of time. On an individual basis, it is beneficial to analyse the meaning of a dream content, but this is a very personal experience that is impossible to do in general terms, and you will see why as we go on.

When we dream, a part of the dream involves taking external stimulation, and incorporating this into our dreams. Sometimes the dream will create the necessary environment for the external stimulation, *before* it actually happens. If, for example, you were dreaming about your house being on fire, your senses would be aroused, and this would be a vivid dream. If you had one of those alarm clocks with the bells on top and it activated itself in an effort to wake you up you would, in your dream, probably interpret this as hearing the fire engines coming to put out the fire. Having woken up and, thankfully, realising that it was all a dream, you would normally get up and put the horrible experience behind you, after all it *was* only a dream and soon forgotten.

In reality, you were lying in bed asleep and having a dream, as we all do, near to the awakening stage. Again, quite commonly, you began to feel warm and this could possibly have been reflected in your dream as being in a house that has caught fire. Subconsciously you knew that the alarm clock was about to go off, and this fact was reflected in the dream as the bells of the fire engine coming to rescue you. It does not matter that fire engines have not used bells for many years now.

The strange thing is that sometimes the dream can create a scenario that incorporates an element of the *future*. In other words, the bells of the fire engine could also, quite easily, have been the postman ringing your front door bell, or someone ringing you up on the telephone. Now, when the dream was created, how was it done with the precise timing, and the precognition, that the postman was going to ring your front door bell at the actual moment required in the dream sequence. It might be appropriate to mention here an excellent book written by J.W.Dunne, and entitled 'An Experiment With Time'. I cannot claim to understand, or even enjoy, all that Mr.Dunne writes about, but the parts that I did comprehend became a great source of inspiration, to a point where it checked out with my own research!

He effectively shows that a small element of your dreams actually contain a perception of future events, and he instructs you on how to access this information. It takes a lot of effort but it does work. If this information is within us then it is more than likely that an unconscious projection could occasionally involve a place, or person, that you have never seen in physical life, *if* it decided to.

Quite how this future element works within dreams is still a mystery, but what *is* certain is that *external* stimuli will also affect the dream content. A well known trick is to dip a finger belonging to a sleeping person into a cup of warm water for a short while before waking them up to discover that, in their dream, they were in the process of maybe swimming a length at the local pool, or struggling against someone who was trying to hold their head under water, etc.

External stimuli can work against projection at one phase and yet be an extremely *positive* factor during another, just the same as emotion can. Upon awakening, always try to recognise the effect of any external stimuli on your dream content. Some effects will be obvious to you and others will need to be brought to your attention before they can be correctly analysed. Purely by way of an illustration, imagine that for some peculiar reason you were to fall asleep in a lift. Every time the lift was activated, your dream content would probably involve the process of flying, or falling, in some shape or form.

Keeping that in mind, I have talked about the specific route that the etheric body takes when leaving the physical body. It will generally rise in a horizontal fashion and, still horizontal, glide to a region of your bedroom where there was some room to become upright in a standing position, or remain horizontal in a resting position, before becoming free of the catalepsy. This is a very common out-of-body etheric manoeuvre, rarely experienced at a conscious level, but this route needs to be thoroughly understood as it strongly affects our dream content and is an essential part of being able to comprehend the whole business of oobex. This type of out-of-body phenomena, for me, is the ultimate state to achieve *because* of its difficulty.

I have talked in depth about etheric projection so I am not going to go over old ground. Here we are discussing vivid dreams and so it is only important, at this stage, to realise the effect that *subconscious* etheric projection can have on an 'ordinary' dream. So now we have another process to look for when we awaken from our slumbers. Did any part of our dream contain a sequence where we were rising in the air and travelling forward, or falling, or floating, for example? See Figure 3, page 51. This could simply entail climbing a set of stairs and walking along a corridor, or taking off in an aeroplane and flying along. These two examples are common, and boring, but look hard at your dreams, the sequence can be very weird and can take some looking for.

In a dream, I recall trying to escape from something horrible that was after me, at one stage I was scrabbling up a steep railway embankment feeling the hot breath of my pursuer behind me and hearing the snapping of its jaws at my heels. I only just pulled myself up in time and I ran, ran with all my might along the road to put as much distance between me and 'it' as possible. Upon awakening, it is usual to be *very* relieved and thankful that this experience was 'only a dream' and it is purposely put out of your mind to be forgotten as quickly as possible. I am asking you to look at all your dreams, however distasteful or horrible and quickly analyse your movements. Look for the 'rising' factor, in my dream I was climbing the bank. Look for the 'forward' motions following the rise, mine was running along the road. They *are* there to be found if you look properly.

According to Freud, dreams of falling, flying and nightmares, have a sexual significance. *This is utter nonsense!* There is plenty of room for sexual significance and stimulation within the dream sphere without promoting this falsehood. I believe that this gentleman was over-

78

troubled by his sexual beliefs and has led, and is still leading, many students along a mistaken path. The immense good that has been generated by Freud is tempered by this sexual predominance. For this I have no explanation.

With these types of *ordinary* dreams we have no conscious control over the content. All we can do is try to induce them and *then* note what happens. Everything has a purpose, and the purpose of a vivid dream is to take us to stage one of obtaining an out-of-body projection while at the same time, it *may,* or may not, also be masking an unconscious spirit journey. What it does do is give us our first choice to say yes, or no, to further development. It is part of the *gradual* understanding of oobex phenomena.

A computer has pull down menus giving us a range of choices, we pick one and a further menu appears, we pick another, and so on until we have the screen that we desire. The steps to *enlightenment* are naturally arranged in much the same way, allowing any person gently, and safely, to understand the real spiritual nature of life, all life, for this is not confined only to the human animal.

So, where are the choices in a vivid dream? I can think of four choices that may appear on this 'menu'. Clicking on one of three options will get you through to the next important stage of out-of-body projection, but only if you wish it. If it is not for you then there is *always* the cancel button, the last option.

I will assume that you have just had a vivid dream, and you are lying there, upon awakening, quickly analysing the dream before it fades away into oblivion. The first things to note are the key points of the dream, where the likelihood of obtaining conscious awareness was possible. Some people advocate writing dreams down, I am not one of them. I think there are better things to do with your time. Come the day that we can plug our brains directly into a recording system and replay our dreams it really *will* be worth doing. Until then..... no.

We are all used to one scene moulding and transforming itself into another scene, within the dream environment. We are also used to having dreams that incorporate people that are famous, or are deceased, or are our friends and family. These are all very normal dream happenings. However, during your vivid dream, can you remember, at any time, visually accepting anything as normal, that during waking consciousness you would find incredible? The examples of this, alone, could fill a book. Animals talking to you, toothpaste coming out of a water tap, and so on.

These peculiar cameos only exist in a dream to enable you to have the opportunity of being able to realise that you are, indeed, dreaming. By regularly looking back over the content of the vivid dream, and recognising all the potential points of awareness, you will begin to programme yourself to become consciously aware of them as they happen during the dream itself. When you *do* become consciously aware that you are having a dream, then you will have successfully turned your *vivid* dream into a *lucid* dream. More on lucid dreams in a moment. This has been your first option.

The second thing to look for, in a vivid dream, is the mishap. If you really analyse the content of the dream while it is still fresh in your mind, you may well find that somewhere you missed your footing, or you had to really *struggle* to open a sticking door, or you dropped a drink, or you saw a child run too close to a sheer drop. Tripping up a kerb is a good one. Again, there are numerous examples of the little accident that we all accept as part of life.

These 'little mishaps' are another way of gaining consciousness during a dream. When any accident happens, even as small as these, we can heighten our normal awareness and become focused on that *particular* incident. But, we have a choice of either accepting the accident, and getting on with the dream, or realising that the accident happened at the right moment for consciousness to manifest itself and take full advantage. This is the second way for you to choose to turn your vivid dream into a lucid dream.

The third option that we have commonly existing in vivid dreams, is the big scare. Being chased by the monster, knives whistling past your ears, incredibly loud pounding on your back door, being run over by a train, tightrope walking across a very high suspension bridge and knowing that you are about to fall. You will, no doubt, have your own personal favourites! Yes, we are talking about the normal, happy, pleasant dream that for some reason turns into sheer terror, or what I will label, the common nightmare. The one thing we all try to do during a nightmare is get out and wake up!

A nightmare is the closest that we get to conscious awareness in a vivid dream. Our subconscious is really getting us by the throat and shaking the awareness into us. So much so that we actually wake up, thankful that we have, *and* worried about going back to sleep again. Certainly, nightmares are so vivid that they can easily be analysed afterwards. But, remember, it is not the nasty content that is important so much as the *movements* and the *sensations* that you felt during your ordeal. This is an extreme way of trying to attain dream awareness and rarely works, because of the severity. But having *had* the nightmare, you will be very wary, and worried, about going back to sleep again.

The positive aspect of all this is that it puts you into the correct state of mind needed to enjoy the disturbed sleep that is necessary for experiencing vivid dreams. Try to look at these nightmares objectively, and I have found that once you do this, and understand *why* you have the nightmares, they moderate themselves. They actually become part of your armoury for inducing out-of-body experience's. These are the three most common ways of obtaining dream consciousness.

I mentioned earlier about recognising the upward and forward movements in a dream, brought about by the external influence of the subconscious etheric body moving away from the physical body. Obviously, it follows that there will be a similar influence when this body returns to the physical. This *can* create a specific and recognisable nightmare, different to ones that we have already covered, where we seem to be powerless to save ourselves. This has been covered in depth when we talked about the etheric body, in all its mysterious glory.

You can see from this chapter, so far, that all these dream events are in existence purely to give you the choice of developing further your spiritual self, if you choose to. These are spiritual, 'mental' gates that can be opened, or left shut. They are not coincidences that just 'happen' to appear at the right time in dreams. The choice is there to be taken, when you have developed the control, the maturity, but most importantly the *courage* to deal with your inner self. This means coming to terms with the real you, not the facade we allow others, and in some cases, ourselves, to believe.

If you decide to pick up the gauntlet, you will not be disappointed, but it can be hard work for all of us that are not natural projectors, and I include myself as one of those. It took me very many years before I realised the structure of the process. I can honestly say that in my case the dawn of realisation often appears around noon! It is my sole intention to bring that enlightenment to you, to do with as you will. I hope it will mean that *somebody* will be able to make further progress into the shady areas!

Practise analysing your dream content in the way I have said and concentrate only on the *recognisable* points that could arouse consciousness. You will now realise the importance of one of the relaxation exercises that involves repeating to oneself 'I must become aware in my dreams'. This is a way of implanting the idea of light sleep, and dream awareness, into the subconscious mind to create the required stress before, and after, going to sleep. Another reason why I say you must read the whole book before you can realise how the complete picture fits together. That exercise appears in the next chapter as part of the relaxation programme and may appear a little silly, but put with something else it becomes important. Like a fuse is innocent without the bomb, but put together.....

Very shortly there will come the time when you realise that you *are* dreaming. The realisation may wake you up and if it does, you will kick yourself for not maintaining control, but keep trying. Alternatively, the realisation could very likely induce intense vibrations throughout your body, and in such a case all you need to do is, idly, wish to rise up. The rest will do itself and you may well find yourself projected. In which case you have just had the good fortune to hit the fast track to oobex.

Lastly, the realisation could give you the privilege of experiencing a *lucid* dream. Often confused, by many, as an out-of-body experience. Dream delusion can recreate personal environments *very* convincingly. Unfortunately, you have to experience a real out-of-body projection before you can admit that, up until now, your travels have only been in your dreams. But you *must* be honest with yourself.

Now, it is essential to be sure about the different types of dream that we are discussing. A *vivid* dream is one that is so real that it becomes a memory and can be reflected upon *after* awakening. It presents itself as an experience in which you play the major role but *cannot* control the proceedings. A *lucid* dream is also very real, but in this case you are *aware* that you are dreaming and can *influence* the content of the dream, if you decide to.

Let us now assume that by instilling the wish into the subconscious mind, you have gained awareness in your dream. You may not have any knowledge of what led up to this point, and it does not matter, for you are experiencing a lucid dream. One of the greatest pleasures possible is to have *control* in a dream. Your own imagination, from then on, is your only jailer.

If you can progress to the lucid dream state, then I believe that you *will* soon have a *real* out-of-body experience. The lucid dream is the launch pad for the spirit-body to release itself completely from the physical body. From this stage it is as easy as a little boy letting go of a balloon string and releasing the balloon. All you have to do is to realise how to let go of that string.

So, there are many choices as to what can be done whilst taking part in a lucid dream. If the dream is one that is pleasurable and fulfils your desires, then the chances are that you will not even think to alter anything that is occurring. This is normal practice and will be similar, in most ways, to a vivid dream. If, however, you *realise* that you have *conscious* control in the dream and wish to change things, you can, whilst still remaining in the dream environment. The temptation to remain in the most enjoyable dream that you have ever had, is sometimes stronger than the urge to project. In a lucid dream complete freedom can be irresistible, a commodity rarely savoured. This is of course another way of camouflaging and, therefore protecting, the *real* experience.

Supposing, in your dream, you became aware that you were back working for a company that, in reality, you hated working for and had left years before, under a cloud. In a lucid dream you would immediately realise that you should not be there and feeling self-conscious, you would quickly put your things together and sneak out before anybody catches you. We behave in these dreams very much as we would in real life, because that is how *real* they feel. Anything is possible in a dream, so we could have just as easily found the boss and wreaked our revenge in any appropriate way we thought fit!

Again, suppose you were to have a party and guests were arriving. There would be the general mishmash that would normally be there, but you could also have famous guests to make your party special. If you wanted the next person to come through the door to be Damon Hill, or Felicity Kendall then, with a little luck, that is whom you will get. Remember though, that this is still a dream environment, so you will still get people turning up that you did not invite, or even people that you *dislike*. It is funny though, for should you meet someone during a dream that you dislike in reality, they often appear more friendly and acceptable in a dream mode and you can find yourself changing your waking opinion of this person.

We have spoken a little about the special attributes of lucid dreaming. There are no achievement limitations within this wonderful state as long as you retain *control* of the dream. The options now are for your awareness to fade so that you slip back into the vivid, or even the normal non-memorable dream state. The other is to go on to have an out-of-body experience.

Do you remember the awareness points that we looked for during a vivid dream that enabled us to progress to a lucid dream? Well they are still here, but now they are easier to find, or to make up, and *certainly* easier to use. With conscious awareness we can make ourselves do anything we want, trip up things, have any kind of mishap, because we already know that we are dreaming. So why do we need to do these things to enable dream awareness when we already have it?

We have arrived at another vital point. Any kind of shock, mishap, or fear will induce a response from our emotional body. That tingle we feel, when scared, shocked, or when we listen to beautiful music for example, is the match that lights the fire. Any neural energy discharge, goosebumps, sadness, etc. will act as a primer to instigate a full vibrational 'rush'. More will be said about the tingle factor later.

If your lucid dream is fleeting, and you are not solidly in control of the dream, then one option open to you as soon as you are aware of consciousness appearing is to fall over, as you will learn to practise. Or, alternatively, induce the tingle by thought alone. What happens now is pretty much out of your control. You will either fail, have a very big fright and decide that life is too precious for this, or enjoy the amazing experience of existing *outside* of your physical body.

If your lucid dream is good and strong, and you find yourself firmly in control, then you have the time to *choose* and get your head around exactly what position it is that you are in. Your mental clarity will give you ability to realise that you are a participant in a dream and that you wish to project your spirit-body. In these cases I look for a suitable place to lie down, I lower my heartbeat, idly think of rising upwards, and I *induce* the vibrations. You could just as easily find the nearest window and throw yourself out of it, whatever suits you. In fact anything will do that really gives those vibrations a racing start. Fear will hold you back, or throw you forward depending on your personal control and understanding. Accept the fear, so that you are really frightened, but *understand* that you cannot be hurt by it.

Should you still fail to project yourself, don't worry, you will remain in control to try again. Remember the 'weaker' the physical body is, the more chance you have of projecting. So remain very calm, allow your heart to beat lighter and slower, and imagine that your abdomen holds a tiny puff of air and it is gently deflating. Repeat this so that even when you are *completely* relaxed you manage to find yet another tiny puff of air deep in your abdomen. It feels as though your solar plexus is giving a final sigh as it gives up the ghost......This is *so very important* that it can easily mean the difference between success and frustration.

I mentioned previously how external influences can affect and influence a dream. Now that you understand how these ordinary, vivid, and lucid dreams work, it is necessary for you to know that light (natural or artificial), and noise disturbance can elevate your dream state. This type of interference can turn an ordinary dream into a vivid, *or* a lucid dream. It can also turn a vivid dream *solely* into a lucid dream. It can even turn a lucid dream into a full-blown projection. If you gain the control to recognise the influence *as it is happening* without letting it wake you up, it will work to your advantage. If it does wake you up, you will stay calm and begin again to lessen the heartbeat, etc.

Chapter Six
Initial preparations

Preparation is the one most important factor, initially, in attaining the first recognisable sensations towards spirit projection, and the very first step in the preparation process is understanding the nature of the beast itself. So, in this chapter, not only have I explained a lengthy relaxation procedure that you can follow until you can successfully go 'solo', but I also explain *why* each procedure is necessary, and *what* is expected to be achieved by doing so. In this way I hope to convey the necessity of order, how the physical body should become entirely relaxed *before* relaxing the mind. In other words, this is not a willy-nilly relaxation process. Everything is done for a reason, and I will tell you *why* as I go.

Through my personal experiments, I have proved to myself, without a shadow of a doubt, that our mental attributes can become detached from our physical body. Clarity of mind is not diminished in any way, memory is not affected, sensations feel real, and we are very aware of what we have achieved. We know that we are projected away, and detached, from our physical bodies. However, we retain bodily substance, feeling as solid as we do on earth and equally solid are the new surroundings that we find when we are projected astrally. Movement, though, takes on a new, and very different, perspective.

I can only describe an oobex as a super-normal occurrence. One feels strangely 'at home', familiar, and at ease, in this environment. But it is losing the earthly attributes that make it so exciting. In this new world, some things are very different and must be experienced to be appreciated, like love without lust, lack of gravity, freedom from stress, freedom from pain, an altered perception of time and distance... I could go on! Of course, some people will go to a science museum and play, some will go to learn, and some will go to do both. You will do the same. For those that go to play, you will never be bored, and never want for more. For those that go to learn, remember that you only have the benefit of your physical body for a limited number of years, so you need to get a move on for the benefit of those that follow, and good luck to you.

Slowly, very slowly, I will now take you through the long, and sometimes difficult, process that you need to conquer. Things that you find irrelevant, *or* very important, will be the issues based on your present understanding. Please try to put this pre-knowledge away for the time being and read everything as having an equal importance. It is sometimes the blindingly obvious that is the most difficult to understand.

Everyone that settles themselves down at night, will go through subtle awareness changes as they move towards the attainment of the sleep state. For the vast majority of us, this is a wholly natural process to which we give little or no thought to, in fact the sooner we can get to sleep the better. And, yes, a good sound sleep pattern is one of the most beneficial promoters for maintaining a healthy body, and a calm state of mind.

To prepare for successful out-of-body projection we must, initially, sacrifice a certain amount of this healthy well-being. A sick, or unwell, person is more likely to achieve an oobex, than a healthy person, because their physical body is suffering a weakened condition. The balance of the body versus the mind has altered slightly in favour of the mind, therefore enhancing the possibility of success. In my own case I have found much success when physically weary, but mentally contented.

There is, of course, another, and far more likely reason for the, apparent, greater success rate of people that are bed-ridden to enjoy out-of-body experience's. When we are confined to bed for any reason, illness or idleness, we are obviously not using up any physical energy, and very little mental energy. Certainly not anywhere near enough to require the normal sleep quota that the body expects. The result of all this is that we are inclined to doze in and out of a very light sleep state, the same very light sleep state that we pass through, when going to sleep normally, and the same very light sleep state that we come out of every time we wake up normally. Part of this is otherwise known as the hypnogogic state, on entering sleep, and the hypnopompic state on emerging from sleep, and are, precisely, the same areas in which we find out-of-body phenomena occurring. These areas, along with others, are also utilised by 'mind therapists' to interface with the human subconscious mind during treatment.

As individuals, we all have varying sensations when entering sleep, from the 'I remember nothing, once my head has touched the pillow' to 'I just lay there and lay there until eventually I drop off.' Please note that here I am reflecting the habits of the majority of the population, and I am not including the very many people that experience other 'nasties', like sleeping problems, that will come later.

So, generally speaking, as we lay in bed, contemplating sleep, our full awareness gradually fades into a kind of daydream in which we might dwell on the happenings of the day or, perhaps, a book that we have read. At some stage, sooner or later, we drift into sleep and whether we have knowledge of it or not, our conscious mind always slips into this, dozing, state as a prerequisite of sleep, even if only for a micro second! It is this half-sleep, this daydreamy stage, that we have to learn to recognise, influence, control and extend, *especially* to create the balance between being aware and being asleep, but only up to a certain point. After that ..... well that comes later.

It is difficult to know what to call the projected body without upsetting someone somewhere, but as it is our essential 'spirit' that projects, irrelevant to where, and on what, we travel. I therefore propose to continue to call it a spirit-body or any other name that feels right for me to use, at the time. It then covers all types of projection, etheric, astral, and any others. I do recognise the likelihood that offence may be taken to this in some quarters, and I sincerely apologise, in advance, for any distress this may cause. My intentions and aims reach far beyond mere words and I suggest that if you do feel deeply opposed to the terminology used, within these pages, then I feel that perhaps your heart and mind are not yet sufficiently open to accept the true understanding that I am offering here.

It is possible to enjoy a 'seemingly' spontaneous projection without any preparation at all, in fact, most first projections, without instruction, are of this type. Not only is this very rare, but with analysis, it will commonly be found that some necessary prerequisites have already been satisfied on a subconscious level, prior to this apparent 'miracle' happening. I have, myself, had many projections on going to sleep, or in waking from slumber, without consciously making any preparations at all.

It is worth noting now, before we go too much further, that the smallest sentence read, and taken as having little importance, can on the third, fourth or even fifth reading, depending on your progress, suddenly impart a wealth of knowledge that opens up the next path of realisation and take you further to your goal. A little like a tiny key unlocking the door to a palace. It will seem like a revelation as this little piece of the jigsaw suddenly slots into position and, behold, a complete picture is formed. Likewise, it is common that some components will be forgotten once you have become involved in the excitement of participation, and will need to be revised.

Once you are fully aware of the whole process, and how it works, you will find that there will be times when you will not need to do a full wind-down to achieve results. You will learn to recognise what the inner sensations are. Conversely, there will be many times when you are really not in the mood, or you are stressed out, when the 'wind-down' process may have to be repeated, at least in part or, if necessary, abandoned completely.

If I explain the *maximum* that you have to do to be able to project the spirit-body, and you *will* need this initially, then as you progress, and develop your skills, you can omit the parts that are no longer needed. It is quite normal to find that some of the things that work well for one projector, at one time, will not work at all well at other times, so a certain amount of self experimentation is not only needed, but extremely beneficial.

Pre-relaxation preparation.

Some of the things that I ask you to do may seem a little strange until you have familiarised yourself with the rest of the book, by which time all will be explained. Try to practise these methods and accustom yourself to the various sensations so that they become *second nature* to you. For example, if you attempt a projection whilst having a perfectly normal dream, the chances are that it will be the subconscious mind that instigates the relevant sensation allowing you to have knowledge that you are dreaming and enabling you to attempt a projection. This last sentence will become perfectly clear, in due course.... I promise.

To influence the *subconscious* mind it is necessary to dwell upon the *whole* discipline of oobex, when the time allows. This means also during the daytime hours, and it is important to try and refrain from talking to other people about it as this *lessens* the effect by releasing the built-up tension. To keep this subconscious pressure built up inside just, purposefully, continue to inwardly think about the subject, bringing the *want*, the *need*, and the *desire* to project to the forefront of your existence. By not discussing the subject with anyone will help to keep the stress within yourself, where it must be restrained. Try to imagine what it must feel like to project, think about the way the spirit-body would feel as it separates from the physical, and what it must be like to have absolute freedom from the material body.

During the day we do many things without consciously thinking about it. Simple things like walking, for instance. This type of action is instigated by our subconscious mind and is accepted as a normal part of life. The projection of the spirit-body is worked in exactly the same way, *without* conscious involvement, and this is the knack. If your physical body is *not* incapacitated it may result in sleepwalking. If the physical body *is* incapacitated the result will be a projection.

At odd times, during the few hours prior to going to bed, repeat to yourself, mentally (or you'll get locked up!), 'I will project, I will leave my body' or 'I will become aware in my dreams' or other phrases to that effect. Try and build a tension in your conscious mind, during the day, so that there is a chance for it to permeate through, and into, the subconscious mind enough to keep it current *after* you have gone to sleep. How many times have you watched a film in the evening, and subsequently had a dream about it. This is what we are trying to achieve. Religious institutions chant and pray, often very repetitively, for exactly the same reason. Try to saturate your mind with the subject of oobex by making it such an integral part of your life that you even begin to have dreams about it.

There is a very important feeling that we all know very well, the feeling of 'someone walking over your grave'. The spine tingling sensation when you hear of bad news, a sad part in a movie, or when someone makes you jump in the dark. There are numerous times when we feel this sensation - how about when we get goosepimples in the freezing weather and the little hairs, all over our bodies, stand on end? We know that science adequately explains this function but what has not been previously understood is the interesting fact that our spirit 'selves' dwell within this nervous system of ours. We all feel our own spirit sensations in this way. As soon as you experience your first proper oobex you will completely understand the importance of this feeling, for it is the same sensation that you feel when you consciously project, although it will be magnified many times. Experience alone can be the only thing that proves my words. I, too, was sceptical until it actually happened.

Now, try to recreate this tingling sensation at will. Use whatever imagery, or thoughts you need to make this happen. With very little practise you will find that you can produce this feeling just by *wanting* to. Do not be fanatical about this, just gently get the hang of it, for once you have, it will always be with you to use when needed, and it *is* a tool to be used.

The energy that we use, every time we induce the tingle, I know as *neural energy,* for want of a more appropriate name. When we sleep, we replenish our store of neural energy and, as we go about our day to day lives, it is consumed, to a greater or lesser extent, and the amount of this usage directly affects the following nights' sleep. It is the need to replace the depleted neural energy that is the *main* reason that we need sleep. So, if you use up too much neural energy during the day, it can work against your attempts at oobex, for you will need to sleep long, and deep.

Sleep and survival, to the subconscious mind, usually takes precedent over a projection. Later you will learn that we, as projectors, utilise this very important tingle factor as a tool to 'kick start' an externalisation. It is necessary to learn how to reproduce it, but not to use it too much that it becomes detrimental to success. If you are a nervous type of person then you will already be using up a great deal of neural energy in your daily activities, and because of this you will be a good subject for out-of-body projection, because the kick-start mechanism is more readily apparent. The problem here, is that nervous people may worry *too* much about the peculiar effects of separation to allow themselves to proceed. There is a balance to be maintained, in every step of this process, and that balance has to be carefully recognised to ensure fulfilment.

I am now going to test your belief in my sanity! Pick your time, and place, very carefully - I want you to stand up and, in a discreet manner, try to lose your balance! Allow yourself to tip over, and fall in any direction that you wish, until you reach the point where it is still *just* possible to save yourself from falling. Please take great care that you don't actually fall! I hope that you will notice that, as you reach the point of no return, the neural energy sensation is felt quite strongly. Every time you fell the rush of this energy, say to yourself, *'astral projection'* or *'I will project.'* Do whatever you can to encourage this sensation to happen.

The whole point of doing this exercise is to become used to the feeling of falling, coupled with the accompanying 'electrical' tingle, and coupled with the association of out-of-body projection. If you realise that you are becoming conscious during a dream, it will either be a lucid dream, or an actual projection, and you must recognise which it is to take full advantage of what is being offered to you. It is most important that you retain your mental equilibrium in order to maintain the quality of the experience to progress the lucid dream, if that is what it is, and turn it into a conscious projection. To do this without over-taxing the mental state it is much easier to simply fall over. This, automatically, induces the tingle factor without any mental exertion at all. The rest of the externalisation is out of your control until, very quickly, you find yourself projected. But that is yet to come.

You must do this exercise often enough for it to become so commonplace that, when you feel the sensation, you will *immediately* think oobex. This is the method that I use to make the majority of my projections, for sure. So really associate coming out of your body with those tingling vibrations, and get it deep into your subconscious so that, from now on, they are inseparable and always there when you need it. Alas, many people experience lucid dreams and believe that they are having an oobex. They are nice, but not that nice!

When you realise that you are having a lucid dream, an experienced projector can, instead of falling over, find themselves a likely spot to lie down, nice and easy, and mentally induce the vibrations that will take them from the dream state to the projected state. Having a lucid dream is a cats' whisker away from having a full out-of-body experience, and it is relatively easy to achieve from this position. It is getting the lucid dream, initially, that is the problem.

Another reason for learning to get used to this falling sensation is so that it can automatically promote the flying mode, which is a marvellous way to travel when projected and is, incidentally, my personal favourite.

Among the many other reasons for constantly rereading this book is the focus it will give you, if read just prior to meditation. You can, of course, read any book that commands your attention by describing the sensations of height, flying, speed and so on. A book that accurately illustrates a method of out-of-body projection is best of all as it focuses the mind precisely on the subject in hand, and deters any troublesome and wayward thoughts from polluting your concentration.

If you are one of the many lucky people that have the power to visualise, as well as imagine, then use the two, in conjunction with each other, to maximise how you think an oobex would feel like, as you read these words. You will invariably be wrong but that does not matter at this stage. We have discussed the different ways that the spirit-body actually separates from the physical, some are gentle, some are very scary, initially all are strange. It is difficult to determine the kind of separation, that you are going to have, until it is too late. My advice to you is, be prepared for the most challenging, and you should be able to cope with all! Keep your mind *open*.

Let me give you a scenario. If I covered your eyes with a blindfold, and led you up a very long ladder into the dizzy heights of nowhere, I would expect you to be somewhat nervous. If I then asked you to leap off into the abyss, I would expect, well... refusal. But if I assured you that I had done this very same thing a hundred times, and your landing will always be so soft that you would come to no harm, I would expect you to trust me. After collecting enough courage to actually make the first jump, and proving to yourself that I *was* telling the truth, you would be very happy to jump again. Can you recognise how much the neural energy element is coming in to play here? Just like the first jump off the high board at a swimming pool - the first one is always the scariest. All the rest that follow, are pure exhilaration.

Some projection's can be exactly like this, they will catch you off guard and have you clinging to your mattress for dear life to save you from falling into the deep depths of nothingness. It took me many years to learn that I should relax and enjoy the fall, thereby allowing myself to pass through the 'doorway' into another world. A 'doorway', or 'gateway', is just a term that is used within this book to mean a specific point where a choice can be made. Usually it is the option of 'no thanks, life is too short!' or 'here goes ready or not, please Oh Lord, look after me!'

It is a general case that you should require the courage to do the opposite of what your instincts tell you to. That is where the progress lies. Now by opposite, I don't mean back the way you came, it doesn't work like that. Like a ball hitting a central pin, in a pinball machine, it can rebound in an infinite variety of angles. So it is the case with spirit separation, if you hit a crisis, like falling from a great height, you must rebound, into the abyss, and fly, or float, or hover, or anything else you can do *except* scare yourself senseless!

I do not expect you to succeed on your first attempt, but armed with my knowledge, I expect your development to be more rapid than mine was and, just as importantly, be able to recognise that progress.

So you have thought about oobex all day, you have repeated, and repeated, your wish to project, you have practised creating the body tingle at will, and you have done your falling over exercises. Make sure that you go to bed tired, but slightly earlier than normal to make up for the amount of disturbed sleep you may experience.

Try to go to sleep in your usual way, but allow your *idle* thoughts to be centred on waking up at a certain time. As a guide, I regularly wake up about four hours earlier than I have to get up. So, yes, we are talking very early morning indeed! To begin with it might be justifiable to use an alarm clock until your body adjusts to waking up at this regular time. You will find that this takes very little time to become used to and very soon you will find that it will happen automatically and without any effort at all.

I must include a general note here about being woken up by an alarm clock. We all sleep in cycles that vary in depth. In the deep part of the cycle we are physically aware of very little compared to the shallow part of the cycle when we can be woken easily. We all know the horrible feeling when the alarm clock goes off to jar us out of a deep sleep, and as a result we often continue to feel tired well into the following day. A good tip is to set your own internal alarm clock, in your head, to go off five minutes before you have set your real clock. If your alarm is set for 7am then say to yourself 'I will wake up at 6.55am,' or 'I will wake up five minutes before my alarm goes off.' If your internal clock does not wake you up then the real one will, but what you have done is to set your sleep cycle to be at its shallowest for awakening.

If I find myself awake in the early hours of the morning, I can get up do some work for an hour or so, and then go back to bed without feeling any ill effects the following day, because it has happened *naturally*. I find that when my partner has to get up early to go to work, and we are awoken by the alarm, I feel wretched for all the following morning, because it caught me at a deep part of my cycle. So I experimented with setting my own internal clock and found to my delight, that it automatically adjusted my sleep cycle to be in accordance with the waking time. Through this I also discovered that there are other internal settings that can be utilised for out-of-body projection, and I will come on to these later.

When you prepare for sleep, and you have confidence that you *are* going to wake up at the pre-arranged time, then you can allow your *idle* thoughts to dwell, calmly, on feeling lighter, and floating with any kind of upward movement, in fact, any movement in general. But try not to use any effort in doing this because it is not necessary, and it could be detrimental to a good sleep.

The situation that we are trying to accomplish is one in which an adequate sleep can be enjoyed, so that your physical body, and all its component parts, are rested and running slowly. When you awaken, at this pre-arranged time, your heartbeat will be slow, your breathing will be shallow, your organs will be rested. The digestive system will have processed the majority of matter, and is settled. Importantly, you will still be tired enough to be able to go back to sleep again. Mentally, you will also be calm and content with the sleep already gained, and this has provided a break from yesterdays' problems and pressures.

Once you have woken up, you may wish to go to the toilet, or go and make a cup of tea, and this *is* allowed as long as it is done in a calm, contemplative kind of way. It is necessary to clear the dream state from your head. If you don't wake up properly, the dream state will remain too dominant and will quickly overwhelm you when you go back to sleep.

So, allow yourself to wake up, and stay awake for approximately an hour, or so, before returning to bed. Whilst you are up, *put a bright light on*, and become *fully awake*, but remain bodily calm. Make the most of this time by reading about oobex, revising the relaxation procedure, drink your tea and induce the tingle factor. Make sure that *only* oobex related topics are concentrated on during this hour of preparation. The golden rule is desire, desire, desire! Do this in a calm contented way, the subconscious mind will want to appease this desire as soon as the conditions are right. You will now be in the correct frame of mind to attempt an out-of-body projection, on returning to bed.

It is always more difficult if you sleep with a partner, as one sniff, snort, snore or movement, at the wrong time, can spell disaster. This is especially so if your projected body has not made enough distance away from your physical body. With time, however, confidence overcomes this hurdle to a great extent.

Keeping the concentration focused, during relaxation, is another problem to overcome and one must learn to be patient with partners. It goes without saying that if you do sleep on your own, or get the opportunity of sleeping on your own, then it is worth making the most of these times to attempt projection. It is also very important to have the inner safety, and security, that sometimes is not possible with company.

Finally, take five very deep gentle intakes of breath, in such a way that your lower abdomen expands on the in-breath. Hold each one for three seconds before slowly exhaling and feel *every part* of your inner body relax as you slowly exhale. This puts oxygen into your bloodstream and allows you to breathe in a shallow manner. It also lessens the strain on the spirit cable. All you have to do now is to fill your mind with expectation and go back to bed!

Chapter Seven
The relaxation process

Imagination is an important tool that we use to prime the various stages that are necessary to promote oobex. We use it to visualise and feel, mentally, how we *think* something should feel like. However, once an external projection has been made, imagination is not present in any greater capacity than is normal during the waking state.

Make sure that the position you are in is as comfortable as possible and it is preferable for you to be on your back, at least to begin with. The majority of my projections have occurred whilst I have been lying on my back or left side. I strongly advise the initiate to persevere with the back position until further knowledge is gained. It is quite acceptable to complete the relaxation procedure in this position, and *then* turn onto your side when you are ready to go to sleep, but only if you *really* have to. Resting on your back actually becomes more comfortable as relaxation increases, until eventually all physical feeling virtually disappears, and *completely* disappears during a projection, although you retain knowledge of your *actual* whereabouts.

If you really cannot lie on your back, do not despair, just pick whichever side is the most comfortable and continue accordingly. For many reasons that include safety, and because of the direction the spirit takes when leaving the physical body, I strongly advise *against* lying on your stomach. It is not important which side of the bed you sleep on, in relation to which way you face when sleeping. Your spirit-body is already well used to the position in which you sleep, and is very familiar with the configuration that makes up the inside of your bedroom.

Now, just to set the scene, *imagine* that you are as light as possible, perhaps suspended under a balloon, and on the verge of floating away. I want you to envisage that your body has, instead of a skin, a hard shell, light like an egg shell, and like an egg shell, *not* pliable. Pretend that this shell, the same shape and dimension of your physical body, lifts itself up in the air to a height of three or four feet. Believe that your consciousness is within this shell body, and that you are leaving your material body behind you on the bed.

Now envisage yourself slowly moving, horizontally, down to the bottom of your bed, and if there is room, pretend to upright yourself into the standing position onto your bedroom floor. If there is no room at the foot of your bed to do this, then *pretend* that your horizontal shell swivels to one side of your bed, before uprighting yourself, once again, to a standing position onto the floor.

Now believe that your shell softens and changes back into a mobile body so that you are able to walk around your room. Continue this *fantasy* by wondering what your material body looks like lying in bed. Use this imaginary body from the other side of your room to have a good look around the rest of the area to visualise as much as you can, just as if you were *really* using the eyes of this phantom body. Pretend that you are *actually* existing in the ether and how exciting it is to travel whilst invisible. Study objects at close range, really use your *imagination* to the extreme.

Once you have done this bring your 'imagined' body back to your physical body, lying in bed, in exactly the same way that you left it. This is another very important exercise to learn, and practise, as this is the path the etheric body takes to leave the material body. Usually, this is done while consciousness is *not* present and is a very common occurrence if we did but know. I have already differentiated between the types of projection in another chapter, and even though this relates to etheric projection, it is *important* to familiarise yourself with this sequence.

The foregoing explanation is a typical example of a spirit loosening exercise. I often extend this routine by *pretending* to wander around the house, picking on things that I would not normally look at and imagining that I am studying it. Frequently I will go outside and walk up and down the road, taking off and imagining that I am able to fly a circuit around the church spire a couple of times. I even feel the air rushing past my ears with a real sense of movement, before returning to my bed. There are some, so called experts, that actually teach other's to do this exercise in the belief that, with repetition, eventually a spirit-body is *created*! This is nonsense. All this really does is influence the subconscious mind into believing that spirit projection is a perfectly normal thing to do, so it is an important exercise in that respect.

There will be other spirit loosening exercises to do as we progress through this ultra important phase of relaxation. If any exercise leaves you mentally tired with the strain of the concentration, then you are concentrating too hard. This is supposed to be *relaxing*, so simply take time to dwell on each phase. All the time feel lightness, height and movement.

While you are lying on your bed, feeling light and relaxed, allow your mind to dwell on relaxing *every* muscle in turn, starting at the feet, and working your way up to the shoulders, down each arm, down the spine to your bottom, back up to your neck, and through to all those fine facial muscles in your head. Spend a little longer on these facial muscles, really relaxing the eyes, temples, cheeks and ears.

Do not physically tense these muscles just *imagine* that they are relaxing like melting snow, gently and easily.

I now want you to imagine that the inside of your body is hollow..... yes hollow, just as though you are an empty egg shell. I want you to imagine that there is a ball, the size of a table tennis ball and it is resting at the bottom of one of your feet. I want you to *imagine* that this ball is going to spiral itself, in either a clockwise or counter-clockwise direction, up the inside of each leg in turn. *Imagine* that you can actually feel the progress of the ball. Round and round as it slowly travels up towards the groin. When it reaches the top, start all over again with the other foot.

Once both legs have been done, allow this ball to spiral its way slowly upward, around the inside of the pelvis, abdomen, and up around the inside of the chest cavity to the neck. This activity may, or may not be accompanied by the tingle sensation, and you might well find that the direction that the ball spirals in, will change from time to time.

Continue this exercise for each arm, in turn, before allowing the ball to wind its way up around the inside of the neck and into the head area. Just let this process come to completion at the very top of your scalp, if you can. There is a build up of pressure that goes before the ball and this, sometimes, will not allow you to complete the head stage.

I sometimes substitute this exercise by imagining that I am hollow and I am slowly filling up with water. On top of the water is a float and as I am filling up it nudges various parts of the inner wall of my body as it gently rises. Either of these exercises is fine, as long as you do one of them. Go as far as you can with these relaxation exercises, but bear in mind that proficiency comes with,familiarity, and practise.

During either of these last two exercises, especially towards the end, the tingle factor can become a major sensation to be observed. It may be very strong, it may not be there at all, but whatever you are feeling, continue with the spiralling ball, only this time make the ball much bigger and make it swiftly encircle the *outside* of your body. Again, work upwards from the feet and allow the ball to spiral around both your legs at the same time. Continue upwards around your chest area, fully encompassing your arms, before finally ending up over your head to finish.

As a substitute for this exercise you can imagine a stream of hula hoops slowly moving up and over your body with you in the centre. Remember that the tingle sensation is, if present, simply *you* feeling the vibration of your own spirit-body. Remember not to spend too long on each exercise otherwise you will be there all night!

If everything has gone according to plan, you should already be feeling a deep sense of calmness and relaxation. Whatever sensations come along it is important to let them happen, go with it and do not worry, this is all to the good. Let these feelings happen naturally, for this is the 'real you' in existence.

I must give most of the credit for this next *excellent* procedure to Sylvan Muldoon, for it has stood me in good stead for many years now. You need to give your attention to your heart, begin by recognising how *fast* it is beating and *where* you can feel it beating. With a little effort you will find that you can feel your heartbeat in any part of the body you desire. I always begin by feeling my heart rate in my solar plexus area, just below where the ribs divide. It is always the area that, for me, feels tense and is in need of extra relaxation. After a few moments of consciously relaxing this area, the heartbeat becomes clear and settled, but wait until the surrounding area feels 'at ease'. It is worth spending time on tricky areas to attain a clear heartbeat to ensure the best quality relaxation possible.

Now go down to the lower pelvic area and feel your heart beating there. At times it is also possible to actually hear the heart beating inside your body. Next, go to your right thigh, on downwards to your right knee, onwards to your calf, then down to your ankles, and eventually to your feet, finishing in your toes. Spend a few moments at each location, until the heartbeat is clear and strong, before moving on to the next spot.

Do exactly the same exercise for the other leg, before transferring your concentration to an easier location, the neck. The heartbeat is usually felt very readily here. Now do the same for your right shoulder, your right elbow and your right hand. Next, do precisely the same operation for the left arm.

Finally, feel your heart beat in your head, beginning with your chin, behind your nose, just above your eyes, at the very top of your scalp, on the inside of your ears and, lastly, at the back of the head slightly above where the top of the back bone meets the skull. This is the point where the spirit cable is normally attached to the spirit-body and can be felt during a projection. In my case, I have *never* felt it anywhere else. The sensation that you are feeling now, of the heart beating in this region, feels very similar to when you are projected during an actual out-of-body experience.

Allow yourself to return your heart to its rightful position, back in your chest, and think about the rate that it is beating. Also feel how strong each beat is. Muldoon suggests that it is necessary to slow the heartbeat down to aid incapacity. I certainly agree, but he also said that it is quite an easy thing to do. I disagree! For me, I allow my heart to slow down naturally during a sleep period, to a degree where it is suitable for projection. A better, and more effective, alternative for all of us that has a similar problem with slowing the beat down, is to lessen the *strength* of the beat, as it has the *same* outcome.

By concentrating on slowing, and lowering, of the heartbeat it can either slow down, *or* become fainter. To achieve either state, it is necessary to tune in to the rate of the thump-thump and consciously hold it back. I often imagine that I am walking through deep water with each step taken in time to the beat. Because it is a struggle to walk through the water it acts as an anchor to gradually slow the beat. Try it, it works for me.

As I am already in a calm state of relaxation, my heartbeat grows fainter. My physical body is so calm that my heart does not need to work as hard and the desired result has been achieved, which is a heartbeat that is almost imperceptible. This exercise is one of the *most* promotive facets of oobex meditation.

Whenever you wake up *always* reduce your heart rate as a first task, without even thinking about it to make this an automatic process. This has the effect of slowing the function of all organs and body systems, so if the idea of movement flickers across the subconscious mind, your physical body will *not* be in a position to instantly respond.

I am assuming that you are still awake at this point! If you are thinking that these exercises are too long winded and unnecessary, I must tell you that a double effect is produced. One is to *profoundly* relax the physical body to such a state that it *safely* maintains existence just within the borders of life, similar to hibernation in other animals. The second function takes advantage of you having to mentally concentrate on remembering the next relaxation exercise.

This allows you to maintain awareness much deeper, and nearer, to the sleep state. The longer you can hold off sleep the more you will have knowledge of certain effects, and processes, that happen as you get nearer to the hypnogogic threshold. This is not always easy, but then oobex is not an easy thing to master.

Somewhere along this process, if it has not already happened, be prepared for a slight sensation of being elevated, just a little floating sensation that happens every night, and quite naturally to us all. For most people, this slight discoincidence happens a little after we have altered our awareness state and we are already, effectively, asleep. We, therefore, can go all our lives without even knowing that it happens, quite understandable then that we also do not know *why* it happens. To some people, of course, it is a commonplace occurrence and does not warrant further investigation. It can be very subtle but definitely noticeable, so look for it. If you have not noticed this feeling before, it can also be quite frightening, but only for the first couple of times, until you are used to it. The sensation felt by this is nothing, however, compared to what will be felt later! This slight separation is the first sign to us of the method used by the spirit-body to recharge itself during the sleeping hours. We need do nothing but observe this as a *positive* sign that we are relaxing correctly. I have explained this in detail, in another part of this book, so it is not necessary to dwell further upon this subject now.

We are now going to do some more exercises. I want you, while you are so relaxed, peaceful, calm and free of pain, to continue to loosen your spirit-body. It is purely your mental self that I am dealing with now, as you will not be in touch with your physical form at all. In an automobile there is a clutch that, when depressed, disconnects the engine from the gearbox, these exercises enable you to, in effect, depress the body clutch to disconnect the physical mass from the mental controller. Concentrating so much on staying awake, while allowing the physical to relax, often means that you can end up being *too* mentally alert. If this is the case, then it is worth letting your concentration relax a *little* during the following routines. Contrary to the above, I am still assuming that you are awake.

Mentally set your mind onto the absolute *need* to project, the fact that you *must* project, how *important* it is, and how *pleasurable* and *exciting* it would be. Saturate your mind only with the thoughts of undergoing a projection and tell yourself that it will happen this time. But even if it doesn't, you are spending your time in training for the time when it *will definitely happen*, and it *will* definitely happen.

If you find yourself dreaming about out-of-body phenomena then you can take this a sign that your subconscious mind has successfully taken onboard your desires. Similarly, if *each and every time* you awaken, the first and *only* thing on your mind is projection, you will be near to success.

It will, undoubtedly, take a few trials before results are attained, so it is necessary to view your first attempts as practise runs and, in reality, that is exactly what they are. This process involves as much a subconscious adjustment as a conscious effort. The driving force must be the promise of eventually enjoying the ultimate experience that can ever be accomplished this side of the after-world. So never regret the failures, it is partly because of the elusive nature of the subject that makes it all the more fantastic when it eventually becomes a precious part of your individual life.

The physical equivalent of a spirit loosening exercise would be spinning oneself around and around until you get that giddy feeling. Also the feeling that one gets when first on board ship, before you become accustomed to the swell. I must say that I used to suffer with travel sickness, as a child, and I certainly can still recollect that same feeling when I am carrying out this particular spirit loosening exercise.

I will talk you through this as carefully and as accurately as I can, exactly as I feel when it happens to me. I am, in my mind, a mental entity, my body being detached and separate. I am a mental 'thing'. I *imagine* that I am gently rocking, as a ship would, but bow to stern. Head and shoulders go up as my legs and feet go down, head and shoulders go down as my legs and feet go up and so on, but *gently*. This feels similar to being on a playground swing, suspended from a pivot located above my body centre.

Now imagine that the rocking becomes, not faster, but more exaggerated, until eventually you rock so far round that you do a complete 360 degree turn. You imagine that you have ended up at the same place that you started from. Now that you have done it once, continue until you can do the full circle continuously, and do so for about a dozen times, depending on how pleasant, or unpleasant, you find the feeling.

I want you to now to do it all over again, but this time I want you to rock, in a swinging motion, from side to side. Exactly as you would if you were lying in a hammock. In fact, it is a good thing to imagine that your bed has become a hammock, and you are gently swaying, side to side, on the perfect halcyon day. As before, work at getting the swing to go further, and further, until eventually you can swing all the way over and back to where you started. Keep this momentum going if you can, or start again, but please do complete several loops before going on to the next phase.

Having now attained the necessary ability to swing full circle in both sideways and lengthways, I want you to be able to do complete 360 degree loops in *any* direction. So, you should now be able to do a full loop in whatever direction that takes your fancy. Really, it is somewhat like being on the inside of a slippery ball, with your consciousness facing towards the centre, and your back against the inside wall of the ball. You can loop-the-loop in *any* conceivable direction, head first, feet first, whatever. Really experiment in gaining the ability to swing complete loops, again and again, to really lose the feeling of lying in bed. You are a mental entity that is now mobile enough to move, at the slightest willing, in any possible direction that can be thought of. If you are feeling seasick then please stop before it becomes a problem to you. I used to get the same feeling following a fairground ride, but oobex has cured me of that, along with my fear of heights!

Now is the time to really instigate the vibrations, these are the vibrations that we previously called the tingle factor. When we now bring on the tingling sensations, having achieved a very deep state of relaxation, they quickly turn into intense vibrations that are of a finer, and higher frequency than the slow, courser tingles, that we previously felt. They will also be felt very deeply, and very powerfully within your very being. Allow yourself to feel these strong vibrations by inducing the tingle factor, and by letting the feelings flow all over your body. Be sure to keep all tension from your mind, and direct these vibrations so that they run the full length of your body, and back to your head, *if* it isn't happening already. It is now that you will notice that all aches and pains, in fact, all feeling is leaving your physical body. For people with chronic backache, as I have, this is a blessing, and a therapy of its own. All of you that have previously found it uncomfortable to lie on your back, please persevere at least to this point, and see if you feel the same.

If you have trouble inducing these powerful vibrations, mentally search the *surface* of your body and find the 'pockets' of sensation. As you did before, let these

112

regional sensations grow and spread over the rest of your body, and *then* induce your vibrations.

Having achieved this 'disconnection' of the senses, you will feel that your mind is pretty much in isolation from your physical body, and you are ready for a projection - if it has not already happened.

The reason I say, if it has not already happened, is because some of you will not have needed to do all these preliminary exercises, and at some previous stage will have lost consciousness. But not all is lost, far from it, for you can go to sleep at any stage, and *still* be successful, as you will see from my practical records. Everybody *has* to lose consciousness prior to a projection anyway. Some say that they have achieved an oobex whilst remaining entirely conscious from start to finish, but this is not my experience. Even if only for a micro-second, consciousness appears to fade prior to gaining full awareness in an oobex.

If you were to go no further on than this, you will have learned a very effective, and powerful relaxation technique. The point that you are at, at the moment, is also ideal for autosuggestion, listening to hypnosis tapes or learning tapes, etc. Not to mention a considerable aid in pain management. But it is oobex that currently concerns us here.

All these exercises are designed to create the right mental conditions but may, on some occasions, need to be done twice, or even three times. At other times, and with experience, they may not *all* be necessary as so many factors are involved in influencing a successful projection.

The real answer, to being a successful projector, is to do all the exercises, every night. Have it cemented in your head that you will do this religiously, a little like saying prayers, every single time you go to bed. Do this, whatever the time, however tired you are, however ill you feel, and however drunk you are, etc. Projections often manifest themselves when you least expect them to, and may appear only once you have learned to give up *consciously* trying, giving your subconscious a free rein at last. These exercises should take between 20 and 40 minutes, as long as there aren't any interruptions, like sleep!

Remember, oxygen in the bloodstream will give you shallower breathing and a lighter heartbeat. This is as far away from an emotional condition as we can be. Emotion means excitement, a faster heart rate and heavier breathing. Emotion will stop you projecting or bring you back.

So, always lessen the heartbeat, and think height and lightness, *every* time you awaken during the night. But, remember to *try* not to move whilst doing this. If you physically move this may destroy the conditions that have been obtained, and you will have to backtrack. Lastly, always dwell for a few moments, as you awaken in the morning, on the events of the night, experience's, dreams and all, to see if you can recognise some of the issues referred to in this book.

Try, if you have a chance of projecting during the day, to make the most of the times when you *naturally* feel tired, mid-afternoon is quite common. It is to your advantage to experiment with these opportunities as often as you can. Your body does not want a deep sleep at these times, it only wishes to dose, making this a brilliant time to try for an oobex.

The final thing to do before sleep comes on is to again use your *imagination* to promote an oobex. I want you to *pretend* to be bored about an action that others would find exciting, like a pilot who spends everyday flying and has become sick of it. What you choose is up to you, but pick something that you will enjoy and find pleasurable. So, with this state of mind, imagine that you are flying, tobogganing, skiing, driving a car, racing, horse riding, fairground riding, or *whatever* suits you and incorporates *movement*. It could be something you used to enjoy as a child, it doesn't really matter. The activity you choose doesn't have to incorporate height, but *if* it does then all the better. The important thing is that you get the movement *without* the conscious excitement, although it could be an exciting activity *if* you weren't so bored with it. Once you have lost consciousness, and your subconscious has taken over the activity, in maybe another form, it is more likely that something will happen to make you scared, or aware. This your chance to put into practice what you have learned so far.

Try and incorporate *all* these disciplines into your individual lifestyle so that they suit you as much as possible. This will help lessen the possibility of failure, and you will never know how close you have become to success until success itself has been achieved.

When you return from an oobex, you will be a changed person, and I will not go into totally what that means because I have no words to describe how it affects your whole thinking. Needless to say, you will also have a calm and easy feeling. This is the time to dwell on what you have experienced, and you must have this time.

On occasions, and they are rare, your physical body may still be in a cataleptic condition *after* you have returned. When this happens, don't worry, take your moment to dwell on your projection and, if you have the time, simply slip back into sleep. The next time you awaken you will be back to normal. If you don't have the time, concentrate all your efforts on moving a very small part of your anatomy, like running your tongue along the back of your teeth, wiggling a finger, that sort of thing. Once the feeling comes back it will spread throughout the rest of your body quickly.

When all this has happened to you it is understandable that you will want to rush and tell someone. Do *not* leap out of bed immediately following a projection, because your physical body is not running at normal levels, and it may make you feel very ill. Gently arise and allow your body time to readjust.

Feel the goodness of the air, oxygenating your bloodstream every time you breathe in, and feel your whole self internally relaxing with every gentle out-breath. Be aware of this action happening, and try to promote all relaxation in your life as far as you can.

Chapter Eight
Practical records

My own natural way of projection seems to go like this - I complete a cut-down version of the relaxation procedure, when I *first* go to sleep. I then awaken at the pre-set time, in the early hours of the morning, when I arise and make myself a cup of tea, which I drink while reading and dwelling on oobex.

After about an hour I go back to bed and carry out a full relaxation procedure and, finally, allow myself to go to sleep. I will then reawaken, at some stage, in a very sleepy condition but with my mind aware that I am ready to project. I then calm myself, slow down my heartbeat, and allow my very insides to 'give in' with a gentle sigh.

For the majority of times this will be enough to induce the head thumping and the massive vibrations, as you have never felt before. Sometimes you may even hear a conversation somewhere, or hear your own name being called. If these things happen for you, then you can expect to automatically project, in fact, you may not be able to stop yourself. If these things happen to you, but you do not project, it will be because the vibrations were not strong enough, or the desire within your subconscious mind was not strong enough.

If your subconscious mind has the 'will' to allow you to project, and your physical body is relaxed enough, then, and only then, do you have the possibility of projecting. However, if all these things do happen to you then, whether you project or not, you can take comfort in the fact that you have successfully reached the launch pad, and sooner or later a projection *will* happen. Also, it is likely that you may now experience lucid dreams, and get another bite of the cherry.

Many people that reawaken, following the relaxation procedure, will do so already projected in their astral body, so it is a good idea to check first to see if you are one of those lucky folk. The easy way of doing this is, without effort (I often use the word 'idly'), try and twist the upper half of your body, or try to raise an arm, do this very, *very* gently. It will be obvious if the physical body remains in its original position and you don't, or if the physical body gives resistance and nothing happens. So try it first and see.

SUNDAY 26TH FEBRUARY 1995

As with the majority of projections I am alone in bed, and this morning I am trying out a revised system that might allow my spirit to leave my physical body more efficiently, always optimistic that it will be etheric but always expecting, and happy, with astral. I am experimenting with using excessive amounts of neural energy during the pre-relaxation, and relaxation periods.

My thinking is that the spirit-body leaves the physical body in order to recoup neural energy that has been lost during the day, or at least, during waking hours. So if I use more neural energy than normal, it follows that the spirit-body will be wanting to discoincide as soon as possible, and it will separate further to recharge at a greater rate, all aids in promoting an oobex.

The deepest part of sleep, in the bowl of the spoon, will be deeper, and because the spirit-body is going deeper and further away, at this stage, it should follow that it will also be inclined to go further later, when I positively induce separation.

I have said that nervous people are more inclined to have troubled sleep, because they use up more neural energy during their waking times. Nervous energy is the same as fear energy, and will be used up very quickly if, for example, you have an exciting day at a fun park on the rides, or you believe that someone is following you, or your job demands reflex actions. Anything where you 'live on your nerves' will use up greater amounts of this precious stuff.

One additional factor that must be taken into account is that the controlling mind will make allowances for any changes in your routine, or lifestyle, within days, so you must make the most of any inspirational changes by spreading them out over a period of time. It is too easy to say that something worked initially, but now it doesn't seem to, and disregard it as unhelpful. This couldn't be further from the truth. It is a fact that you have to keep the process stimulated or it will all revert back to nothing. Playing 'cat and mouse' with your own mind is a strange game.

This morning I managed to have a good five hours sleep. During the day I consciously used up neural energy by instilling a sad feeling, pretending to fall over, remembering loved ones that had passed away, anything to make that tingle happen. During the relaxation period, following sleep, I really overdosed on the tingle factor, just to see what effect it would have, if any.

I became aware that I had been asleep and was now in the throws of awakening. I quietly relaxed my insides and slowed my heartbeat down. It is already slow at this stage, so I am only talking about fine tuning, I am not affecting anything drastically.

The vibrations hit me hard, and with great power, greater each time than I ever quite remember. The pressure seems to be concentrated mainly behind my nose, and in

119

behind my ears. Suddenly, my inner 'being' ripped itself away and I lost all adhesion, and became weightless. I tumbled, and tumbled, cartwheeling out of my body, with a distinct feeling of what it must be like to be blown about hither thither in the wind, with no obvious control.

I found myself standing beside a road, in a residential area, surrounded by an array of fairly nondescript houses. I approached the first house that was nearest to me and gently pushed myself against, and through, the fabric of the front door. Immediately I came across a glass panelled inner door that I dealt with in the same fashion. Walking down the hall passageway I noticed a lady in the kitchen, so I made my way up to her and tried to speak. She turned away from me, and I tried to speak to her again, but she seemed unaware of my presence. I felt the usual feeling of not knowing quite if I should be there or not, so I decided to leave the woman alone, and make my way outside. I left the building the same way as I had entered, however as I passed through the front door the power to concentrate left me and I found myself back in bed.

There are many projection's similar to this, and they can become quite boring, in their content, to you the reader, so I will only give examples where there is something to be learned. Here, for instance, I used up a lot more neural energy, prior to projection, as an experiment to see if it aided projection. It may very well have done so, as the projection was successfully accomplished, but we must be careful not to believe that it was this influence alone, it may have been a coincidence, or a contributing factor. The important thing is that it happened at all. It is interesting to note that the lady was either unaware of my presence, or didn't want to acknowledge me. This is quite unusual for astral projection.

Your astral locale is influenced by your physical life experience's, like it or not. This is for the very good reason of comfort and acceptability. I, more often than not, find myself projected to an estate of houses, or sometimes to an architecturally interesting building, all because of my years as a professional architectural illustrator. I have drawn thousands of houses, over a very long period of time, and this is an influence in my own particular astral environment.

It is very easy to look back over a projection and say, 'Why didn't you fly to the Empire State building, or Buckingham Palace?' 'Why did you waste a good oobex by walking into a strangers house, and walking back out again?' I completely agree, and these are things that I, also, say to myself. The fact is that it takes many failures before you achieve a successful oobex, and when it does happen it can take you a little by surprise. Once projected, your perceptions and priorities alter in subtle ways. What seems important, or interesting, during the normal waking hours, can hold no attraction in your astral world. Also, it is better to explore what you *have* in the hope of prolonging the projection as much as possible, then to try something spectacular and risk an early bath! A bird in the hand, etc.

The sexual act becomes unimportant, for that is a basic, *physical*, animal urge, and only exists to allow us to multiply our own human kind. It is love, and intimacy, that is the real pleasure, and can be found in abundance, in the astral world.

Likewise, our daily problems with finances, our employment problems and so on, all fade out of existence. We are left feeling the same as we do here, in our physical bodies, but without any pain or stress. As far as going into someone else's house is concerned, it appears to be acceptable behaviour, in the main, as long as your conscience thinks fit. But the only real reason for wanting to

121

go into that unknown house, is because you can. And you 'can' do whatever you like. There always exists a curiosity about who lives there, and the amazing reality that, whichever house you pick, holds a person, or family, going about their business.... can this all be only in the mind?

The ability to pass through seemingly solid objects and being nosy is very powerful and is one of the most enjoyable parts of this astral projecting business. But, like the employees of the chocolate factory, you are allowed to eat all you possibly can because it is known that you will eventually become fed up with it, so the practice itself becomes self-controlled.

The initial feeling, once projected, is just how normal you are. The scenery is also very normal, so normal, in fact, that you do not immediately consider the possibility of flying to another location. It would be similar to you saying 'Hold on a second, I'll just put this book down, for a moment, and fly to Spain, or Uruguay!' It doesn't occur to you to do so, until you have done it many times and make a conscious effort to do so. Even then, it is a case of controlling your emotions to avoid an early return, so simply walking into a house, and exploring, is quite a safe and natural thing to do and surprisingly pleasurable.

If this system, of over-using neural energy, proves to be reliable then I hope to have more control in producing projections at will. This has been the very first projection of the year, so you can see that the gaps between excursions can be extensive, and as such it is important to note any possible improvements that can possibly aid regular success.

TUESDAY 28TH FEBRUARY 1995

Two days following my last projection, I have been successful with another. I am still using the discharge of neural energy to aid projection, exactly as I did before, during all phases of priming the spirit-body. I am hopeful that this is the primary cause of two astral outings in quick succession.

On becoming aware, I found myself in a cataleptic condition, my very self was being exteriorised, interiorised, exteriorised, etc. I was also experiencing a massive electrifying buzz as I was going through the process of leaving my physical body. This 'in-between' stage continued for a time, elongated because my conscious mind kept taking an interest in what was happening, which slows the exiting process down. Eventually it became obvious that I was too aware for my subconscious mind to allow the separation to happen. This is unfortunate, but not an uncommon occurrence, and in this situation I always break the deadlock by turning over onto my side and going to sleep. This doesn't mean that you have given up, far from it, even though the disappointment of being so close to success is great indeed. I may have changed my sleeping position, but I continue to imagine that I am leaving my body, and my heartbeat is slow. *I must have fallen asleep because the next thing I know is that I am aware of being in a dream.*

I found myself at the top of a flight of stairs, in a house that was not known to me, and as I felt myself becoming more aware, I began falling from side to side (previously described) and I was under the belief that I was drunk. I was unable to keep my footing and I had an overwhelming urge to accept the fact that I was drunk and lie down, as one does! I happily laid myself down on the stairs and immediately came out of my body, consciously existing in my astral body.

For the first time ever, purely on an off-chance, I put my hand to the back of my head to see if there was anything there, and to my great surprise and consternation, there was! Up until this stage I had only glimpsed, what I assumed to be, the spirit cord during some of my brief excursions in my spirit body. I have, on most occasions, felt the effect of 'something' but exactly in what form it took, I presumed, was well beyond my grasp. Not so! The cord felt hard and solid where it joined my head, and I would guess at being approximately 2.5cms (one inch in English) in diameter. This is a strange feeling to touch a part of myself that I was hitherto unaware of. I very carefully looked around, over my shoulder, to see a long, off-white, cord disappearing into the darkness behind me. Proof at last, to me, that a link exists between the two bodies that I inhabit. I turned back again and was immediately pulled back into my physical body.

Many people claim that the cord does not exist, because it cannot be seen. But there are many things that firmly exist in this world that are invisible to our eyes, the important thing is to *feel* for it! Put your hands behind your head, grasp your own spirit cable and satisfy your own curiosity. This was the first projection where I had even thought of *feeling* for a cable, and from now on I will be investigating this phenomenon as often as I can. Since this occasion, I have rarely had a projection where I have put my hand to the back of my head and the cord has *not* been there.

FRIDAY 3RD MARCH 1995

This is my third success, in a row, at inducing an astral projection using the neural energy method. I dare not allow myself the thought that I have found a foolproof way of projecting. I would dearly love to find this sort of consistency with etheric separation, and this will remain an aim for the future, how ever long it takes is immaterial. I am sure that it is simply a case of 'the grass is always greener' and I am sure that people, who only project in an etheric body, must wonder about this fabulous place, called the astral, and wish that they too could have a taste of life in 'Utopia'. I really am not disappointed, or moaning, but I must continue to strive for understanding and knowledge about how this all jigsaws together as part of life, if only for my own gratification.

I am very aware that astral existence is at the mercy of the non-believers, I was once one of them! All this can only, and I believe *should* only, be proven to yourself. If everybody proved to themselves that this is *reality*, it would become commonplace, and no longer be under suspicion. I value the immensely important role that scientists play in our world, but even a scientist would not be able to prove that they had travelled to the astral plane, but they would be able to prove the truth of it to *themselves*, and gain their *own* inner conviction. This must be a personal thing and we must let our personal experience's be our common ground to speak for all people, all ages.

My only reason for recording this next projection is really because it has been the third in a row using the neural energy method. *A very short and 'ordinary' projection, I left my physical body in a normal rush of vibrations and found myself back in an astral estate of houses. I often wonder whether there is any information to be gained personally, by finding myself in these particular surroundings, and bearing that in mind, I had a good look around, passing in and out of various houses. I found a main street but immediately began experiencing dual consciousness. This is something that needs to be explained but, firstly, let me say that the projection terminated, and I found myself awake, at home, in bed.*

When you are projected in your astral body you are, all the time, very aware of exactly where your physical body is resting, and you are very aware that you are projected away from it. When dual consciousness occurs, you have

125

the strange experience of the combined senses telling you that not only are you in your own bedroom, but *also* in your astral environment. Even though your physical eyes are closed you will 'see' your bedroom one moment, and then your astral surroundings the next. By intensely concentrating on the astral locale, the bedroom environment fades, by relaxing the concentration on the astral locale, the bedroom location very quickly overwhelms everything and brings the projection to a permanent end. Here I found the dual consciousness very strong and, in the wink of an eye, I was awake at home. If you can realise in time that dual consciousness has begun, by using deep concentration, it is possible to delay the return two, or three, times and extend the projection.

In an effort to maintain clarity, there is another type of dual consciousness that you ought to know about, and that is *etheric* dual vision. Because the spirit cable carries the sense perceptions between the two bodies, some strange anomalies can happen. In etheric projection it is possible to see from *both* bodies at the same time, and therefore you can be in the confusing position of being able to look at your spirit-body from your physical body, and able to see your physical body from your etheric body, *both at the same time*. Because this is etheric it is a rare occurrence, but something you should know about. I have talked about vision, but these sense currents work the same with all the senses not just sight.

Having projected three times out of three attempts, I am allowing myself to consider my future plans regarding oobex. Instead of projecting etherically, straight from my physical body, which I find extremely rare, I want to try and find out if there is a way to project to the etheric plane, via my astral body. The answers, to most of my questions, would be discovered in regular, and consistent, out-of-body experience's. I need to obtain more control of my mental abilities, especially in lengthening the period of exteriorisation. Deep concentration combats dual consciousness, but too much interest, prior to the onset of dual consciousness, will terminate the trip. So, mental control means keeping an idle interest, generally, during a projection, but also knowing when to use intense concentration to prolong it. Odd things begin to happen after forcing a projection to last longer than it naturally would. I believe that the superconscious mind is happy to let you roam around, and do your own thing, as long as you play within limits, very much like a mother with her children.

By stretching the projection to its limits I am entering unexplored territory that 'mother' doesn't like me being in... why? I would like to find out if this is perhaps another area for choices to be made. These could include returning to the physical body, projection to the etheric body, projection to another, hitherto unexplored spirit-body, and let us not be forgetting death itself. I hope that I will get to know what the choices are, before I make them. This unexplored territory, being just out of the reach of normal endurance, reminds me of that area between complete relaxation, and projection, you know, the head thumping, voices calling, etc. The 'feel' to it is very similar, difficult to obtain, difficult to maintain, and it dances just beyond your finger tips. These are fulcrum points, or cross-roads, that allow different directions to be taken. These fulcrum areas allow the vibrational changes to take place, taking you from one body to another. Yes, I am talking about projecting the spirit-body, whilst already projected! As if it isn't difficult enough to do the first one!

Have you ever found in life, how, when learning something new, e.g. a musical instrument or maybe a college course, etc. great strides are made initially, interest is high and progress is being made, to your personal satisfaction? One just begins to get a grasp of the subject when it goes off the boil! You hit a foggy patch, where progress slows to a terrible pace, or even ceases altogether. Try as you might, it only gets harder. Frustration sets in and you begin to analyse why am I doing this, and why am I doing that?

Eventually you hit the stage of 'why am I putting myself through all this' or 'why am I here, life is too short'! This is the point where a lot of people give up, believing themselves to be not suited or capable of the discipline, whatever that may be. However, the enlightened, stubborn, or single minded person perseveres through all this, no matter what, and is rewarded. For some reason the light comes back on, the interest is regained, and great progress, at last, can be made.

It is my belief that the initial progress comes from the conscious part of our minds, all the interest and the intense desire to learn is up front in the part of our consciousness that, in the long term, is limited. A two-way link has to be forged with that part of our subconscious mind that allows access to retrievable information. Persevering through the foggy patch establishes this link for the specific task that you are trying to achieve.

Having confirmed this connection, the subconscious can allow thoughts and actions to be made, in conjunction with the learning conscious mind. If you are learning to play a piano, for instance, your fingers will begin to automatically play certain keys, leaving you free to improve your technique, or to read the bar ahead, and in so doing, make much greater progress.

Having eventually made this connection, it will be with you always, to use as you wish, or when you need to. I hope that enough of you can recognise this phenomena to give it credibility, surely it can't happen only to me! If this is common to us all, as I expect it is, then why hasn't it been recognised for what it is and dealt with as a serious issue in our education systems.

Every child should be monitored to make sure that all the initial hard work isn't going to run away down the drain when the enlightened stage is so close. The standard of education could rocket, with very little extra effort. Once the link has been made, we will continuously suck up information about the particular subject for the rest of our lives. Leaving a child in the foggy stage can actually leave the child in a worse condition, convinced that they are not capable, and closing the door on that subject for good. What do you think?

Obviously the same applies to out-of-body projection and persevering through this particularly confusing patch is most difficult, but very necessary. It will be your subconscious mind that will be the main instigator in determining whether, or not, your future projections will be successful. If the subconscious mind can be made to accept out-of-body travel as a perfectly legitimate thing to do, then the majority of your problems are over. It is up to you to get to that stage first.

SUNDAY MARCH 5TH 1995

My fourth attempt to project by over-using the neural energy discharge, has failed. I had reached a satisfactory state of relaxation, I charged my spirit-body with neural energy and lost consciousness. Unfortunately I stayed that way, at no time did I regain consciousness in order to project. Let us look at a few possible reasons why the outing failed. I may, of course, have been successful with an *unconscious* projection, but who knows!

I am sure that there are other factors involved in oobex that I do not have knowledge of, and I suspect that our natural body cycles will affect completion, either helping, or hindering, depending on the timing. I have checked my own record of out-of-body experience's to see if the lunar cycle had an influence, and my findings were negative. Even so, when I see that great big yellow ball smiling down on me, I always think 'tonight's the night'. Expectation does play a great part, always expect to project, always be positive, even in the teeth of failure.

Another major factor is how much sleep our body needs, if we are over tired, or under tired, the balance of our relaxation preparation becomes unbalanced. In other words, we can prepare all we like, but if our body needs sleep... it will sleep. If it is not tired, it will be restless. Both will act against successful projection, and this all comes back to being aware enough to live the kind of lifestyle that is conducive to oobex. Of course, if you find yourself *too* tired to attempt a projection, it is in itself an indication that you need more sleep generally.

Being members of the human race we also have problems, interests, relationships and a myriad of mental stimulation that will occupy our mind at night. We have health concerns, we watch television programmes that rivet our interest, we vote for politicians. What about the late nights, the occasional drinking session and love making? Not necessarily in that order! All these things will affect regular projection and must be taken into account so that, when the time is right, the projection can be attempted.

To be *really* good at all this, you must take yourself off and live on your own with no worries. Give yourself a strict routine, go to bed at dusk, get up at dawn, drink only water, eat simple food, toil on the land all day, allow yourself a couple of hours to think about spirit projection, and repeat over, and over, the wish to project so that it permeates the subconscious mind. Does this ring any bells? Well, *they* do.

'They' being the special religious people who give their lives to their Saviour by living exemplary lives in the employ of God. Without being fully aware of *why* they lead the lives they do, they nevertheless actually live the perfect lives that would enable them to experience a religious experience, or in other words, an out-of-body experience. As my astral locale, within the astral plane, is influenced by my earthly life, the astral locale of a monk, or nun, would be made up of churchly, religious and holy trappings.

An astral trip for one of these good people would be evidence indeed, and justification, for all their beliefs and endeavours. If these people understood the *true* meaning of what they do, and why they do it, they would be able to make more, and get more, out of their simple, but perfect, lives. Living this existence would give them the control to upset their routine whenever they wished. A strict routine works against spirit projection.

SUNDAY 19TH MARCH 1995

I find astral projection a very private affair. The vast majority of out-of-body experience's have happened whilst I have been in bed on my own. It isn't that I don't trust my partner, it is simply one less thing to have in the back of my mind. If things happen at the wrong moment, it can be quite unpleasant, just a cough, a touch, another persons' nightmare, can wrench you with great violence away from your desired destination. Now, the fear, or awareness, that it *can* happen, is greater than the actuality of it, and is something that I am trying to conquer.

This morning I managed a projection whilst Linda, my partner, was there. I managed to put the risk into context, for so many opportunities are lost when projection is only possible if you are on your own. My projection again, this morning, used the neural energy method. I have found this to be a full, and permanent asset to successfully projecting, so much so, that it is this method that I have given you in the relaxation preparation section of this book.

Much of this spirit projection is about getting to really know yourself, a journey along a path of personal discovery, not always nice, sometimes surprising, but overwhelmingly honest. You can fool anybody, everybody, but never *ever* yourself. Feeling uncomfortable never wears well, even on the best of us. There are also many very simple things, some of which you have already come to recognise, that once meant nothing and were unworthy of notice. Yet, suddenly, they become seen for what they really are. Simple things *are* necessarily 'simple' to avoid detection, to avoid attention, and it is these simple things that we must train ourselves to be aware of.

My projection this morning, was astral, even though my bedroom appeared to be exactly the same as it is in the physical sphere, and my house seemed to be exactly as it should be. I knew that it was an astral projection because of one simple change, and that was the fact that my bedroom door should have been open. In my projected body my bedroom door was closed. It is sometimes only these simple things that will give you the initial clue to where you are. I passed, effortlessly, through the fabric of the door, and made my way down the stairs and passed through the front door. I love passing through solid objects. Outside, I made my way along the High Street from Ivydene, my house, to the church where I was amazed that everything looked so normal. It was only the fact that my bedroom door was closed made me keep to the fact that this was astral.

When I reached the boundary of the churchyard, the High Street had 'morphed' into a single lane country track, which I followed into a foreign, and very beautiful, setting. I had never seen such glorious countryside, such intense colours to take your breath away. Even so, I was regretting that this was not etheric, what am I like? I wandered through this syrupy landscape, overtly real, wondering why I should be in this fantastic place, when suddenly I found myself fighting to stay. Once again I found myself awake, at home, in bed, just as conscious as I had been in my projection.

This is a point to note, and a point where you must be totally honest with yourself. After a projection has finished, usually, but not always, you will find yourself awake, in bed where you started. The reason that you are awake, is because you were awake in the projection. Therefore your conscious awareness should be exactly the same, after the projection, as it was whilst you were in it. If it is at all different, then I suggest that what you, probably, experienced was a lucid dream, very real, but not real *enough*, and *so* very tempting to call a projection. That is why you must be very honest with, if no one else, yourself. On the odd occasion, consciousness can be lost, and leave you to the mercy of the dream world, but this usually happens when you join the projection late when nothing much is happening, and you are very tired.

SATURDAY 25TH MARCH 1995

We had a very rough night, last night. Sleep came and went, but never stayed long enough to allow a beneficial recharge. To cap it all, the alarm clock went off at 5.00 a.m. because it hadn't been switched off from the previous morning. I took this opportunity to rise, drink a glass of water, and begin my relaxation procedures. In due course I

133

reached the correct depth of calmness and lowered my heart rate a little, in order to stimulate the vibrations and the head thumps. What followed is an example of unpleasantness that can sometimes happen. Having successfully entered the fulcrum area, I began experiencing the usual head thumps. I normally feel one, or two, really as a sign that all is going well. *This morning I found that I could not progress any further on from this stage, my head was receiving a continuous stream of thumps. Without warning, the effect became magnified and spread to my whole body. I was extremely uncomfortable, every tiny part of me was jumping and vibrating, my teeth were banging together, and my eyeballs felt as though they were loose in their sockets. I could feel my brain sizzling, like a burger on a barbecue, my body was wracking itself out of control.*

I remained in this condition, I know not how long, desperately expecting to project out and away from it at any second.... It didn't come. I was locked in this horrible condition. With all my remaining sensibility I concentrated on lowering my heartbeat further, because it felt as if it was 'going like a train' and, thankfully, it worked. I found myself projected into my bedroom, alive and grateful!

I will finish telling you about the projection first before going back to that awful experience. I immediately put my hand to the back of head in order to feel the cord. It has a root system before it combines into a single cable. On this occasion I, very gingerly, felt what seemed to be three thick strands, originating from three different parts of my brain. These were extending from my skull for approximately 5cms (two inches) before gradually coming together and combining into one cable-like structure. Rather like the end of a thick rope, when the individual strands are coming undone. At the head end the cable has a feel to it similar to a cucumber. See Figure 4, page 135.

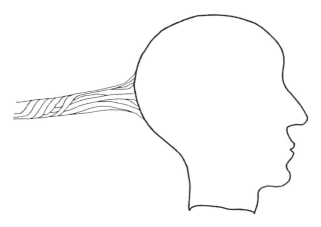

Spirit body close to physical and showing root system.

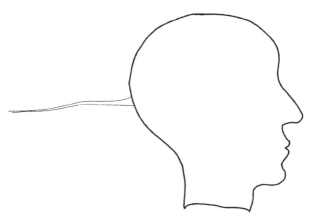

Spirit body away from physical, showing no root system.

Figure 4.

My bedroom was exactly as it should have been, as was the stairs and front door. It was only as I passed through the front door, to the outside, was it confirmed as being astral. This was because Braunston High Street had completely changed out of all recognition.

Because of my previous experience, I still felt very shaken. I wondered down this strange road in a slightly different mood to usual. With no great surprise I returned to my physical body as the shock caught up with me. I wish never to experience that again!

Lying back in bed, afterwards, I wondered exactly what had happened to cause such severe reactions from my body. Which body? Obviously, I had become caught in-between 'in' and 'out', with one mechanism unable to pull me back, and another mechanism not strong enough to pull me clear. I also wondered what the whole episode must have looked like from the outside. I believe it may have appeared as though I was having a fit, of some kind. Indeed, was I? Having never had one I wouldn't know, but I have witnessed, on two occasion's, human beings having epileptic fits. I have also seen my Irish Water Spaniel, Roxy, have them on many occasion's until we got them, medically, under control. Well I *felt* like, what *they* all looked like, while it was in progress.

If, indeed, I actually was fitting, then is there any possible help that I can give existing medical authorities, expert in this field. Did I, in fact, voluntarily put myself in a position where these convulsions, or seizures could occur? And do these other people, unaccountably, go naturally to the same set of conditions. If so, my knowledge could very well help them to understand their problem, and control it, without the use of drugs.

Epilepsy sufferers are often of a nervous disposition and therefore use up a lot of neural energy in their day-today lives. Their spirit-body is in constant need to detach itself in order to recharge. Is the seizure condition, in actual fact, the spirit trying to detach itself at an inappropriate time? Many epileptics sleep at the end of an attack, of course they do, for they are desperately in need of neural energy. The obvious difference is that I was *conscious* during the convulsion, whereas I believe that suffers of epileptic fits *lose* consciousness during an attack. Was it my expertise for projecting my consciousness that kept my awareness during the fit? Surely this is worth investigating, I would be very willing to help.

Now, looking at this from all angles, was it possible that the whole incident happened in my spirit-body and didn't affect my physical body at all? Certainly possible. Linda was asleep beside me, at the time, so wouldn't it have woken her up? I do know that she was extremely tired, and it is possible that she had hit the deepest part of her sleep pattern. My instincts tell me that, at least in part, it was physical, I remember feeling the bed on the back of my body, during the ordeal. All in all, a good example of what can happen if you are unlucky and, please believe me, I have only had this happen to me once, so far.....

You will also note that I investigated the spirit cord and found a root system, see figure 4, page 135. This gives rise to the likelihood that each strand begins in a different part of the physical brain, and carries one particular sense function, along its entire length. All these 'sense' cords then wind, and combine, outside the skull, to make one complete spirit cable. This root system is sometimes not apparent, the cable seemingly abuts directly to the skull. This could be due to the tightness of the winding cable, the condition of the cable, or the distance between the projected body and the physical body.

MONDAY JULY 31ST 1995

Be prepared to go long periods of time without projecting. When it does happen, it seems to happen again, quite quickly. Also, many times you can successfully project, only to return immediately. On other occasions you will find that you will somersault around the room, desperately trying to grab something, in order to remain out. There are so many variables to the norm. At times you will find that all you have to do is sit up and walk away. My view is that any projection, *however long*, is a successful projection as it confirms that you must be doing it right.

Only yesterday, I had a perfect separation, and I was so determined to stay out for as long as possible. Too determined it seems, for I managed to get 100yds along the High Street before it ended. Yet again, a victim of my own emotions playing a major role in a balancing act between achieving the wish, but not to the extent that it commands your deep interest.

This morning was better, my awareness came after separation, and a found myself in a place that was strange to me, but definitely English. I found myself standing on a pavement, on one side of a road, that ran between a fine collection of mature, Victorian, houses. I resisted the temptation to look around inside any of them, opting instead to make my way to the bottom of the street and explore. I passed a lady walking her dog, she glanced at me, but took no further notice. Having reached the end of the road, it became clear that I was near to the centre of a small town. Walking towards the centre, I chanced to see a diesel powered goods train rumble over a bridge near to the heart of the place.

The choices that have to be made, in these situations, are almost too numerous, because you can do practically anything. Because it feels so real, it acts as a

138

restraint, until you project enough times to come to the real terms of it. Not knowing where I was, I called into a shop and asked how close we were to London. If I had asked where were we, and what was the name of this town, they would have thought I was nuts! That is how real it is!

My thinking was that if I could get to London, then I would have a confirmed point of reference. The silly thing is that if I had managed to get to London, it would have been my astral London that I love and know so well. I do not remember the reply, for I was already awake, back at base. I laid there for a few moments, reviewing the projection, before settling down and, to my surprise and delight, I projected again. Back to the very same street as I went to before!

It was early morning and the air felt cool and fresh, you know, the sort of morning where you have made the effort to get up early and have driven to a place that you have never been to before, so you really notice everything. I wandered down the same road, just as I had done previously, but this time, instead of going into town, I thought that I would go into one of the buildings situated right at the bottom of the street. It was a large, imposing, public looking building that probably once was a single Victorian residence, but now, like so many, looked as though it had been converted into offices.

I had to ascend a half flight of stairs to get to the front door, which I passed through easily, to find myself in a large and beautifully tiled hallway. I heard some noises coming from the basement area, so I made my way down the carpeted stairs to investigate. I walked in to meet two gentlemen, in their working environment, and introduced myself. To deflect any kind of criticism, concerning my uninvited entrance, I immediately proceeded to tell them where I had come from, who I was, and gave them a demonstration of my 'powers' by walking through their wall, and back again, twice!

My impromptu show caused them some amusement, but not great surprise. I suspect that it would be nothing like the response that would have been received if this were to happen on the physical plane. I felt a little self-conscious as the thought came to me that they were perhaps more capable of executing these tricks, than I was. Perhaps their amusement was a little at my expense. It must have seemed a little like an Englishman visiting Paris, only to rush around pointing out the Eiffel Tower, to Parisians! The Parisians might also find that mildly amusing, in a humouring sort of a way. The important thing, to me, was that I was making contact with other people, in an astral environment, so what the hell!

These two gents then introduced me to their team of people, two other men and four women. They were all involved with designing and the manufacture of miniature helicopters, that carried equipment, or cameras for aerial photography. One of the gentlemen picked up a half completed helicopter to show me the detailing, and began to explain the features, which I found very interesting.... I had actually forgotten that I was projected, until I became aware that I was in bed. No dual consciousness that I was aware of, at least that gives you a chance to stay longer.

Looking back over this good, and long, projection, it seems daft to me to be making helicopters for aerial photography *if* the astral inhabitants can fly up there and do it for themselves. So perhaps they can't. I must admit, that I have never seen anybody else airborne within the astral environment. I must also say that I haven't met another projected earth human whilst I have also been projected, but I have been told by astral inhabitants are we are not uncommon visitors. So I live in hope, but unless they are acting in an obvious fashion, like flying, I would not recognise them as such, or them me. My conscious mind expects to see other people flying and passing through solid objects, my subconscious mind does not, because it doesn't happen here on physical earth.

What amazes me is the vastness of the astral world, and all it contains. It more than matches the content of the physical earth. Astrally, I can travel to any part of the globe, pick a house, pick a room, pick a cupboard, pick a box, and see what is inside. The art of astral projection reigns supreme above all other experience's.

Something I haven't mentioned before, is the afterglow following a good projection. That sublime feeling is a treat in itself. Success is a great confidence booster that stays with you for the days following the oobex. It is a secret that you hold, and is very difficult to keep to yourself, for once you have told somebody about out-of-body experience's, you begin to water down the in-built tension that you have accumulated, it is that that helps you to project, so beware. Talking to another projector is OK.

THURSDAY 3RD AUGUST 1995

This morning I had another astral projection that began unconsciously, with the awareness only coming later, after the projection was well under way. What happened in the first part of this projection I will never know, but then again, think how many other unconscious astral trips we must all have enjoyed without having any conscious knowledge at all. Just think, for all these years we might have been having a great time!

I found my awareness whilst walking along an extremely busy thoroughfare, my initial impression was that it looked, and felt, like busy London. It was a warm, sultry evening and I noticed a 'pub that had an open

141

frontage, with people spilling out onto the street, all enjoying the convivial atmosphere so common to Central London. I picked my way through the bodies to discover that it was a typical London 'pub, in full flow, with lots of different rooms nurturing the full cross-section of society. All the world was there to see.

As the projection continued, I became increasing aware that I was being followed by a girl. Existing in my conscious mind, I knew that I had never seen her before, but I wondered if I had ever known her, in my astral counterpart. You see, everybody that you meet astrally has the status of an acquaintance, someone you know well enough to approach, and talk to, if you so wish. One simply accepts all without question. Oh, if it could be like that on earth. Anyway, this girl, for some reason bothered me.

She came closer, definitely making a bee-line for me, in the noise and the crowd she began shouting and reaching out, in a pestering fashion. I thought, is she drunk? or deranged? or what? I didn't want to talk to her, or know her, and I asked her to go away. I said that I was not looking for company and how ever much she pestered me she would not succeed. But to no avail. I thought that this was spoiling the whole projection, so I endeavoured to get away. In the crowded bar I pushed past a group of people in my haste to escape, and heard the sound of breaking glass. Whether it had been dropped, or I had knocked it, I don't know because I was so desperate to get away from this bloody woman.

I eventually managed to get outside, back on to the pavement where, to my deep concern, she caught up with me. I remonstrated with her, I tried to walk away, but all to no effect. I became convinced that she was mentally unstable, as she was not able to justify her actions. It is difficult to know quite what to do in these circumstances,

142

especially when you are perfectly aware that you are projected, and all you want to do is to be left alone to get on with things. I could have terminated the projection, but they are so rare, so difficult to come by, that I have to resist this option at all times. I must admit, I was surprised that I had lasted this long already, many times I have been pulled back for an awful lot less.

In the end, I became so sick and tired, I ran towards a high wall, and leapt at it, scrambling over the top, to leave her behind. I experienced dual consciousness, seeing my bedroom through my 'physical' eyes, and my astral world through my astral eyes, both at the same time. I really didn't want to give in to the bedroom scene, but short of strangling the woman, I thought it might be the best thing to do.

In retrospect, I cannot be sure if my physical eyes actually open up, when dual consciousness intervenes. I certainly do see the interior of my bedroom as clearly as I view the astral environment. So maybe my eyes do open before I am properly back in the physical body. In that case, it would be sensible to try and close my physical eyes, every time dual consciousness appears. The trick will be to remember to do it, when the time comes. The alternative to this surmise is, perhaps, that I am looking at my bedroom scenery through the flesh of my eyelids, which I believe is not possible. Yet another, and far more likely alternative, is that I am using the sight belonging to my etheric body, which has remained at rest within my physical body, leaving only my astral body projected.

Being pestered like this, has never happened before, well not in a projection, anyway! It was also very strange that I could feel myself getting agitated, my emotions becoming aroused, but without immediately being returned to the physical. I also experienced a peculiar, but fleeting, sensation whilst projected, and I will try and relate that feeling to you in the best way I can. Again, using your imagination, can you think of your body as a raw egg? Now, imagine if it suddenly set firm! On two fleeting occasions, during this projection, my astral body suddenly set firm, solid, cataleptic.

You remember we talked about events happening, during a dream, that arouse your awareness in order for you to recognise the opportunity to project? Well, I think that this was exactly what was happening here, only on a more advanced level. I believe these opportunities are sent to see if we are ready to go further and, if that was the case, yes I failed. The astral body 'setting firm' was an example of the spirit-body altering its vibrational rate in order for consciousness to exist at another level, possibly, probably, etheric. The longer the astral projection lasts, the more chance you have of things happening. The important thing is that it has happened, and hopefully I am one step nearer to recognising this phenomenon the next time it occurs, if indeed it ever should.

The experience with this woman was purely, and simply, another gateway of choice. That choice was to bale out, as I did, or recognise the signs for what they are, and progress. I should have gone opposite to my natural instincts and embraced her, there would have been a good chance that she would have disappeared, leaving me on a higher plane of existence. This business is full of missed opportunities that leave you feeling very frustrated with yourself. It is a slow process, and must be, for your own sanity is at stake.

SATURDAY 12TH AUGUST 1995

Have you ever said to yourself, last thing at night, 'I will wake up at such and such a time,' and found it successful? It is almost as though we have a built-in alarm clock for our personal use. OK it is not 100% reliable but flesh and blood isn't. This morning I had a projection that I had to terminate, as it seemed to me to be out of control, and my only reason for recording this is to relate the *method* of projection.

The last thing I did, after completely relaxing, and before losing consciousness, was to say to myself 'I will project my astral body within half an hour.' Now, what I have omitted to say, is that I have been trying this idea for the previous two mornings, without success. What did give me encouragement, though, was the amount of vivid dreams it produced. It was obviously having the, beneficial, effect of not letting me go too deeply into the sleep environment. This enabled me to prolong the time that I had to play in the quality dream world. I presumed that this was worth pursuing, and my persistence was rewarded this morning, to a certain extent.

I cannot swear that I had my projection within half an hour of going to sleep, because there is no way of telling, but who cares? I was off, with awareness coming as I was in the process of separation, so I got the usual high velocity fire-hose treatment. Bouncing around, upside down, every which way, as the cord pushed me further, and further away from my dear old physical body. I was hanging on, safe in the knowledge that once we had reached a certain distance I would regain control. Also it seemed that, so far, the projection was etheric, so my fingers were patiently crossed in expectation. It wasn't to be, my spirit-body suddenly took off like a rocket, at tremendous speed, and kept going. I hung on for awhile but my instinct told me that I was out of control, so I terminated the session by concentrating on being back in my bedroom.

Not really a difficult thing to do, because you know where your physical body is residing at all times, contact is never lost. Consciously returning to the physical body, from the astral, is a lot easier than docking from the etheric, or should I say, not so beset with possible discomfort. I did not experience the repercussion I was expecting, therefore my projection had been astral.

FRIDAY 25TH AUGUST 1995

A projection that lasted only seconds! I tumbled, and rolled, out of my physical body, unfortunately the actual exit was quite severe. Have you ever had a bad cold and felt pressure behind your nose, as with sinus trouble? and have you ever experienced pressure inside your ears, usually accompanied by earache? Try to imagine only the pressure, without any of the accompanying discomfort. A little like someone has cut a little slit in your skin and pushed cotton wool up into your face, right behind the bridge of your nose, and continued on by cutting a little slit in front of each ear, similarly pushing cotton wool inside each ear.

The effect I had this morning was one of a normal, easy separation, but with my spirit-body unable to separate from the physical in two strategic places. My ears and my nose felt all the force of the pulling pressure as my spirit-body tried to elevate from the physical. It felt, to me, as if the front of my face was being pulled off, with the additional delight of my ears bursting and my nose bleeding. It didn't come to that, in fact the separation didn't happen at all. Often I have felt pressure in these areas, during the process of separation, and I think that it is something that should sensibly be taken into account if you are a sufferer in these areas, and are contemplating participating in this field.

I will just say that at the time of this attempted projection, I was not suffering with any kind of nasal, or ear trouble, but that doesn't mean that perhaps there *was* a slight congestion that I was unaware of. Another theory, of mine, is that the astral cord is connected directly into the receiving areas of each of our physical senses, so that we can enjoy the same sensitivity whilst projected, as we do in our physical bodies. Perhaps the connection to the hearing and olfactory sensors are different, more basic, more sensitive, located in a different area, or something that makes them a more challenging connection for the spirit cable. I can honestly say that even, in a good projection, it is often those two areas that you feel separate the last.

FRIDAY 29TH SEPTEMBER 1995

It has been a little while since my last projection, and I always begin to worry that, for some reason, I will lose the ability to project my spirit-body. The thought of that happening fills me with abject horror, a whole part of my life would be missing. So, after awhile with no success I began to turn up the screws, just in case. I read more about oobex, I imagine myself walking around my bedroom as though I *was* projected. Always trying hard to impress upon the subconscious mind that it is OK, and perfectly normal, to be fully conscious outside of the physical environment.

I began my preparations a full day before the proposed projection to give me time to absolutely saturate myself with the want, the need and the sensations necessary for an out-of-body experience. Right up to the evening, as I was giving my dog her final walk of the day, I was repeating the will to project, just like the chanting of our holy folk. Astral projection, astral projection, let nothing else fill your mind other than astral projection, for if it can saturate your

147

consciousness it will stop all other rogue thoughts from leading you astray.

I am glad to say that all the preparation worked. I wouldn't have told you about all this if it hadn't! Not a fantastic projection, but they all count, and the important thing is the personal reassurance that the system still works.

My first projection, this morning, was very short due to the fact that it took me by surprise and, to a greater or lesser extent, they all do. However I found myself already projected, and in the process of wandering around a High Street shopping area in a pleasant sort of market town, with no idea where I was. I must get used to the fact that this location aspect is unimportant. Unconsciously it doesn't matter and, consciously, I must learn to shed my earthly concerns and simply enjoy it for what it is.

A lady was walking towards me, and I thought to myself, if she should see me, I am astral, but if I am invisible to her, I am etheric. Well, she saw me, everybody saw me, as though I was just one other facet of the life that was going on around me. Without warning, or reason, I returned to my physical body. I felt a little short changed and deflated, so I composed myself to try a second projection.

My projected awareness made itself apparent with loud crashing noises, the sort of noise a plate, or glass, would make if it fell from a table and shattered onto a solid floor. My immediate reaction was that my cat, Daisy, had been shut in the bedroom and was creating havoc. My common sense told me that could not be possible, as she is not allowed upstairs at night, and I must maintain my composure. So my second impression, that followed, was that this must be something to do with my projection. Even though it was so real that I wanted to check the house, I had to hold back. Of course, I checked later, I had to, but these noises were definitely inside my head.

I am not one to unduly experience these severe noises, and it did remind me of the experience's of Oliver Fox, as related in his compelling book. I did *not* suffer his accompanying flashing lights and other effects. For me the separation process can be far more exciting than the projection itself. A little like a trip on all the rides in a fun park, followed by a walk around the nearest town.

The projection itself was most depressing. I found myself in a very run down part of town, with empty building sites, badly maintained roads, scruffy children pouring out of school, on their way home. Children of all ages, dishevelled, grubby and resigned to their lot, were wandering along as though each had had their spark extinguished. To be truthful, I felt a great sense of desolation and loneliness. The more I saw, the more I lost contact, and I wasn't sorry to be back home.

Looking at this afterwards, I should have risen up and flown away to explore somewhere more exciting. I suppose I needed to know that these places exist even in the astral world. It is because that you feel sorry, and have empathy with the situation, that it doesn't cross your mind to fly away. One almost feels a sense of apology, and it is the least you can do to not rub in your advantages by desertion. Again I must learn not to get so involved.

SUNDAY 12TH NOVEMBER 1995

This morning I am not very well, my throat is swollen and sore, I have a terrible cough, a bad headache and I am feeling generally lousy, Apart from that I am OK. Although I don't feel like it, I am continuing to attempt an out-of-body projection in the belief that the weaker the physical body becomes, the easier it is to separate. If the

149

physical body continues to weaken, without stopping, it will result in death. As the body gets weaker, the resistance to projection lessens. Obviously, at the point of death there is no resistance at all, it is at that stage that all the sceptics realise the truth of this book. A little late to say I'm sorry, but that isn't a worry, I'll catch up with them later!

It is interesting to note that the greatly respected Sylvan Muldoon, was very ill indeed during much of his experimentation into the etheric phenomena. In fact, if it wasn't for his illness, I believe that we would not have the benefit of that vast knowledge to work with today.

The only real worry I have, when projecting in this condition, is if I become caught again during the separation process. Having the inside of your face pulled out is not very pleasant. It was my concern that having a congested ear, nose, and throat, condition could put additional pressure into these areas, and cause problems. If we don't try these things we will never know.

I am happy to say that I did project, missing the separation process completely, and also losing all my feelings of illness. What relief, I felt, to be free of the aches and pains that accompany a heavy cold. I am also sure that had there been a problem with the separation, the projection would have been aborted. Time will tell but I am looking to discount the congestion theory.

My consciousness came to me, clear and complete, as I scrutinised my astral surroundings. I was in a house, not my astral house, but a strange house, and my feelings were that I was a little uncomfortable about being there. Choosing the nearest wall, I pushed myself up to it and permeated through to the other side, to find myself outside. As I wandered around to the back of the house, I could see in the distance a wooded area and I decided to make my way in that direction. I began to experience dual consciousness, seeing my bedroom clearly, and yet still walking along towards the woods. I stood still and concentrated as hard as I possibly could on staring at the view, trying to notice everything about it, absorbing the vista in as much a complete form, as I was able to. My conscious 'will' triumphed as my bedroom scenery faded away completely, as though it had never been there and I was, once again, 100% back in my astral body.

It would be easy for me to miss this out but, in the interests of honest research, I must say that I put my hand to the back of my head and felt nothing. This was my first knowing experience of having no cable, just the curve of my skull. I was solid enough, I stamped my feet, twirled around and convinced myself that I was as 'normal' as I am here on the physical plane. I decided to fly back to my home so, simply by thinking of it and having the confidence to launch into it, I took to the air with the greatest of ease.

Flying is fantastic, yes the height, the speed, the exhilaration, can take your breath away, and yes you actually feel the rush of the wind as you travel, but no it is never noticeably cold. Temperature has never been an issue that I have ever taken any notice of, only in the way of sight. Places have *looked* hot, or *looked* frozen over, but I have never actually felt the temperature when I have been projected. *I made the most of enjoying my flight by swooping very low to skim along the surface of a large lake, before gaining height to clear some trees. I continued over the tree tops, missing the very tall ones, eventually coming to a business park where it all faded away to reveal my bedroom.*

MONDAY 20TH NOVEMBER 1995

This morning I successfully attained the necessary depth of relaxation required to stand a chance of projecting.

Sometimes sleep will just naturally happen immediately following relaxation, sometimes sleep will happen before you have done all the things that you need to do. This morning, as is often the case, the relaxation procedures are finished and you are in a kind of limbo state, too alert mentally to go to sleep, but completely relaxed physically. In this situation, I allow it to continue, to be sure that nothing is going to happen, and when I am satisfied of that fact, I turn over and go to sleep as I would normally. Remember, the job of setting up the spirit-body for a projection has already been done, during relaxation.

I look at it a little like a racing car transporter carrying a race car inside, travelling to a circuit for the purpose of testing. As the transporter travels along, the mechanics, inside, work on the race car, getting it ready, checking the fuel, tuning the engine and getting it warmed up and ready to go. There is no point in wasting time, and money, at the test track if all this can be done on the hoof.

Once the transporter has arrived at the correct test track (relaxation), the race car (spirit-body) is ready, and primed, to speed off in the most efficient manner possible. The more we tweak, and tune up the spirit-body during relaxation, the more chance there is of a projection manifesting itself.

As I turned onto my side I noted the time by my bedside clock, I reawakened exactly one hour later, lying in the same position. When relaxation to this depth is achieved, you will notice that very little body movement happens during sleep. I quickly realised that I was at the imperceptible gateway to projection. This is the condition where you feel totally normal in your, sleepy, physical body but, in actual fact and unknown to you, your astral body is just waiting for the slightest nudge to release it from the physical anchor. The great temptation is to roll over and go to sleep again, we have all done this hundreds of times.

What we should do, is precisely what I did this morning, and that is to firstly recognise the possibility of being in this state. There is no way of knowing absolutely and, therefore, it is good practice to be aware always upon awakening. This also serves the purpose of creating a habit, on awakening, of doing nothing for a few moments, to allow the sleep to clear just enough for realisation to appear. This a state of mind known to hypnotherapists, and sleep analysts, as the hypnopompic condition and is a naturally occurring condition that can often be accessed by a competent practitioner, but the details of this will be found elsewhere in this book.

So, having established the possibility of me being in this state, I immediately concentrated on lowering my heartbeat, or the strength of it, *either* will work. I relaxed my insides, by that I imagine that my solar plexus gives a final sigh of resignation, and I induced those, indispensable, vibrations. This is akin to lighting the blue touch-paper and standing back! The very second that I did this, I was hit by a massive 'rush' that ejected me from my flesh and blood. *I was on the end of that hose again! It felt like a rider in a rodeo, riding a particularly spirited steed, but without the advantage of being able to be thrown off. I was cavorting around the bedroom trying, in vain, to grab hold of something to steady myself. A fight ensued, I did everything I could to force myself away from my physical body and reach calmer waters.*

While I was ricocheting off the bedroom walls, I put my hand to the back of my head and found the cable. Importantly, the diameter of the cable was much thinner than I have ever known when being in such close proximity to the earthly body. Instead of a healthy 2.5cms-3cms (one to one and a half inches) it was a mere 1.5cms (five eighths of an inch) in diameter. I lasted a few more minutes before bowing to a greater adversary and giving in.

I think it is obvious here, that the condition of the cable is extremely important, more so than anybody before has given credence to. A strong, thick cable, will allow a longer, more extensive, projection that, in itself, will give further opportunities to progress into uncharted territory. A measly, frail, withering thing can give cause to hope, but not much else.

This, also could make sense of all the times when projection should have happened, but for no accountable reason, failed to develop. It could also explain why some projections last longer than others. So what *does* affect the condition of the cable, and what can we do to maximise the 'health' of the cable? The possibilities are, physical health, diet, sleep, or mental condition.

The answer will, hopefully, appear with time, but I think we can discount health, for astral projection is a natural occurrence and however healthy we may be, we still will be able to enjoy out-of-body experience's. Diet, I believe, is in the sole domain of the physical body, and affects the personal health of that body. Again, if we didn't eat properly, it would aid projection, not hinder it. So, once again, a healthy eater will still be more than able to take part in the natural act of oobex.

Mental condition is a vast subject that must have an influence. For myself, I find a greater success when I am not under undue stress, or pressure, in my daily life. The one greatest influence is sleep, that's where my money lies. It is the strength of the recharge, how much charge has been used up during the day, how much charge was made during the sleep period, prior to the possible projection. This is something that routine, with the important ability to break the routine, can only control. Those of us that lead varied and colourful lives will not be able to take advantage of the 'routine', and 'broken routine', aspect. Unless we *do* live our lives by routine, it will be difficult to use this method to control the 'health' of the cable.

This morning I enjoyed a good five hours sleep prior to my projection. But that alone doesn't guarantee the quality of the recharge, or take into account whether, or not, I was in a run-down condition before the onset of the projection. Have you ever noticed that if your sleep pattern is broken, let's say by a very late night, it may take a couple of night's sleep before you return to normal? This is because your depth of sleep will not immediately cater for the sleep lost. It will still be recharging at your normal rate. When that normal rate doesn't quite cut the mustard, the recharge has to be strengthened, which it does the following night. That is why you need two nights sleep to recover from one late night. It is the night after, the night that follows the late night, where the lost sleep is found.

If medical science could find a way of testing the level of neural energy held at any one time by the human body, indeed any physical body, it would go a long way to curing many ills. Quality sleep will, definitely, *assist* recovery from many illnesses, if not all. This must also be evaluated from the other side of the perspective, in that a *lack* of sleep can enhance illness or slow recovery.

Nocturnal sleeping habits can be so strong as to render the unfortunate person, practically useless to society. Neural energy should not always be high, that would prevent sleep. It should be sufficiently low, in the evening, to promote a good deep sleep, and, therefore, sufficiently high, upon waking, to promote a healthy mind to help you through the day. Problems arise if, for some reason, this is knocked out of sequence. The worst scenario, are those poor people that live on their nerves in their high pressure jobs, and sleep badly, for they are surely heading for lots of trouble. Nervous illnesses, stress, skin complaints, ulcers, piles, bad backs, headaches you name it.

There is a phrase 'a healthy body is a healthy mind', yes that is true. If you can exercise during the day, to physically tire the body, beneficial hormones are released into the system that make you feel good. This will, hopefully, encourage you to do it on a regular basis by getting into a routine of working out. Naturally, a physically tired body, needs to sleep to *also* rest the tired muscles, and in so doing it will give us the opportunity to recharge the mind. In the morning we are rested, mentally alert, and confident to meet the challenges of the day. If we do nothing, during the day, to tire the physical body, then sleep is only required as a mental necessity, and is at the mercy of all kinds of mental stimuli and influence. A ship needs a rudder to keep her steady, take the rudder away, and she becomes quicker, but uncontrollably useless. The mind (ship) needs the physical body (rudder) to rest soundly at night, so that the mind can sustain a regular controlled recharge. By breaking the routine at the right moment, when the physical body needs sleep and the mind is expecting a deep recharge, a projection is more likely. You have in effect caught the system on the hop.

TUESDAY 21ST NOVEMBER 1995

I am suffering with 'flu. This morning I went through the normal routine and went back to sleep around 5am. I became aware that I was dreaming and my consciousness, within the dream, strengthened to allow the dream to be lucid. At this point, some people, Oliver Fox included, would instantly be projected into that dream, and off they would go on their travels. It is slightly different for

156

me. I realised that I was taking part in a dream and, therefore, I have the choice of staying in the dream or projecting on. Being in a lucid dream is a real treat, and is an experience to enjoy in its own right. Many people do not realise that achieving a proper projection is so easy in this condition. It is the fact that the lucid dream is so good, that they don't even give oobex a thought. Yes, this is another gateway where a choice can be made, but only if you know.

In the dream I found myself in a busy city environment and I had to cross many main roads that were full of fast flowing traffic. My concentration was honed in on avoiding cars coming from all directions, so I had to be very careful. I eventually reached the house that I was making for, and entered the building. The house contained many people milling around, and I seemed to be doing the same, a sort of dream socialising. It was at this juncture that it dawned on me that I was dreaming.

Being 'experienced', I know that all I have to do is to induce the vibrations, and I will be off. I found myself a spot to lie down, not really necessary, but best to be prepared, and did the usual. Nothing! I couldn't believe it. I induced the vibrations, but they didn't activate the 'rush'. I got back to my feet and tried falling over, again to no avail. I could feel that I was losing my composure as I became more and more frustrated with the situation. I knew that I was so close and yet in severe danger of allowing it all to slip away. In desperation, I dropped to my knees and, as I did so, I heard the clonk of my knees hitting the wooden floorboards. I recoiled from the noise of the movement and, with an upsurge of energy, I came straight out of my body.

That dream seemed very 'real' and turned out to be very hard work in the end. But it was, nevertheless, only a dream. I had managed to use that dream as a method of projecting my astral body, and I *completely* regained my conscious mind. Unusually for me I found that, projected, I had remained in the same house as the one in my dream. Another example of a dream shadowing an unconscious projection. My, unconscious, astral body was already in the house as the lucid dream became apparent, and prior to fully projected consciousness.

I made my way downstairs and entered the living room, the decor was nicely done, but a little old fashioned. This suited the style of the house though, as it was of a mature age, not posh, but comfortable. I located the back door and passed through it, into the rear garden. There were shrubs, and flower borders, either side of the central path that led down to a little back road that served all the properties in the street. Once onto this, I turned right and headed off, keeping to the road, not having any reason to go this way, but it was as good as any.

It was early morning, and as I walked past the other houses that also backed onto the road, I could see the signs of people getting up and preparing to go to work. Some windows were dark and curtained, in some I could see the electric light through the curtains and, in one instance, I watched the silhouette of the inhabitant tucking into their breakfast.

My little road had come to an end save for a driveway that led off to the left, and sloped down to a pair of old garage doors. I began to fight dual consciousness and at the same time I realised my mistake of walking down a driveway that goes to nowhere. I fought to stay in the astral environment, but this thing is usually stronger than me, and so I caved in and returned to my physical body.

Analysing the projection afterwards, it would have been so easy to *fly* away and rekindle the interest, that was waning, when the road ran out. In my defence, I must keep emphasising that this place is so real, that it doesn't cross your mind to do so because it isn't something we are *used* to doing.

Earlier on, in the projection, I mentioned that I had to cross some very busy main roads with fast flowing traffic coming at me from all directions. You will recall that, at this stage, I was still dreaming, however, it was the serious concentration required, to safely cross these roads, that began to bring my consciousness into play. By the time I had got to the house it had arrived enough to turn an unconscious projection, experienced as a dream, into a lucid dream, so that I could then choose to turn it into a conscious projection. Simple, isn't it....

If at any time, during a dream, you get to a spot that requires concentration, the same thing will happen more often than not. I remember one dream, where I was walking along a tree-lined avenue, and I noticed that the trees had become seriously large around the trunk. I stopped, and stared at one particular tree that must have been a good ten foot across. As I scrutinised this tree, thinking about its age and how much damage the root system must be doing to the surrounding properties, I became 'there', completely conscious, in my astral body. It was something 'catching' my attention that, coupled with the subsequent concentration, caused me to become aware of my already projected body.

Please do not think that all dreams are unconscious projections, because they are not. It is only a percentage of dreams that will truly reflect an actual astral or etheric environment. But of course, this percentage will rise considerably when we use our specific relaxation procedures, and positively enhance the odds to a much greater extent.

TUESDAY 5TH DECEMBER 1995

I have a last, and very short, experience to tell you about for this chapter. After a long and extended relaxation I happily dropped off to sleep, prepared and ready.

It seemed like, in no time at all, I was leaving my body. My awareness had come to me after the 'rush' had subsided, but I was still close to the physical body. My spirit-body was in the air, over my physical body, and falling sideways, down to the floor beside my bed. As I hit the floor, I bounced like a blown-up balloon, gently rising up in the air again. I was seeing my bedroom as it actually was, without any alterations at all. I floated down again and bounced on the carpet, and out of the corner of my eye I saw a long, off-white, cable. On the third bounce, unfortunately, I returned to my physical body with a jerk.

My last projection of the year has given me much hope, and optimism, for the future. My relaxation was more streamlined, and efficient, I had the confidence to project whilst my partner was with me, *and* the projection was etheric. All positive, and very important aspects of making progress.

Chapter Nine
The religious factor

At some stage it does become important to look at how, and where, out-of-body experience fits in to the big picture of religion and this is as good a place to start as any. I have split the section of the book containing practical experience's into two sections so that I can insert this chapter on what *I* refer to as religion. I believe that you will be better able to understand the rest of my experience's with the benefit of having absorbed this chapter first.

At the beginning of the book, you were asked to keep a completely open mind regarding the contents of this book. This is especially important when discussing such an emotive subject as religion, and I accept that it is very difficult to put aside beliefs that have been deeply held for many years. I am not going to try and challenge those beliefs, or threaten them in any way, that would be wrong and counter-productive.

My only aim here is to clarify aspects of religion in a way that relates, specifically, to out-of-body experience's, some of which is already known, and documented, but looking from a relevant perspective. This book will be read, hopefully, by people whose views range across the whole spectrum of belief, from those who regard themselves as having no religion at all, to those who live their daily lives in the service of God. With that in mind, please excuse me for beginning at the beginning, in maybe a simplistic manner, for it is my wish to be understood at each step. I would sincerely hope that a good person is recognised, and valued, in our society as a good person, whether they 'have' religion, or not. Similarly, out-of-body experience's can happen to anybody *irrelevant* of their spiritual, or religious nature, it really makes no difference.

We have already hit two difficult words, religion and God. So many contrasting meanings to confuse the mixed assortment, we call the human race. For now I would like to put them to one side and start with the one word that unites everybody in the world, regardless of everything, that word is *faith*. Even people who believe that they have no religion at all, have experienced faith, in some form. So let us use faith, a word we all understand, as a foundation stone on which to build our hypothesis.

Through all the confusion of the past, *somehow* intelligent human people came into being, and prospered. One view has it that we all managed to grow from a single celled amoeba. Another, is that a man and a woman were 'created' by God, and we are all descended from them. Yet, another, is that space travellers are using us as an experiment, our planet was viable for sustaining life, so they have created us in their image. There are many more 'theories', but here we have three, typical, examples incorporating a scientific view, a religious view, and a science fiction view. All possible, and all have their weaknesses under scrutiny. I mean, can anybody tell me how a single cell can develop and create an eye, for instance? What was the eye before it developed into the eye? I am saying that none of us have the answer, for sure, so that is why I am beginning with basic, intelligent, humans, and not getting involved with *creation*.

We all sit and idly muse over things that happen in our individual lives. The next time you do this I want you to subtract the *material* content of your thoughts and see what there is left to muse over. Take away all thoughts, and related thoughts, of television, radio, computers, cars, books, reading, writing, fashions, finance, etc. What do you have left to think about that isn't materialistic? It really wasn't all that long ago that this residue was all that *most* human beings had on their minds, over and above basic survival. It is very likely that, in those days, we were more in tune with our spiritual selves, our intuition, our instincts, the weather, the seasons, and our beautiful Earth.

The human race of animals are territorial hunters that have learned to grow crops, and are intelligent enough to realise the advantages of being a part of a social group. To remain an accepted member of this group means behaving in such a way that is agreeable to the others. To behave in any other way would force you to either lead the group, or leave the group. Here we have the seeds of society forming, group safety in defence, group efficiency to hunt and provide food, group members to trade with, and the establishment of a figurehead. Essentially, we are still exactly the same now, as animals we have not changed that much. In times of war, for example, our true colours are not all that flattering.

Throughout history, humankind has left evidence of religious belief. Even isolated tribes, existing on remote islands, or living in darkest rain forests, have all found the need for religious belief. The sticking point is, exactly *what is it* that they all believe in? All our emphasis has so far been concentrated on this point. We have, for example, fought wars to stop people worshipping the sun in an effort to force people into worshipping one God. We tried to make them cease believing in something that keeps them warm, helps them to grow their crops, and gives them light. In exchange we gave them something they can't see, an intangible 'something' that they must take somebody else's word for, or suffer the dire misfortunes that will befall them.

But we have been looking at this religious aspect from the wrong direction. It is not *what* we believe in, that is important. What *is* important is *why* we believe. Humanity has always believed in something, why? Because belief, and faith, is as much an ordinary part of us as an arm or a leg. We cannot *not* believe, and the reason 'why' is because of our *feelings*, our *emotions*. The one thing that unites everybody, throughout time, is the strength of belief, their faith, in *something*. We are all a spirit living in a physical shell, we all have a soul, and that soul lives within our spirit, and that is a fact of life.

When we feel emotion, it is within our spiritual selves that we feel it. When someone speaks the truth to us, or we hear beautiful music, a gentle wave tingles through our body. A person standing on a cliff top, gazing out over a magnificent sea, a thousand years ago, would have felt the same *kind* of emotions as someone doing it now. For example, I doubt if the emotion of fear has changed very much, if at all, over the years.

Jesus Christ was a man, the son of God, as we *all* are children of God. Jesus was a great individual, an enlightened person, and He was needed at that time, for many reasons. He gave religion foundation, rules to live by, standards for other's to achieve. He had to prove to the people that he was someone special, otherwise no-one would have taken any notice of Him. He carried out miracles, he was able to levitate and he was able to, not only project His spirit-body, but recognise others doing the same. He gave people a religion they were able to see, and see working. A religion they could have faith in, a real religion to love, fear and respect.

Many groups of human beings had their faith and beliefs well on the way to being out of control, and in danger of conflicting with the universal law. Human sacrifice was

164

one such act. If Jesus had not come along when He did, I would doubt that we would be as civilised as we are today. We must all be thankful for the influence He and, of course, *all* other great religious figures have given us, so strong that we still feel it today and, I suspect, forever.

There are many allusions to spirit projection, within the Bible, indeed I need only refer to the precious Holy Spirit, itself. Most of these references have been prised out, and aired, mainly by authors who purport to be experts of astral projection but, in fact, have no personal experience of the phenomenon. So they fill their books with references to the Bible and include other projector's experience's. These books are a waste of time and money. Would you buy a cook book written by someone who couldn't cook? No, of course not.

I will refer to just one example, and that is of Jesus going into the wilderness, for forty days and forty nights, all alone, and without food. For what purpose?

Fasting is one of the surest ways of inducing spirit projection. On this occasion, I suspect, Jesus did not go to project astrally or etherically, but to a finer, higher, plane. One that is very difficult to access and a privilege seldom granted. It is feasible that Jesus went to perform a special projection, one that would allow him access to a guiding authority. I have resisted the temptation to use the word God, so far, and for now we will keep this as a word only. By depriving Himself of nourishment, Jesus allowed His body to become weaker, by depriving Himself of company, He gave Himself enough time and space to concentrate, to relax nearer to the point of death. By cutting out food, He had effectively cut off a vital source of body energy. He was also in a place where he was well away from temptation, and the others who, fearing for His safety, would also tempt Him, and try to influence Him. Worst of all, they would have tried to support Him, by doing as He did. Jesus did not want that responsibility, for He knew that what He had to do, no other man could have done. Jesus went for guidance, and needed privacy, for what actually happened we will never know, but I suspect that it got quite interesting.

As His body became weaker, the physical resistance to hold on to the spirit-body dropped dramatically. He had no need for deep sleep as He was not tiring His physical body, so His body would have *appeared* as though he had died with life signs being virtually nil, another solid reason to be alone. In His dreams He may have dreamt of food and water, and it is possible that this helped His spirit-body project to a place where food and water would have been in abundance. This would have brought arousal of the conscious mind and clarity to the projection. He would have then gone on to commune, I suspect, with a higher knowledge, His spiritual guardians. The information He gained, must have been greatly needed, and put to use.

So what *is* God. Again, we spend all our time trying to work out *who* He or She is, or *what* He or She is. God is a *three letter word* that means the source of all things spiritual. One God? Yes of course, you can only have one spiritual source for everything. Our link with this 'source' is maintained through our spirit-bodies, and it is this 'source' that we use every night when we recharge ourselves with neural energy. So, God is omnipresent, God is everywhere, God is within us all, God is the common denominator that connects us all. God is part of the universal energy and without it we would all die. I am very sorry, but even if you do not believe in God, it is still with you, you breathe it, eat it, and invite it into you body, every time you go to sleep. When you feel deep emotion that causes your eyes to weep, it is God that you feel deep inside your soul. Like it or not!

It is said that we are the children of God. This needs a little explanation because it has been said so many times that we take it for granted without really thinking about what it means. We all have a soul, and each soul resides in a physical body living on earth, so many souls are waiting in the wings to reincarnate on their cycle of development, and so many souls have done all that and have progressed to, I presume, the *true and final* heaven. What the percentages are of each category must remain a mystery, but I suggest that they have always remained fairly constant. Since the time of Jesus, the earth population has indeed rocketed, therefore the number of souls in the other two categories have rocketed too.

The whole *simple* system is designed to improve the quality of the soul so that eventually we all will exist in the final place that, for want of a better word, we will now call *heaven*. This is the true meaning of the word as opposed to the erroneous label given, sometimes, to the astral type environments. It takes us a long time to achieve heavenly status, some longer than others, and it all depends on our learning the necessary spiritual values that make us worthy of such a place.

Back in the time of Jesus we humans led a simple, basic existence. It wasn't all sweetness and light, I grant you, but simple *compared* to today. Our survival depended on our physical abilities, our instincts for survival were sharper, and life was incredibly harder, we were most definitely not wrapped in the safety sheath of cotton wool that we are today. The real essence of life was easier to see, today these basic essentials of life are often masked by technology, modern stress, medical/non-medical drugs, peer pressure, fanaticism, etc. We take relaxing holidays that go a little way to rediscovering peace and contemplation. We never quite get there but we feel better for it, and I agree that we have little choice but to be a part of the 'rat-race' and fit the modern mould. The many that have been able to 'drop out' *and* survive will know the tremendous benefits that come from getting back to simple natural pursuits.

The more the basic issues of life are masked, the more difficult it is for our spiritual souls to learn and to develop. The more we plummet down the road of technology, or addiction, in all areas, the more difficult progress becomes. Real life is becoming substituted by virtual life. Taking things to extremes, *eventually* I can see the likelihood of someone being able to live a completely false life where no spiritual advanced will be made at all. The backlog of souls unable to progress will be the downfall of humanity, as the world will eventually be populated by too many, new, base souls that are not gaining any spiritual development or learning, at all. The percentage of these souls on earth will far exceed the enlightened ones and the problems will be many. I believe that it is already happening but in a small way, technology tarmacs a long road.

It *doesn't* have to be this way, and I sincerely hope we realise in time, but it is important to understand that should the soul ratio become unbalanced *real* havoc will certainly ensue. These underdeveloped souls will be influenced by each other in the absence of mature sources. What makes this dangerous, in the modern world, is the sheer population numbers involved, the increased technology involved, and raw education. For a soul to achieve its final destination may take many more lifetimes that it actually ought to. We are *already* moving in the wrong direction.

Back in the time of Jesus, the population figures were much easier to comprehend. When a soul has completed the cycle of learning, maybe only having to return six or seven times, it goes 'somewhere' and I have called it *heaven*. There are far more intricate stages that I know little

168

about, and they do exist, but I am purposefully keeping this as simple as I can. Over the thousands of years the body of souls that have attained heavenly status has steadily increased like a slow drip of purity at the end of a spiritual processing plant. Once it was small and had a small population to regard. Now it has increased in size, as has the population also. If we upset the balance this heavenly body will be stretched so that its influence will be diluted across these new, base, souls.

For those that have still to grasp the significance of what God really is, let me make this statement: We have the physical environment that sustains life, this is nature. Part of the life it sustains has the benefit of containing a spiritual cycle where we, eventually, progress to an enlightened state. From the very beginning this final state of heaven has been growing as a body of total knowledge and wisdom. It is this exalted echelon that actually is our 'God'. From now on whenever I mention 'God', it is this high body of knowledge that I am referring to. When we pray, and our prayers are answered, it is because we have transmitted our deep emotion via our own spirit through the spiritual system to God. God can advise us, God can also affect our fate pattern, via other spiritual means, to help us. But God will be able to see further into the future than we can, and ultimately God will know best. God is part of nature as everything else is, but it exists as a separate entity, albeit closely entwined. God, therefore, cannot prevent natural disasters and catastrophes from happening, just as it cannot advise those that are blind to His/Her/its existence or give any kind of acknowledgement when served by lip service alone.

A sad fact of life is that it often takes absolute despair before people will address God, and acknowledge the possibility of God existing. Sometimes a seemingly cruel turn of fate will cause whole families to begin to pray and reappraise their lives within the reflection of God. I am not a religious fanatic, I am just explaining the simple fact that if you understand that there is a real purpose for being a good and caring person then you *will* be. And the point of it all is to become a good spirit in as little time as possible, so that you will become a part of the final 'God', a part of heaven, a part of the ultimate blissful peace.

I first mentioned, during the relaxation procedures, a little feeling that I called the 'tingle factor'. I wonder if you then realised how important this link was going to be? We sleep at night to recharge ourselves with spirit energy, the 'tingle factor' is us, consciously, using up a little of that energy. When you have become a projector, you will understand the truth of this. By the way, if we are out of our body and induce the tingle it shows up as light.

My dearest wish would be for enough people to experiment with out-of-body existence on a personal basis, and realise the truth about how the system works, so that they can tell, and teach others. Humankind would, at last, begin to re-evaluate its religious principles, revise its current thinking, but more importantly, it is the *realisation* by the human race that they can touch, feel, and integrate with what it is that I call God. At last, we all can take responsibility for our actions in the full knowledge that what we do *will* affect us for all time, and not just while we are on this physical earth.

One hears the phrase 'the day of judgement' banded around as some kind of mysterious threat, as though someone will, at the gates of heaven, judge the life you have led and punish you accordingly. What actually happens is this - the *quality* of your afterlife is determined by the quality of spiritual development gained on earth. In other words, we are self regulatory. If we are well intentioned, and have a clear conscience, come the day we die we will reap the rewards of a good life. There is no such thing as complete privacy, for everything that we do is known to others, *everything*. I repeat, it is our duty to become good, caring, and balanced people whilst we inhabit a physical body on the physical plane. To commit a crime that goes against humanity, is to commit a crime against God, against the universal energy, and against ourselves. Our punishment is our conscience, always there to remind us, plus the realisation that one day you will have to return to earth, and try again. We carry God with us wherever we go, just think.

By the way, everything I have said in this book, is personal to you, between you and yourself. I am not one of those people that organise weird religious sects, and brainwash you into believing me! I want you to get to know *yourself* by using my simple, and very normal, procedures. Oobex is actually the missing link between science and religion, an area where we can all understand each others viewpoints. How can we ever understand anybody else when we don't properly understand ourselves?

Isn't it interesting how technology has created virtual reality machines to thrill us into experiencing flying sensations, and getting us to believe that we are somewhere else in this world, or another. How very perverse when we all have this ability anyway, and much, much more. I do worry that we make things too easy and once again, by creating this technology, it continues to take people further away from reality. We are losing our finer senses to shallow entertainment and easy amusements. Somewhere, somehow, the understanding of these words, must find a place in our personal education, for this is *important*. When do we ever spend time in silent contemplation? This world has speeded up and left our consideration behind. The time it takes to respect each other has reduced itself to a minimum, so much so, that in some cases it has ceased completely. When that happens society is easily broken down and very difficult to repair.

Oobex is a 'religion' personal to each and every one of us, because we are all different, with differing values, which allows us the freedom to be *individual*, and to care for our fellow kind in the full knowledge that if we *do* commit an offence, it will not go unnoticed. Fear God? Yes indeed, for all your sins are laid bare to decide your future existence, not here, but sometime following death. It is right to be afraid. If you have done something wrong and you pray for forgiveness, you must be able to forgive yourself first. If you can do that, forgiveness will be granted, but if you cannot, *honestly*, forgive yourself, then you will suffer, to a greater or lesser extent, for the duration of your life on earth, and beyond....

Should your sins be of a nature where they were committed unintentionally, you will be forgiven, because we are allowed to make mistakes in this life. It is mainly due to these mistakes that we learn about ourselves, and grow. Accidents do happen as a fact of life, and are not always part of a fate pattern or can be foreseen. Most real accidents are random, and nothing at all to do with fate, God, coincidences or anything other than bad luck. Whoever says that all life is mapped out, and out of our control, is barmy. We have fate lines, some strong, some weak that we naturally work within. Very generally, these are made up from a combination of genes, education, life influences, spiritual guidance, past life influence, etc. Over and above all this future likelihood, hangs the sword of accident, the killing scythe of natural disaster, the random killing element that prunes the incestuous growth of complacency in the evolution of human kind.

Let the common man and woman come together and unite. Let the educated learn that there is more to intelligence than being able to remember facts. Real intelligence comes from being able to do something useful with those facts, in order to help others. Many people will learn from life, and from their family and friends, far more than they will ever learn at school. Education systems are often not able to cope with individuals, unless they are *very* clever, or gifted, and that is perfectly understandable. But, we should *all* be educated to a standard where we look to ourselves, before looking to other's.

The importance of knowing how to realise our own strengths and weaknesses, in an honest fashion, would be a start. I'm bumping my gums about all this, as though it is difficult, and it isn't. It is simply getting back to a state of mind where we value *ourselves*, impossible when our teachers, and parents, haven't got this understanding. Why on earth are we trying to teach logarithms, rainwater levels in tropical rain forests, and the sex life of a mayfly, to someone who doesn't know that it is wrong to hit people, to steal and abuse our fellow human kind. If nothing else, shouldn't the common, and basic, life values be taught first?

Let us educate children to be concerned that life is precious, and to be respected and cherished. Children unconsciously look for guidance, they have underdeveloped minds that suck everything up within a *comparatively* short time-scale. Massive amounts of information are retained in the first three years of life, even prior to being able to speak children are already understanding language. If that influence could be monitored, regulated and censored to a healthy standard, then we wouldn't have children that harbour deep dark thoughts, and bad attitudes, without possessing the knowledge from whence they came. Do parents watch objectively, the programmes, and magazines that are accessible to children these days? What ever happened to common-sense parenting? The *pace* of life has put an end to this, and I have just travelled in a full circle. For all those good, and caring, parents out there that *are* enlightened, and I suspect that there are even more grandparents (sense really does come with age!) I salute you and encourage you, for you *are* the future.

What does the common man, and woman, living anywhere in the world, want from life? This question is a little like percentages. If you give everybody that works in a factory a rise of five pounds a week, it sounds fair, evenly shared across the board, no arguments. The sweeper up is a happy man, the dispatch manager is angry. If you give everybody that works in a factory a rise of five *per cent*, everybody is happy, because everybody has got the same and been treated fairly. If you were to ask the layperson, what their priorities are, you will receive a common answer over all, irrelevant of the colour, creed or religion. Those three things are no barrier to oobex, however, identity and tradition, in any walk of life, are important contributors to animal instinct, and should, on no account become confused with it. Yes, I am generalising, yes I am talking about majorities, in a book like this you have to.

So, these people would answer the question with a broad response. Good health, first and foremost for the immediate and extended family, enough work to provide enough money to keep the immediate family, and themselves, in food, and adequately clothed, secure and warm. The common person is not greedy, they are not naturally hurtful or inclined to harbour dark thoughts about their neighbours and friends. They naturally have enough knowledge, however they came by it, to live within their own status, and enough gumption to box within their own weight.

A common example is the boy that rejects mathematics as an anathema and yet can calculate a running total of points scored during a darts match, with lightning speed. If you mention mathematics, he has trouble making the connection. The common person is a good person, but often influenced by those that they 'believe' to be more intelligent and more worldly wise. Of course, nothing could be further from the truth.

Problems arise for those that fall outside the category marked 'normal'. We are born, we grow up, we fall in love, we marry, we have children, we watch them grow up, we become wise, we watch their children grow up, we make the most of our lives, we die. We spend our lives, within society, living within these restraints set by man, in an effort to suppress the *natural* instincts inherent in the *animal* that we are. I am simply stating a fact, I am not complaining, I have no wish to be clubbed around the head and have my woman dragged off for whatever reason. But what about the few that do fall out of the 'normal' category? How do they fit in with what we now know about life?

The physical body, and all its component parts, is simply a vehicle for the spirit. Let us teach oobex to people that have brain disorders, that are paralysed, blind, have muscular wastage, the range is immense. Let us teach oobex in prisons and remand centres, both excellent places where time is plentiful for personal study.

The incentive is freedom, the by-product is finding the truth of goodness. Anyone that can understand language can be taught to disassociate their true selves from this physical shell. Once these people can project to the astral plane, they can *begin to alter their perceptions*. A blind person on earth will, I suspect, also be blind on the astral plane, and the reason for that is because their astral world has been influenced by that person during their lifetime, for a particular use. And that use is needed for when we die. Once that is understood, and they realise that there is no need to be spiritually blind, any longer, they will begin to see, astrally.

A spirit cannot physically suffer with cerebral palsy, multiple sclerosis, paralysis, bad breath, stammers, liver disease, heart attacks or any other such malady. We still must be cognitive, astrally, to be able to shed our earthly apparel in order to benefit from perfect freedom in our astral locality. Can you imagine what it must feel like to be severely incapacitated, bound to a bed or a wheelchair during the day, but at night able to fly like an eagle, with the strength of a bear, and the grace of a ballet dancer? What must that be worth?

Women that decline to have children, for whatever reason, are failing to produce the new human beings necessary for spirit occupation. This is only one of the reasons we have to live an earthly life, the other is to educate, by experience, our spiritual selves. It doesn't matter if we don't have children as long as the reason for that is fully understood. Similarly with homosexual folk, the same applies, to the letter.

I mentioned earlier the word death, so let's talk about it. This happens for many reasons, usually because a part of our physical body, vital to life, has become so old that it has worn out, or it has become diseased, or it has been damaged. Some of us will die quickly, some slowly, it all very much depends on the cause, and we die *via* oobex phenomena. Just as we project in different ways, and to different environments, so do we die in *exactly* the same way. Should we die by accident, or murder, before our time, the transference will be sudden, but no different to normal. The tragedy is that the immature spirit will need to return to complete its maturity.

Dying naturally, we pass through these different states on our way to the after-life. We will either 'death project' through a 'lucid' phase on our way to the etheric, or we can by-pass the etheric and go straight to the astral. If we do enter 'death' via the 'lucid' stage then it is very likely that the subconscious mind will conjure up something quite strange, like visions of past relations and friends, to induce the consternation needed to raise the vibrations that carry you onto *either* the etheric, or astral, plane as quickly as possible.

We can go immediately to the etheric plane *or* the astral plane, following death. It may be there that we perhaps enter the well-documented tunnel to yet a further environment. If we should die suddenly, it is quite common not to even realise that you are, indeed, deceased. It will be the scenes around you, or the sight of your own dead body, that will tell you the truth of it. If, for example, you see your own body lying in its *true* circumstances, then this is an etheric death.

The 'tunnel', just mentioned, is something that I have not experienced in out-of-body projection, and appears to be a sensation confined to near death experience's. Remember, oobex is *not* a near death experience, but *some* near death experience's are out-of-body phenomena. There have appeared many possible explanations for perceiving the 'tunnel' ranging from, gas in the bloodstream to, a throwback to the birth process. I cannot throw light on this except that, contrary to popular belief, during hypnosis the subconscious mind is capable of revealing the intricacies of the patients birth process, the conscious mind however is not.

Stored in the subconscious mind is a record of each birth process that that person has ever undergone. The subconscious mind is mature at each subsequent birth and is cognitive of the situation. The poor physical body is weak and terribly underdeveloped. The conscious mind is new to the process of soaking up information and therefore is not capable of recall. A hypnotised subject undergoing life regression will often go through a period, or 'passage', of darkness between lives. My only comment is that I am not surprised to read of a 'tunnel' experience at the moment of impending death.

Now it is unfortunate to those of us that have a *terribly* strong attachment to *someone*, or *something* earthly, for they are bound to roam the earthly plane, stuck between two worlds, unable to leave, unable to go forward. A tie can be made as strongly through hate as it can be through love, but it *has* to be very strong.

We all know how much we love the people that we would leave behind if we died but, let me tell you, normal love would not nearly be strong enough to keep us in touch. The link, good or bad, has to be verging on the fanatical, our feelings for whatever, or whoever, must be etched onto the core of our subconscious mind, to allow us to remain. Our death at the hand of someone extremely wicked, who might go on to hurt our remaining family, is the sort of thing that would keep us locked within the etheric plane.

Another tie, that could hold you there, are secrets that your family have no knowledge of, illicit love letters, nefarious dealings, or any very deeply held worries. I told you that the spirit environments are so real that you don't even think of the possibility of flying, well these poor deceased persons feel so normal that they are resigned to their new circumstances because they cannot see any way to go anywhere else.

If, for once, they would release their interest over the earthly business, and relax, they would see the way forward very clearly, to their immense benefit. The beauty of dying and attaining the etheric level is that, at least, you can see what is going on and understand the circumstances of your death. Being able to visit loved ones, and relatives, is a comfort to you, which is often all you need to leave the earthly plane behind. Of course it isn't healthy to remain in contact with the physical plane, who needs the upset, who needs to see the grief, or even, perhaps to see, the secret dancing for joy that you are no more!

This is purgatory, you can't go back, even though you can see your loved ones grieving, and you can't go forward, because of the ties that bind you to earth. Your environment hasn't changed though. You will think, well! this dying lark is just like earth, no shocks, no St.Peter, no heaven, no difference. An easy transition from life to death, it is *supposed* to be that way. It is meant to cause you as little disquiet as possible. *Death is meant to be user friendly!*

The other alternative, is to project directly onto the astral plane. This is more likely to be the destination for the majority of us. We spend our lives *subconsciously* creating an astral familiarity that will be a home from home, specifically there for us to enjoy when we retire from our earthly existence. It will have all the attributes that we subconsciously admired in our physical term, but without the downfalls. In death it is infinitely much healthier to be astral, than etheric, for there we *understand* that loved ones are simply out of reach and, in a sense, it is *us* that have lost *them*, rather than *they* who have lost *us*. By being caressed away from the physical, minus pain, suffering, and torment, we can see the unfolding of a beautiful world. A place where we can adjust to the fact that we are no longer earthly, to reach that correct conclusion without too much stress or worry, and to meet people, maybe even old friends...... to be happy again.

How long one remains existing here in 'paradise' is, I believe, variable, and depends on many factors of which I have no knowledge. Spiritual development is probably one, and peace of mind is probably another. I do believe that at some time you will enter a yet another state, which involves the process of losing your familiar, earthly looking body, and you will continue to exist in a kind of a pure mental condition. Not everybody has to return to earth, but those that have to, do so for a reason, and somewhere along the line, consciousness, the working desk-top of the mind, has to be sealed away and a new conscious awareness will begin to accept the new knowledge. Where that happens is anybody's guess, I, personally, think that it happens at the moment your spirit connects to the unborn baby, whilst still in the womb.

This new conscious chapter doesn't always leave everything behind as it should do and some knowledge gained in the previous life, or lives, is sometimes retained.

There is much controversy over whether, using hypnosis, another life *can* be accessed. This may sound obvious, but a lot depends on whether you *have actually lived that other life*. A lot also depends on your subconscious mind releasing that information. Some of us, subconsciously, are 'open' types, that will tell you everything about ourselves, some of us are 'reserved' and do not want all revealed. If you *have* lived before, and your subconscious mind has no problem in releasing that information, this can then be quite easily accessed using hypnosis. Indeed it is very satisfying to help people in this way.

When this other life is accessed, it is not necessarily the most *recent* life that comes to the fore. These lives will be accessed in the order that the subconscious mind decides is correct. When successfully achieved, the subject will often speak in an altered fashion, ladies will suddenly develop deep gruff voices, as near to their previous voice as their current vocal box will allow, and vice versa.

Which brings me to another point, because you are the gender you happen to be, now in this current body, it doesn't mean to say that you have always been that gender. If you have lived a good few previous lives, then it is extremely usual to have been male and female at different times. This is another very important reason that the conscious mind must begin a new page, prior to birth.

Now, when some people retain a degree of conscious knowledge of that previous life, it doesn't always have to be a visual recognition of the locale and, perhaps, family. It can be any aspect of that life. Children, especially during their first few years before their, current, conscious mind becomes fully developed, will come out with some very strange things. These are well worth looking for, and recognising them for what they are. At such a young age they can be drawn to strange objects and utter foreign words. All this has been copiously documented elsewhere, and in a superior fashion, but all parents of young children should look for these clues.

Is this not why we produce child progenies? Has anybody thought to regress a great violinist who, for some unknown reason, could play beautifully at the age of four? Could this be knowledge, and ability, that has been retained from another life? To a lesser extent, we all have interests in life that could very well have been influenced from before. Some of us would give our eye teeth to live in a seventeenth century cottage, because we feel more at home, other's crave for a new house, all spick-and-span, upright and square. It would be very interesting to regress a proficient projector into a previous life, and then allow him, or her, to spiritually project. Would the astral environment also be dated?

Now, let's bite the bullet on another gritty subject. Homosexual people are *born* homosexual. A gay man is different to a heterosexual man, and exactly the same applies to women. A heterosexual person should never fear their homosexual friends having 'designs' on a relationship, because you are *not* the right gender for them. A gay person needs another gay person to live a full and complete life. I am only saying this for the sake of clarity. As different a man is to a woman, is as different as a homosexual person is to a heterosexual person.

The reason that I have laboured these facts, is because we have in our society a whole range of inbetweenies! These include, for example, bisexuals and cross dressers, some happy, some desperately confused. I think that it is very probable that these people have lived before as a member of the opposite sex, and have retained too much conscious knowledge of it. If one is a woman she would naturally have spent a lifetime dressing, very correctly, in women's clothing. It means that a lot of time has been spent on buying clothes, thinking about clothes, looking after clothes, choosing underwear, washing and ironing. In fact, women get great pleasure from wearing the correct clothes for the occasion to look nice and feel good. I am simply picking up on one, typically, positive aspect of a lady's life, for the aim of this illustration.

When this person dies she will continue to be that lady with the retained memories, and feelings, in her mind, just as she had when alive, for a period of time. Now, should the lady have a new life, and properly inhabit the tiny body of an unborn boy child, she, or rather, he, would grow up quite normally, with all that knowledge stored safely away in his subconscious mind. This is healthy for the development of a balanced soul, and should also be an asset to him, in coping with his life as a man.

Using messages from his subconscious mind, it might enable him to appreciate, or even advise his spouse on her apparel. He may think to buy her flowers, because he knows how much she appreciates them, and so on. You see how the experience of previous lives, especially lived as an opposite sex, eventually makes you a good, rounded, capable person.

We know these people, we may even be one ourselves, an old head on young shoulders, calm in crisis, not easily thrown off course, all those things. Of course it happens exactly the same, the other way around.

You may be sitting there reading this, as a woman, but one who, for some reason, *understands* that your man enjoys wearing nice, smart, clothes, but doesn't have any interest in what these clothes are made of, or if they wash well. You may understand the pleasure he gets from time spent, in an old shed, taking things to bits and ending up filthy dirty, or being part of a pack of lads that enjoy a good laugh and a drink, on their own, without female company.

You may well understand this, or things similar to this, because you might have lived before and, without necessarily doing these things, know what it is like to behave as a man behaves.

I am always amazed when people are quite ready, and open, to accept my teachings on out-of-body travel with all that that entails, but when it comes to the suggestion that they have lived before as another sex, oh boy, does that rattle the door of self security! I am threatening their sexual foundation, how dare I suggest that they are not quite a 100% woman, or a 100% man. Often I get, 'yes, that may be the case for others, but I have *always* been a (whichever) and I would certainly know if I had lived any differently.' *No you don't*, that is why it is a subconscious influence.

The sooner we realise that it is the importance of being a *'good person'* the better, and it doesn't matter a jot which sex we are.

I have spoken about the lady, who after living a normal life, died, and in the course of events, gained a new physical life inhabiting the body of an unborn boy child. I have also spoken about how healthy this is for spiritual development. Healthy, that is, as long as the 'old' conscious mind has been stored away efficiently, and the 'new' conscious mind has begun afresh. This term is quite correct because you actually start with a new, but blank, section of conscious mind, when you are reborn. A little like having your last conscious life all in a box, bundled up, and labelled for storage, and you have been given a new empty box for use in this coming life.

The natural instincts of being a man, or a woman, that has already lived a lifetime, are of course very strong. In some instances, during the process of beginning again, a fresh conscience, and consciousness, can be polluted by knowledge retained from a previous life. How much of this information and emotion, that is carried over, varies from person to person, but can be little enough to rate you as, slightly troubled sexually, or large enough to cause you full blown confusion.

To go back to our example, if our little boy begins his life with a polluted consciousness, all aspects of his new life will have to fit around what is already there. Like clothes on a skeleton. He may be drawn to certain fabrics, silk may hold a fascination for him, in the softness and the way it feels when rubbed between his fingers. He may be completely heterosexual, but find certain men very attractive, in their attitude and mannerisms, but not physically. Sexy underwear may be a real turn-on to him, *especially* if he wears it himself. If this knowledge retention

184

is strong enough, it could affect his prospects of a normal relationship, and he may find comfort, and understanding with others that are also sexually uncertain. It is possible that he would feel unable to have a normal relationship with a woman and, not being gay, unable to have a normal relationship with a man.

Instead of being treated as having a mental problem gained in this life, these people should be taught to know more about how this, unfortunate condition, has occurred for them. Of course this is not specifically a sexual problem, it can relate to all aspects of your life, but I talk about sexuality, as an example, because it is such an important, and prominent, aspect of life. It could, just as easily, relate to health issues, or the reason someone has irrational habits, or just about anything. Remember, this doesn't mean that all the ills in life, or peculiarities, stem from a polluted consciousness, or from a previous life, not at all. But, on the occasion where this *is* the cause, and quite frankly, we don't know how many people are affected in this way, we should be cognitive of these facts.

People are better off when they understand how a situation has come about. For a sufferer of a polluted consciousness to comprehend the bigger picture, is a big step towards relieving the confusion and stress of the problem. They become *normal* human beings with a *fully* understood problem that manifests itself, in a common manner, to many other people in many differing ways. Their particular problem, is caused by no fault of their own, and they realise that they are one of thousands, instead of the individual freak, they often feel. Once people learn to recognise their finer feelings by studying my relaxation procedures, with a view to experiencing an oobex, they can convince themselves of the truth of the life after life cycle. I'm not saying that it is necessary for everyone to project

185

their spirit-bodies, but I do say that if you begin to go down the oobex path there will come a time when you will believe the truth. Once you have convinced yourself, you can then see clearly the problem and deal with it in much more effective manner.

If many people, in the world, practised the art of spirit projection, they would be united by a *tangible* religion. The 'real' meaning of life. United by truth, but each with their *own* unique spirituality in direct contact with the universal energy force. Of course, these people can continue to follow their existing religions, why not? When you have been privileged to the ultimate experience possible in life, you understand a much wider picture. When the pieces slot into a jigsaw puzzle you gain the realisation that all religions are trying to do the same thing, but misunderstanding individuals have, over the years, convinced us different. Armed with the inner confidence of 'truth', we can all continue to attend our religious centres, and use them for our own spiritual development. You now know that God is everywhere, because it *is* within each of us, it has to be or we would die.

Any holy place will be a comfort to you, a projector can sit in a mosque, church, chapel or a mighty forest, for the God within us will be felt everywhere. Any place that is peaceful, contemplative or awesome, will also be good for feeling the tingle factor naturally functioning within us.

I do not have all the answers, so help me. The more projector's we have, the more we can build up an even bigger picture of life. Also it will enable me to spread the flack! Having achieved spiritual peace and contentment, I really am not looking forward to spending the last years of my life arguing about it. That is why I say, try it for yourself and see. Could you imagine if we all became happy and secure in our private faith in God? If we all knew how our actions in life affect our own soul for the future? If every act is known to others, no matter *how* secret and we all became responsible for our own actions, how this world of ours would change!

I feel very uncomfortable with how our precious world is being finance driven. The people that make decisions, on our behalf, don't seem to me to be too in touch with common values. People that can *influence* other people are the ones that run countries, whether that is by the word or by force. Because of this we end up with a very peculiar mish-mash of odd bods in power. Do we not have enough *educated* men and women on this earth that *are* responsible and sophisticated enough to run our planet in harmony?

We live on a natural planet, a simple benevolent ball, in space, that sustains life. Why are we taken in by people that do not appreciate how fragile we are, and how careful we must be? Why, because we are not sure of ourselves, because we do not know ourselves, because we have not looked deep enough to understand how each of us works. We have never before known how to look at ourselves, or where to start, although the clues have always been there. Nobody has the power to be the human voice of God. That is only to be found within each of us, for our own personal use, and for *us* to abide by.

We have not got to go to the extremes of living a monastic life, to maintain a good link with our own spirit hierarchy. We should be able to incorporate that in our modern situations, if we can't, then we must put ourselves into the situation where we can. If you are too busy for your self, then you are too busy in life. It only takes a short period of time each day, spent in silent contemplation, to maintain a healthy contact. A time to re-evaluate the situation, to gather your thoughts, to centre yourself and calm those wayward urges. If we ignore our finer feelings, we will not be able to recognise them in other people, or be able to teach our children the art of discovery.

How many children have to sleep with the light on, because of their fears? This book gives you, the parent, an understanding of exactly what is happening, so that you can communicate with your child in a, hitherto, impossible way. Nature presents to you the perfect opportunity to teach your children the finer values of life, and how life really works, but instead, we switch on a light, effectively suppressing their access to the mental playground. To understand and enjoy oobex, as a child, means that you will always have easier access to it, throughout life. To ignore this religion, will make it always harder. A bit like a serious version of happy now, pay later.

Walking into a church, to confess a terrible deed, and expect forgiveness, is perverse. Who has forgiven you? Let no-one be under any doubt, that the only person who can forgive your sins is yourself. If you do something that you feel was wrong, it will sit on your conscience. If it was something you did unintentionally, by accident, it will not sit for long. However, if we intentionally do something, knowing it to be wrong, then it will stay on the conscience for ever. To expect a priest to clear this conscience for you, is an impossibility. That deed will stay with you for the rest of your life, and beyond, and it will affect the quality of the environment you live in, following death. You *will* reap what you sow. A good deed will never cancel out a bad deed, but realising that the bad deed was wrong, and learning from the experience, especially if you can help others, will help you immeasurably. If a bad deed eventually helps to make *you* a good person then you will have succeeded in turning it around, we *all* have a chance to be good.

I have seen hell, or at least what I believe is *my* hell. But first, what is hell, and where is it? A good, happy and healthy life, lived with joy and understanding, will create an astral environment to die for! This is what we usually regard, erroneously, as heaven, I'll talk more about that later. If we live less than perfect lives, the quality of our astral status lessens. If we inflict terrible deeds on other people, attacking them physically and destroying them mentally, shattering their emotions, we are truly creating a bad astral environment for us now, and following death. If we continue this type of behaviour in subsequent lives, without learning or improving, then we must expect to know hell. But it will be our own *particular* hell.

For want of knowledge to the contrary, I have always perceived hell as a place of furnaces, hard graft, no breaks, and some nasty so and so, with a whip, wandering around making sure that you don't falter in your work. I guess this may be the common perception for most people. Well I don't mind hard work, the pay is lousy, but you are warm and dry, so if the worst comes to the worst, is it really so bad? As I said, that was my vision of hell, until I had an experience that *radically changed my thinking.*

It happened a few years ago, prior to the time that I kept records, on an ordinary night of relaxation that culminated in vivid dreams and restlessness. *I became aware that I was dreaming of being in London, not busy central London, but somewhere in a town centre within the London area. Perhaps just south of the river, it was familiar to me, but then most places are, in dreamland. The weather was warm and sunny, people were roaming around in tee-shirts and shorts, smiling, joking, and generally enjoying the perfect day. I recall the moment that the dream ceased to be vivid and became lucid, it was as I was about to cross a busy road junction. I was happy to gain the extra awareness in this place of sunshine and goodness, it really was a very pleasant place to be. I crossed the road and walked along the pavement, past the shops, thinking about where I was going to find an appropriate place to project my spirit-body. I knew it was going to be easy, as I had done it before, so many times.*

All of a sudden, the ground opened up beneath me! I felt myself falling, projecting into what seemed to me to be the bowels of the earth. Further and further, faster and faster, until my descent eventually levelled out and before me I perceived a terrible spectacle. I was flying low over rows, upon rows, of naked people. Men and women standing naked, and frozen, in lines that stretched as far as my eyes could see, in every direction. They were alive but lifeless, holding hands in some semblance of unity, their faces drawn and blank, their bodies shivering in hopelessness. Between each row was a mere eighteen inches of space, their skin was a horrible shade of white, and a kind of blue mist swirled around them.

I flew low over this desperate scene, and with the vision of the lines of bodies stretching into infinity, I rose up in a soaring fashion, to make my way back to the place from where I had started. I stood on the pavement in a state of shock, and bewilderment. Looking around me I saw the perfect scene as I had left it, as though nothing had happened. As though nobody knew the desolation below them. I sat down on the edge of the pavement, with my head in my hands, and felt myself immediately back at home, in bed. Needless to say, this experience is as fresh in my memory now, as it was when it happened. A clear illustration perhaps of how 'hell' can be personal to each of us as 'heaven'. I believe that I was given a glimpse of what my hell destination would look like, and what I saw worried me deeply. I would sincerely fear becoming one of those cold, isolated souls, at the end of my life.

Hell is the antithesis of all that has been good in your life. It comes as the result of everything you hate, from your guilt, from your vengeance, from your small minded nastiness. Oh yes, even the good and the great will evolve and create a tailor-made hell as their individual life unfolds. Hell is as much a reflection of you as heaven is, and will subconsciously grow within you, like a waste bin of your mind that contains the dregs of your mental processes. It is impossible to escape, but if you live an honourable life, a *good* life, then your individual hell will be small, in proportion, and firmly left where it should be, weighted down by goodness.

It serves as a control, in our daily lives, that should be more effective than any manmade law could ever be, once we know *personally*, of its existence. I believe that out-of-body experience is a natural thing that we all should strive to achieve, and those that are successful may, at some time or another, also be given the privilege of seeing what their own hell will look like. The natural, universal, law must be obeyed, but we can only do that by understanding it first.

Some people would rather not know. Why? It will make you think twice, about all that you do in the future, and would halt the most hardened criminal in his tracks. Knowing that hell exists *does* make you a better person, it *does* force you to go into yourself and find that extra compassion that is in all of us. So I have seen my hell, and I am all the better for it, I hope. No more can I use ignorance as a shield.

Little by little I hope that a much larger picture is emerging for you of how life is and what it means. It is a fact of life that no matter how much light is thrown over this subject, there are those that will always look at it through stained glass. It is not until the big picture is realised can we really make progress. Each part that I explain to you, can be, and no doubt will be, pulled apart by scientists, and will be discounted on the assumption that it cannot be proved. Very many of these scientists go to church, and believe in God........ I *want* my teachings to be investigated, I would very much *like* scientists to take up the challenge, to personally try oobex and, in *their* language, teach others that I can't reach, because I have no professional foundation. Let us be positive and take this further, for the sake of us all we need to be going in this direction *as well* as in the direction of technology. I am greatly aided by technology, but not to the detriment of my soul.

Oobex is the missing link, as I have already said, and has eluded mass discovery since time began. It is so important, and powerful, and yet so difficult to uncover and define, but once this has been achieved, many mysteries are seen to be understood. The shadows of oobex have created dark stories of ghosts, demons and the like. All serving to ensure that the real truth remains hidden behind misunderstanding and fear. If we can raise the canopy of prejudice, and superstition, the answers can be revealed for all to see.

Just as in a dream, a monster is the reflection of your own fear, an emotion that has to be recognised, and conquered, to attain advancement. Once done, the monster will disappear for ever. If you can allow yourselves to accept the contents of the whole book, with an open mind, *before* making judgements, then you will have a chance to appreciate the final canvas. Oobex is the one common denominator that can link all people, from all disciplines, if we choose to. It will open a path to enable you to establish your own personal religion, far stronger within, than without.

Life is all about choice. To have choice is to have more than one option. In the West, especially, we are so lucky to have so much, there are many people in poorer countries that have none. Choice is a mental function, and is at the core of successfully being able to achieve out-of-body experience. If we choose to look into *ourselves* then other processes will come to help you in your journey, but that decision has to come from you first.

Our spiritual superiors love us unconditionally, it is *us* that do not reciprocate, it is *us* that are ignorant unless we *choose* to find out, and finding out about ourselves gives us greater choices in a greater life. How can we be, in our lives, our own judge and jury, and make these choices if we are not fully aware of the facts in the case. Oobex helps you to make more of your life and reveals these facts to you.

Chapter Ten
More practical examples

THURSDAY 4TH JANUARY 1996

Following a normal relaxation process, I lost my conscious awareness and through a dream, that I cannot now remember, I gradually became aware that I was existing, and at a distance from my physical body. I had walked through the centre of a town, and back out the other side, when I decided to check the cable. I put my right hand to the rear of my head and, very gently, grasped the astral cord. I had no idea what the real distance was between my spirit-body and my physical body, but I was half way through a normal projection and, therefore, I would have been out of close range. I still get a tremendous thrill every time I touch this most elusive part of my anatomy.

The cable diameter felt as if it was about 1cm (between a quarter and half an inch) thick, at the head end, and it did not have a root system. See Figure 4, page 135. *I brought my left hand around to feel the cord further along its length. It felt like a very thin polythene tube full of pulsating water. It was very soft, and pliable, with a throbbing feeling inside, not the outer cover, but a feeling similar to a moving current of water within.*

It appears that, as the spirit-body gets further from the physical body, the width of the cable diminishes, and the root system disappears. In this instance, the cable appeared to be flush to the back of my head. I cannot bring myself to be anything else but gentle with the cord, I look upon it in a similar way that a mountaineer must feel when he, or she, is hanging over a precipice dependant on a single lifeline.

WEDNESDAY 17TH JANUARY 1996

A strange occurrence. Without any *conscious* preparation, at all, I projected. It was halfway through the night, and I found myself 'rushing' out of my body into oblivion. For sure, you know that you are going, but you never know to where, until you get there. All these decisions are made for you, by your superconscious mind.

I found that I had astrally projected to an upper floor of an unknown house. Feeling a little guilty, I tiptoed downstairs and exited the building through the back door, and I mean the material of the door. I came across a dog that was kept in the backyard, so I quickly made a dash for the six foot gate that led to the road. I passed through the fabric of the gate and turned, making quite sure that the dog didn't also pass straight through, with me. It appears that astral walls are capable of restraining astral dogs!

Looking around I saw a very neat, and tidy, estate of houses with pretty gardens and manicured lawns. As I stood there, deciding what to do, a gentleman drove up and parked his car in his drive. I made my way over to him, as he was locking his door, and asked him the time. In a very pleasant manner, he said that it was 'eleven fifty-five, nearly twelve o'clock.' I thanked him, turned around, and found myself back in bed.

The astral environment is so *real* that it is easy to understand that it exists even when you are not projected on to it. A parallel environment, constantly existing in another dimension. In other words, I maybe back in bed thinking about what I have just done whilst, back on the astral, some poor so-and-so has walked into his home and told his wife that a stranger had just asked him the time, before disappearing into thin air! Or did I? Perhaps I am still unconsciously there, I will talk more about this possibility later. And yes, it looks like you still have to do the garden, and lock your car, just as you have to on the physical plane. When the day comes that I die, and my astral world is there to live in, I expect to lose this precious ability that I have to fly.

I tried to project myself again, but only reached the head banging stage, no further. You do become used to the head bangs, and the distant conversations, so don't worry. Like many other things, they are more severe early on in your learning, but as you become more experienced they fade in intensity, and they become nothing more than a good, and interesting, sign that progress is being made.

SUNDAY 21ST JANUARY 1996

I have read that some projectors, Oliver Fox included, find that when projected, the scenery becomes super vibrant and the colours more intense. I have only found that to be the case in one early experience, and it is yet another variant on the theme. My astral, and etheric, environments have always been as beautiful as they are on the earth plane, to the eye, and to the touch. Of course, the astral environment is only one of many, so perhaps these people were elsewhere in this intriguing universe. Anyway, until I had experienced it more frequently myself, I could not really pass judgement. This morning I had that opportunity.

I was dreaming, very vividly, that I was ascending several flights of stairs, within a tall block of flats. For some reason, I had a conviction to reach the top, which eventually, I did. I stood on the very edge of the roof looking out at other, similar, blocks of flats, and down to the squares of grass and parking areas far below.

196

It was at this stage that my dream became lucid, and I thought to myself, I know that I can fly, I've done it before, all I have to do is jump off. Believe me, this takes great courage, because as I begin to really weigh up the enormity of what I was contemplating, my conscious mind kicks into the next stage, and I became fully projected. I heard people screaming and shouting at me as I hurled myself over the precipice, and out into thin air. My heart was in my mouth, my breath was taken away from me, as I found myself plummeting towards the ground at a tremendous rate.

I noticed that I wasn't falling in a true vertical fashion, but rather more at an angle, and as I continued to fall, this angle continued to increase to around 45%. Just as I was giving up all chances of survival, I swooped out to within inches of the ground, and flew horizontally along the surface. I kept this up for a while as I was adjusting to the fact that my superconscious mind had allowed me to do this jump, and timed it to perfection, with inches to spare. I felt a great sense of exhilaration at having survived and able to tell the tale.

All of a sudden I felt myself slowing down to a dead stop, turned around against my will, before being pulled backwards extremely fast, so fast that all was a blur to my eyes. After a while it all slowed down enough for me to see forests of trees, and lovely countryside. The most amazing thing, that I had never experienced before in such abundance, were the colours. The brilliant, vibrant colours, the richness of the scenery and the glowing reflections. I remember thinking that this reminds me a little of the film 'Fantasia', only what it must be like to be a part of it, and not just a viewer. The colours were cartoon like, seductive pastels, deep subtle hues, intense greens, the like I had never known. I had just decided that this was the most fantastic thing that I had ever seen, when I had to return to my physical body.

I remained as still as I could, my eyes closed, and extremely relaxed as I went over in my mind the visions that I had experienced. With the possibility of projecting again still viable, I thought of elevating my body, quietening my mind, and lowering my bodily processes. As you know, I perceive mental imagery all the time, should I wish to watch. At night though, and especially with my eyes closed, I can't *help* but watch what goes on, I wouldn't choose to have it any other way. *Following this projection, the visions were different to normal, instead of my usual dreamlike scenes, I was seeing patterns. A whole series of beautiful patterns interweaving themselves, evolving from one shape to another, intricately coloured with every imaginable hue. This is the sort of in-house entertainment I like, I need no virtual reality machine to enhance my life!*

At the end of this magnificence, appeared a trail of fantastic monsters, creatures emerging from the sea and roaring as they swung their beautifully ugly heads around, phenomenal demons with quick eyes that lock on to you should they see you staring. I held my breath as these creatures appeared and disappeared, safe in the knowledge that all I have to do is open my eyes, for sanctuary.

I wish all projections were as long and varied as this one. Looking back over the experience, there are a couple of observations that need to be recognised. When I became aware of my dream content, my spirit-body was already in the throws of having a subconscious projection. As my spirit-body was rising from my physical body, my dream interpreted that action by making me believe that I was ascending the stairs in the block of flats. Had my consciousness not intervened, my dream would have continued by interpreting the horizontal movement of my spirit, possibly by getting me to walk along a corridor, until it was far enough away from my physical body, for playtime. Then my dream would have been a good one, probably vivid, possibly lucid, masking my true astral projection, that in turn, could be masking a subconscious etheric projection. Do you see the veils that have to be lifted, in order to get to the core operation? It never ceases to amaze me.

However, because my awareness came when it did, I made the decision to look at the view, as I would in physical life. Now, all my life I have had a fear of heights, if I get too close to a cliff edge and look over, it sucks me. My head swims, my knees buckle, and in my mind, I am already over the edge and smashed to pieces on the rocks below. Since I have had the advantage of astral flying, my fear of heights has largely disappeared, even if my memory of that fear has not. I cannot help but retain a healthy respect for it still, which makes it all the more incredible that I should consciously launch myself into thin air, from the top of a tall block of flats!

Many times in this situation I would bottle out, but this is one of the 'gateways' that I describe in this book. This was the time to choose whether I should go down the corridor within the safety of the dream-life, or whether I should choose fear, the *guardian* of the astral plane. Had my awareness not intervened I would not have jumped, I'm sure of that. Because my consciousness had partially connected, as a lucid dream, I was able to realise that I had jumped off high buildings before, and I could do it again, *if* my courage would allow it to happen. Nevertheless, it is *the* most scariest thing to do, because your consciousness *has* kicked in, and it becomes serious reality.

Apart from the buttock clenching, heart stopping, lunacy of the jump, it is really exhilarating. The fall is real in the fact that you feel the air rushing past you and pushing your facial skin back to your ears. I even feel my hair straining at the roots, (what hair I have that is!) and it makes my eyes water and the hairs stand up all over my body. Yes, I believe the sensation is as real as reality can be.

I mentioned that, with my minds eye, I perceived a procession of fantastic, monster-like, creatures. It has been noted by other projectors that these creatures can play a part in out-of-body projections, I must say that, touch wood, they don't play a part in mine. They are there, however, in my mental vision (a type of clairvoyance), and in my dreams, but never during an oobex. I might suggest that should one encounter a monster, it will be for a reason, and that is to make you aware that you are in a dream. It could also come to you whilst you are having a lucid dream, to frighten you, and thereby inducing the vibrations needed to project your spirit-body.

I have also found that by befriending the monster, loving it, smiling at it, etc. it transforms itself into a friendly entity. This is a completely daft thing to do, on my part. OK it effectively gets rid of a terrifying beast, but it also means that I can't take advantage of the opportunity of getting really scared enough to raise the vibrations, and project. These monsters used to scare me, years ago, so I found this a good way of dealing with them, but this was before I knew the reason why they were there, in the first place. Now, I have to re-teach myself to be scared again! This is called *control* and now I can choose to be scared and welcome the fear, or I can opt to love my 'enemy' and effectively throw a wet blanket over the proceedings.

I cannot shed any light on why the colours appeared to be super-real during this projection. One answer could be that this was another type of projection, not astral. Another answer could be that the strand of the spirit cable that carries the sight/colour messages was more sensitive than usual.

This morning I slightly changed my relaxation procedure, prior to my projection. I think that this helps, from time to time, to make the relaxation more effective by holding your attention a little longer. I have never been an advocate of the relaxation method that gets you to tense a muscle before you can relax that muscle. I am sure that I have many happily relaxed muscles that do not wish to be disturbed in this manner. What is the point of any kind of tension, if the outcome of the exercise is relaxation? But I did do something, this morning, in a similar vein. During my normal run down procedures I *imagined* that I was tensing each muscle. I worked my way down from the top of my head, to the tips of my toes, purely imagining what it would feel like for that, particular, part of my anatomy to be stressed, and then imagine it to be stress free. So this has the effect of negating any tension without physical intrusion, a great part of physical passivity is mentally induced. It seemed a good thing to do, whether I would still have projected had I not done this, I will never know. It really doesn't matter as long as it works, slip it in every so often for a change.

WEDNESDAY 7TH AUGUST 1996

Don't get disheartened if you go a long time without projecting, It isn't something you lose once you have got the hang of it. I usually manage to project, at least, three or four times a month and that's with living a fairly normal existence. I am certain that if I lived a solitary, monastic life, I would project a lot more frequently. Having said that, I have had five projection's in one week, and nothing for three months, so anything is possible. I am talking about conscious projection of course, and I would love to know how many subconscious projections I have had, and missed, very many I suspect.

I awoke, this morning, at 4.30 and went about my usual practice of busying myself for an hour or so, before going back to bed, primed and ready. My relaxation procedures went without a hitch and I duly fell asleep, only to awaken an hour later. I was too conscious to attempt a projection at this stage so I simply imagined that I had height, and that my body was twisting and tumbling.

To imagine any such action, is a very positive loosening exercise. Any sensation that *feels* as if you are in motion while, in actual fact, your physical body is stationary, is good for loosening the hold the physical body has over the spirit-body. One example is being dizzy, you feel movement but are physically still. Making yourself twirl round and around in a frenzy, and then stopping, is used by some cultures as a very effective way of ejecting the spirit form. Much too harsh for me.

Having spent a few minutes on *really* loosening my spirit-body, I lightened my heartbeat, relaxed my inner body, and slipped back into sleep.

The very next thing I knew, I was out-of-my body, completely conscious of who I was, where my physical body was, and the fact that I was conscious in my spirit-body. In my mind, as always, was the wish to bridge the gap to the etheric plane, because if I could project etherically, I would be able to prove my case a little easier. Anyway, this morning I had projected into the heart of a town and, for some reason, I felt particularly relaxed and well. Perhaps a little too easy with my myself, as I quickly began to experience dual consciousness. Three times I nearly lost my projection as my bedroom environment exerted its' influence over me, and three times I fought back with intense determination to remain astral. Successful in my

202

endeavours, I made my way past many houses, some blocks of flats, some converted buildings, the normal array of architectural styles found in any English town of character. I spent some time walking through the many busy market stalls, with colourful people abuzz with activity.

Sometimes I feel a little guilty about looking into other peoples homes and sometimes I do not. If it was the etheric plane, I *should* feel guilty, but I don't think it matters on the astral, I am usually made welcome and accepted.

This morning I was in the mood to explore, and I find great enjoyment in being able to wander around and seeing how other people live. *I chose a house, a house I liked, and I pushed myself through the fabric of the front door into the hallway. I made my way upstairs, observing the decor en-route, and found a lovely sunny sitting-room. This room was beautifully decorated in light colours, immaculately clean, and boasted a huge pair of french windows at one end, where all the light came flooding in. Passing through these doors, I found myself on a verandah that was attached, at the side, to another property, so I continued my journey into this other house. The feeling of being able to go wherever you wish is fantastic, especially if you are a little nosy, and who isn't the least bit curious?*

In the house, I encountered the people that lived there, and it really isn't a big thing. Nobody is ever surprised to see me walking through their property, and I am always accepted without question, but in a matter of fact sort of way. We spoke in passing, 'How are you? Isn't it a lovely day,' that sort of thing, just as you would on the physical plane, no different. Then a strange thing happened, I went to pass through a solid wall, to go into the adjoining room, but found I couldn't. The wall was solid to me. This immediately aroused my interest, so I did a little research on what I could pass through and what I could not. Two of the side walls, in this room, were solid to me and, as I pondered the reason why, I found myself pondering back in bed!

My wish to project etherically, I believe, often inhibits the complete freedom to enjoy the astral environment. If I could master the regular art of etheric projection, I could prove many theories a whole lot easier, as it is, I must rely on you, and other's, taking up the gauntlet and passing on the 'proof'. Etheric projection is possible, as I know by experience, but it is the controlled ability to project etherically that must, at some stage, be achieved.

One reason is to bring the truth nearer to the sceptics who are determined not to understand, and secondly, a personal wish to control my own death, so that I may express my last ever chapter, from the other side of life. I am practical enough to realise how slim my chances of success are, but success exists solely to be achieved. However hard I wish to conquer the etheric projection, I am sure that we are not meant to access that plane for all the reasons I have given elsewhere in this book. Should I project etherically and, for example, enter a sealed room to report the contents to a waiting audience, would demean the process and open it up to being ridiculed, copied by magicians, and used by government agencies. No, I think that individual experimentation, that leads to *self* belief, has to be the only way to go. Etheric projection, *if* it comes regularly, will remain a private achievement for me to use in my personal research for my own ends.

The projection, this morning, was the first one where I had any trouble passing through, apparently, solid objects. I am not used to having to walk around anything other than people, and I don't even have to do that. A vibrational change has to happen within your spirit-body, before any physical separation can take place, so if, and when, your vibrational rate drops, you will return to the physical. During a spirit projection there is present a certain amount of fluctuation in this rate of vibration and, when that happens, it follows that *should* a vibrational rate be encountered that is similar to your own, it will impede passage. Because of the dual consciousness problems, the to-ing and fro-ing from physical to astral, it would seem that my vibrational state *does* fluctuate during the course of the proceedings and, on occasion's, will cause a problem.

I have often heard voices calling me, prior to a projection, when I am in the head thumping area between the two worlds. Some projector's have heard voices, apparently emanating from their partner calling them back from a projection, and I am happy to say that I have never had that experience. Oliver Fox, in particular, used to experience what sounded like his wife's voice pleading him not to go, or calling him back. This morning, something very similar *did* happen to me, which may be akin to Olivers' observations.

Whilst I was projected, I spoke to people that I encountered, in the usual way, as I would in any circumstances. Up until now they have all replied, as you would expect, in the normal way. This morning's projection was also normal, but it was one of those, increasingly frequent, examples where Linda was asleep beside me. The strange, and totally unexpected, thing was that as I spoke to the inhabitants of my astral environment the voice that I heard coming back to me seemed to becoming from Linda! Although I was projected, I have a perfect sense of where my physical body is, unlike in a dream, and where the person that I spoke to was a man, a deep, gruff, reply appeared to emanate from my partner. It sounded so real that, the first time it happened, it stopped me in my tracks. Of all the people I spoke to, none replied in a voice that I could recognise as being remotely similar to my partners. I think that, if it had of been, I would have interiorised immediately.

Because of the connecting cable, any sound, or movement, felt by the physical body is also felt by the spirit-body, at the same time. It is not unusual to feel, in your astral body, the effects of your partner turning over in bed, for example, and one becomes accustomed to this. But what about the other way around? It is much less usual to have something affect your astral body, and feel it in your physical body. So, when I am projected, but alone in bed, and I have conversations, nothing untoward is experienced. When I am not alone, and have these conversations, I hear with both my astral ears and, because of the cable, the effect is that I hear through my physical ears also.

With the physical senses being so strong, it is understandable that I would notice my physical hearing as being unusual in these circumstances and to *assume* that these sounds are very real *and* coming from the only source possible, my dear old Linda. Which, of course, they are not.

THURSDAY 12TH SEPTEMBER 1996

I have a record showing a lucid dream this morning and an oobex tomorrow morning that might prove of interest to you.

Oobex is all about dealing with the subconscious mind to achieve what you *consciously* want to achieve. You have to cajole it, appease it, reason with it, catch it unawares, that sort of thing. It is like dealing with a separate person rather than a part of yourself. But it *does* know best. It terminates your projection at the first hint of anything untoward happening, and when you slow your heartbeat down, it stops it from stopping altogether! Just two examples out of the thousands of controlling functions used by the subconscious mind to keep us safe, and very well protected, in our lives.

I hate to labour the point, but it is fear that has to be conquered. Even now, when I close my eyes to meditate, I often see an array of disturbed, and contorted, multiple headed monsters with evil eyes, so fantastic that they defy description. Their mouths froth with the saliva that mixes with the blood that drips from their teeth and a fierce, fiery, hunger blazes in their eyes, desperate for you to succumb. And then I sometimes have to be careful of flashing knives that buzz as they fly through the air, just missing my ears...... Of course, you the reader, will now easily recognise this as a dream interpretation of the head thumping. Often this head thumping manifests itself as a string, plucked inside your head, or a buzzing sensation. All these peculiar events have ceased to bother me now that I have, eventually, worked out why they happen.

I now know that the 'knives' signal a possible excursion onto the astral plane. I now know that it is fear that raises the vibrations necessary to allow my spirit-body to evacuate my physical body. But, it doesn't stop these things still giving me a heart stopping scare when they suddenly happen. These are illustrations of my own head thumping sensations as my blood pressure falls, yours will be similar, in some respects, but different in the detail. The *important* thing is to recognise them for what they are as they happen.

Dream awareness comes in stages, and consciousness within that dream, depends on the degree of realisation. During the day, if you think about dream awareness, believe that it is possible and *will* yourself to *positively* become aware in your dreams, you will stand a much greater chance of grasping the opportunity when it arrives. It will come naturally, but what we all do is enjoy the experience as a vivid dream, instead of doing what we all should do, which is to recognise it as a lucid dream. How *ever* the recognition comes is not important, as long as it does come.

This morning I realised that I was dreaming, but instead of raising my vibrations and projecting, as I normally would, I decided to try an experiment. I concentrated on the dream environment and willed myself to be part of it. All of a sudden I was part of the fabric of the dream. This experience was akin to watching television, getting really engrossed in a good film, and suddenly finding yourself part of the movie! I have tried this before with no luck, an illustration of perseverance. Just because something fails on one occasion doesn't mean it can't happen on another.

Flushed with success, I decided to try and do the opposite, which is to return to the state of realisation I first became aware of. By relaxing my mind, and not concentrating on my environment, I suddenly found myself outside of the action again. I concentrated again, and again I became an integral part of the dream. Again I relaxed my concentration, and I was back out. I found that I could access this dream environment pretty much at will. I did not get the chance to project further, as this little piece of research was significantly different enough to hold my attention. Had I gone on to project I might have lost some of the detail, so I returned easily to my physical awareness to record this experience.

In all probability, my astral body was on an unconscious trip anyway, and all I was doing was jumping in and out of the spirit-body with my conscious awareness. I do not believe that this can be done with just any old dream that you may be having. I have certainly projected my consciousness before, and found myself part of the dream that I was currently dreaming. More often than not, I have projected from a dream awareness to a completely different astral setting. The interesting thing about the experiment this morning was, firstly, the ability I found that enabled me to step into the setting and actually become an integral part of it and, secondly, the ability to let it go and return to the lucid dream. It is rare that such control can become harnessed. Having said all that, it was an extremely enjoyable experience, and the power to achieve this transition felt quite awesome.

FRIDAY 13TH SEPTEMBER 1996

This morning my adventure began in a similar vein as my experience of yesterday. In that, I was having a dream where I was talking to a couple of friends, in a living room, the television was on and all seemed perfectly normal. I had never seen the room, or the people before, in earthly life, but in the dream I felt completely at home in these surroundings and with these people.

I was in mid-conversation when I realised that I was beginning to feel ill. I tried to put it to the back of my mind but without any success. As the conversation continued, the feelings of illness increased, and eventually got so strong that I began to worry for my safety. It started in the pit of my stomach and worked its way outwards in all directions, increasing steadily, until eventually I felt as though I was losing control. I tried to convey my dilemma to my friends, but only felt the desperation of not being able to talk anymore. In this dream, I began to feel physically sick, I was losing the ability of movement and I felt so dreadful that I contemplated the serious possibility that I was actually dying. I gave up hope when my vision became blurred and my hearing muffled. The sight and sounds of my concerned friends faded away from me and I began to drown. I could not breathe, see, or hear. Whatever was happening to me was smothering me, the 'water' closed over my head and my limbs became paralysed and numb. I would have liked to have panicked, but I was trapped and could not. All I could do was give in to death, resign myself to my fate. I actually found myself accepting the end. I felt as though I had been given a lethal injection and, 'bye bye' world.

Slowly, very slowly, I found that I was thinking, realising that I was somewhere, but I had no feeling and, definitely, no control. Once this realisation had come to me, I was able to relax, for the frightening part of the experience had ensured that I was now operating with my conscious mind. Happy that fate had spared me, I remained calm and let whatever was going to happen, happen. I still could not see, or hear and had no knowledge of my whereabouts, but I was alive, and thankful.

I emerged, like a butterfly from a chrysalis, into a beautiful scene, the vista was superb. Majestic trees murmured and moved in the breeze, a wondrous array of flowers carpeted the ground. I felt strong and healthy, very secure and exhilarated. I moved with the smoothness of cream, all the glories shone out at me to notice, I was so powerful that I felt I needed to be gentle with everything, nothing could threaten me here. This environment did not give me any indication at all of being astral, and it was definitely not etheric, I was somewhere that must be regarded as a plane of existence perhaps several steps on from the astral environment. I trolled through this 'paradise' drinking in the splendour, what had I done to deserve such a privilege? Why me? I sat down with my back resting up against the trunk of a lofty, monumental tree, dwarfed and humbled by its magnificence. I gazed out, contemplating my journey through oblivion (death?) to *reach this paradise, and at that moment I really would not have cared if I had actually died, if it meant a guarantee that I could be here. And yes, as I drank in my ecstasy I relaxed, and in the blink of an eye, I found myself back at home.* I was relaxed, calm, confident, happy, pain-free and euphoric. I had achieved something that I had never achieved before, and at some time, I will return. I *must* return.

The memory of that experience will never leave me, it is impossible to convey to you, the reader, the splendour of the feeling, and the beauty of the place. I will never take this privilege for granted, all I can do is to try to impress upon you the truth of this existence, so that you too, may experience the ultimate freedom. I lay on my bed contemplating my travels with an extremely calm countenance as the afterglow of such an experience is euphoric, and in itself a treasure to savour. I eventually went to sleep, to dream away the remaining hours, a very happy and contented man.

However, it was not to be, I became aware that I was dreaming that I was in a modern office and talking to a gentleman about oobex, and especially about what I had experienced earlier. *I said to this person 'I can prove to you that I am out of my body, at this precise moment.' I enquired as to which floor we were situated on, and he told me that we were on the sixteenth floor of this office block. I went over to the window, opened it wide, and proceeded to climb out onto the window cill. I looked down at the ground, far below, a knot tightened itself into the pit of my stomach and my heart leaped into my mouth, At this point my consciousness became fully developed and I knew that I had done this before, also that I had become fully projected.*

211

I took all my courage in both hands and leaned forwards into the vast expanse of nothingness, sweet fresh air. I spread my outstretched arms into an aeroplane fashion, not that there is any need, but it seems to be appropriate behaviour for the exercise, and glided into space. My stomach had now joined my heart in my mouth and, once again, I was seeing the good earth hurtling up towards me, I don't mind admitting that I was scared. I wished that I was rising up into the air, rather than falling towards doom. No sooner had I thought of rising, when my descent flattened out, stopped, and I began to elevate. Not only that, but I realised that whatever manoeuvre I thought of, I could achieve. Everything and anything was possible, looping the loop, rising turns, barrel rolls, you name it, I could do it. I was having unsurpassed fun, my only problem was that I enjoyed myself too much, and I allowed my excitement to get the better of me, because I found myself back in bed, physically conscious.

As I was returning to my physical body, I distinctly heard my name being called. Where or from whom this voice emanates, I am not sure, but just as I can see visions within my head, there are people that can hear sounds from within. This clairaudience is used to transfer communications from our spirit guides, or advisers, for our benefit. I must say that I have never, knowingly, seen or conversed orally with anyone that could *definitely* be recognise as my spirit guide. I do believe that they *may* exist, but until I have proved this to myself, I cannot be completely sure.

THURSDAY 5TH DECEMBER 1996

A record of a very small, but strange projection. I had awoken early and spent about an hour reading about out-of-body experience's that other people have had, or claimed to have had, and really trying to saturate my mind with the subject. I returned to bed and managed to complete my usual relaxation procedures fully, before dropping off into sleep.

I want you to imagine a trap door that is suddenly released. It swings down and the momentum carries it onward, all the way up and around again in a complete 360 degree circle, only to snap back into its original position. Well, that is exactly what happened to my spirit-body! It was as though my spirit-body was hinged to my physical body, at the feet. *As I separated, I felt the intense vibrational rush, and also felt the snapping of the thousand threads that binds the bodies. Before I knew it, I appeared to be falling downwards out of my physical body, my head swinging down under, all the way around, with my feet remaining anchored. My whole spirit-body did a 360 degree swing and I was snapped back in, solid. I have seldom ever projected downwards from the physical body before. Everything up to that point had been normal.*

MONDAY 23RD DECEMBER 1996

I was having a vivid dream that I was in my bedroom, upstairs at home, and somebody that I didn't particularly like, was trying to peer through the window to see if I was at home. I was hiding and holding my breath and, from my hiding place, I could see this big face bobbing outside the window glass, like a moon balloon, frantic to find me. It was this very action of hiding, and holding my breath, being careful not to move or make a noise, that concentrated my consciousness.

I became aware that I was dreaming and, immediately, I felt the rush of vibrations as I projected from my physical body. The very first thing I did was to check that I had a spirit cord, and yes, it was there, intact.

213

I proceeded to walk out of my bedroom, down the stairs, and I passed through the solid oak front door, to the High Street. I began toying with the idea that this could be an etheric projection. My bedroom was correct, as was my house, as was the little wall, outside my house that I sat on. As I looked up and over to the old house opposite, it was no longer there. Everything else was correct but for the fact that this house had disappeared, and with it any idea that my projection was anything other than astral.

In the place of that house was a long straight road stretching way out in front of me, obviously inviting me to sample its delights. So, obligingly, I began to walk along the road. I walked, and walked, but there was a distinct danger of becoming bored, so I decided to fly to the end, to help hurry the process along a mite. It is impossible to hurt yourself, on the astral, so the best way to launch into flight is to throw yourself forward, and if the ground comes up to hit you, put your arms down and give yourself an extra push off. Which is exactly what happened this morning, I maintained a flight elevation of between three and five feet from the surface.

I arrived in a little village, and had a good look around, in and out of the shops. Everything here seemed to be perfectly normal, as normal as it would have been on the physical plane. There didn't appear to be any reason for me to be there, as is usually the case, and so I returned to my body.

Because the astral environment is mirrored by the image of the earth, it can be as mundane as the earth plane. It all depends on the mood you are in, where you find yourself, and how confident you are about holding on to the projection. It is the *anticipation* of these experience's that is the real magnet for the astral plane!

This morning I had completed my relaxation procedures, before going to sleep, and as I felt myself slipping into the realms of sleep, I pulled myself gently back into awareness. Not full awareness, but just this side of unconsciousness. If you keep pulling yourself back into full awareness, you will lose the intention to sleep entirely, and the whole exercise will be made ineffectual. I managed to do this about three times, idly thinking about out-of-body projection, effectively allowing me to go deeper into the hypnagogic state, and in so doing aid projection. There is a fine balance between staying awake, falling to sleep, deepening the hypnagogic state and projection. The nearer you can consciously get to an unconscious projection the more chance you will have of success.

I did have a second projection, this morning, but it was not different enough to warrant recording here.

SATURDAY 28TH DECEMBER 1996

No projection, but I did have a dream that goes some way to illustrate what you must be looking for, as you sleep. A silly story, as most dreams are, but relevant to our subject. The scene is set on the top deck of an English double decker 'bus, as part of an outside fun event. *I dreamt that my partner, and I, were talking to a famous television presenter, who was naturally clowning around with different things, and he asked us to name the puppet that he used to perform with. During the dream, prior to him asking us, we had known the answer, but the very second that he asked the question, we both had completely forgotten. We stared at each other in expectation, we racked our brains, it was on the tip of our tongues, but could we remember? Not at all. I knew that it consisted of four letters, so I got a piece of paper and drew four short lines to represent the individual letters in the hope that it*

215

would jog my memory. You see, I knew that I knew it, I just could not bring it to mind.

Can you see what is happening here? By concentrating so hard on this silly subject, it was supposed to do the job of arousing my conscious awareness to let me know that I was, in fact, dreaming. This was all conjured up for the purpose of allowing me to project my spirit-body. Exactly the same as the time that I was hiding in the bedroom from the person peeping through the window. In that particular event, it worked. Here, for some reason, it did not. Can you see how the system works?

In the dream, we continued to try and think of this blessed puppets name. We knew that the name was also a verb. The intensity of thought was so strong that it woke me up! Only then did it dawn on me that there had never been a puppet, at all! If there had of been, in all probability I would have known the answer, and so it would not have concentrated my mind.

Can you also see the similarity here with the stage hypnotist? You see, I was dreaming whilst my mind was in the hypnagogic state of sleep, the same state that is often used for hypnosis. If I had been on stage, the hypnotist would have said something like: 'I want you to imagine that you had a puppet, it was a dear possession of yours, and you kept it beside you, everywhere you went, for many years. You really loved this puppet, but, when I ask you to tell me the name of this puppet, it will go completely from your mind.'

In the dream, an idea was put into my head that there was a puppet that had really existed, and boy did I believe it. This was the trick. This was the falsehood, for as long as I believed that there was a puppet, in the first place, I was hooked. All the emphasis was put on trying to remember the name, and as long as I was doing that, it

216

would not cross my mind to question whether there was really a puppet at all. I was tricked into trying to remember something that did not exist, but because I *believed* it did, my concentration would, eventually, be so intense as to succeed in bringing awareness. Unfortunately, this morning it brought me waking consciousness, instead.

These are the times when you lay in bed, thinking about what has just happened and getting very angry with yourself for not realising what was being presented to you in order for you to take full advantage of the situation. I mean, my subconscious mind had gone to all the trouble of setting up this farce, for the sole purpose of allowing me to project, and I was so dumb that I woke up instead!

Like catalepsy, the stage hypnotist is accessing, and making use of, a natural phenomenon for entertainment purposes. The real reason that we have the hypnogogic and hypnopompic states in existence, is for our own internal usage. It is these areas that allow us to mask the true movements of our spirit-body, and to harness, should we wish, the inner power to project. The hypnotherapist can at times help you to access these states, and communicate with the subconscious mind, in the same way that our own conscious mind does at night.

SUNDAY 19TH JANUARY 1997

I, again, managed to retain consciousness until I was deeply relaxed, and I was able to maintain this state for longer than normal, letting my mind adjust to my conscious wishes as I slipped into unconsciousness. I do this, confident that my subconscious mind will retain the desire for projection and, allow that projection to happen through dream awareness, or allow me to awaken. If either of these two things happen, I am a very happy man.

This morning I awoke and, immediately, lowered my heartbeat. I hardly felt a head thump before the body rush enveloped me, and shot me out into an oobex. This is my favourite way of projecting, if the separation is clean. Guess where I found myself? Yes, I was in, yet another, estate of houses! I checked that the cord was there, and having satisfied myself that it was, I leaned forward into flight. I kept my body about two feet above the ground to increase the speed sensation, and to tickle my adrenaline.

I am getting a little tired of projecting to a similar astral locale, so I am making an effort to leave the area as soon as I arrive. With this end in mind, I flew out of this 1930s estate, passed through a more modern '60s estate, and managed to find open countryside. Not only that but, in the distance, I could see the sea, and it was getting closer. By the time I found the coastline, my elevation had risen to about 30ft above land. There was nobody around, so I followed the coastline along, keeping myself with the landside to my right, and the seaside to my left. In places the cliffs were deep and sheer, and in others the land softly undulated down to curtsey to its watery master.

I began to feel the pull to return, so I summoned all my effort into remaining projected. It will always win in the end, but it is worth trying to extend the projection if possible. Sometimes you are successful and sometimes you are not. This morning I was successful, but I experienced a pain in my head for my troubles. It occurred in the very front, and top, of my head and only continued whilst I was fighting the return. Once I became free again, in my projection, the headache ceased.

My reprieve was short-lived however, for after about five minutes, I felt the pull again, and had to say goodbye to the wonderful scenery, the freedom, and one of the most enjoyable projections that I have had for a long *time*. I am convinced that it is necessary to fight the return at every opportunity, for it is *there* where another gateway will be found. I did, in fact, have another projection later the same morning, but it was too short and too ordinary for inclusion here.

THURSDAY 30TH JANUARY 1997

An interesting slant on the relaxation procedures, this morning. I got up as usual, and did all the usual things, up to, and including, the relaxation procedures. At the very end though, instead of going to sleep, I turned my closed eyes upwards, and inwards, to point at my third eye. Whether there really is anything to this third eye business, or not, is something that I, personally, cannot vouch for. So let's say I looked, with my eyes closed, at a spot just above my eyebrows and in the centre of my forehead, and I concentrated *hard* on this for about a quarter of an hour. It doesn't sound a long time, but you just try it! Only then did I turn onto my side, reduce my heart rate, and allow myself to go to sleep.

I succeeded in obtaining five astral projection's, in succession. It was impossible for me to unravel what happened in which individual projection, so I am not even going to try. Every time I returned to my body, by reducing my heartbeat, I managed to project again. Oh! that it was always this easy! The contents of the projection's were all normal fare, except for one part. I was talking to a family, in their home, and I requested permission to touch them, to see if they had any substance to them, and they did. They felt, to me, as solid as we *all do* here on earth plane.

Getting back to the subject of the third eye area, it would seem that, on this occasion, it had a good, and beneficial, effect on my out-of-body experience's, by assisting me to revel in the success of multiple trips. Maybe it did, and maybe it didn't. My own opinion is that by concentrating on this part of my body, for that length of time, and following an already extensive relaxation process, did actually take me a lot nearer to the sleep state. I also had the will to project firmly imprinted on my mind, so the set-up, for the projection, was far stronger because of the combined concentration. Whether the actual 'third eye' spot was essential for this, I don't know, but my mind *is* open for it to be proven either way. If it wasn't, I would not have got this far.

SATURDAY 19TH APRIL 1997

I had been out with some like minded colleagues for the evening, and had returned to 'Ivydene' at approximately 1.45 am. I was very, very tired and got to bed as soon as I could, fully expecting an uneventful night, certainly I had no time for meditation, or relaxation. I awoke at 4.30 am, feeling dreadful, but I managed to prise myself out of bed and I made myself a cup of tea, and managed to read for, about, an hour, or so. The desired effect had been achieved, which is an alert mind that has slept, and a very tired body. On going back to bed, I relaxed my heart, relaxed my very insides, and imagined that I was miles high up in the sky, with the agility of an eagle, before losing myself to slumber.

Almost immediately the vibrations racked my body, firing me up as though I had plugged myself into the mains electricity system. It lasts only as long as it takes to separate your spirit-body from your physical body, so usually a couple of seconds, or so. This morning my shoulders, and head, appeared to be anchored to the bed while the rest of my body was flapping around, in all directions. And by flapping, I *mean* flapping. This was not a slow motion, ghostly, sort of experience, this was serious flapping up and down, right and left, twisting crazy flapping!

This was severe, and just as I thought separation was not going to happen, I fell out of bed, and bounced onto the floor. Such a strange experience, and so real that I thought the motion had physically thrown me out of bed but, in fact, I was in my spirit-body. To be honest, I was shaken and a little confused. I stood up and was immediately pulled back into my physical body. I lay there, unsettled, disappointed, but also, encouraged. I did no more than quieten myself down again, to have another go.

I felt my feet begin to flap again, only this time it was slowly. I could feel a slow vibration spreading over my body, and as this vibration increased in intensity, so the speed of the flapping increased. I was getting a little concerned that I was in for a repeat performance, when the vibrations exploded into a massive 'rush'. *I was lifted up, put over to one side, and placed upright onto my bedroom floor.*

This was an astral projection, because my bedroom was not my earthly bedroom, but it felt very familiar, so I think it must have been my astral bedroom, in my astral house. I made my way downstairs, feeling very much at home and familiar with the comfortable surroundings of this place. So familiar, that I expected to see the High Street, as I pushed myself through the front door. What I did see was a completely different street scene that, to my knowledge, I had never seen before. I wandered around, being nosy, and thought about what the next thing was to do.

I felt for the cord and found it to be approximately 2cms (three quarters of an inch) thick. I gently felt each individual root, where it entered my skull through the back of my head. I then proceeded to run my hands over the outside of my body to check for any other strange protrusions, and I found none that should not have been there!

I returned my attention back to the spirit cable and pulled it round to have a proper look at it. I wouldn't have dared do this at one time for fear of damaging it, but familiarity promotes confidence, and it is something we need to know more about. Obviously I cannot see the root structure but I can confirm that the cable is multi-stranded. It is difficult to count the strands for they are twisted together, as is a rope, but I would guess at around five, maybe more. The cord itself, was soft, pliable and peculiar to the touch. I would not call it silver, as some have, but more like off-white, you know, when hard egg white just begins to be tinged with black.

I then decided to try another experiment, I thought about rising vertically into the air, to see what would happen. As you think 'travel', then so it happens. I rose up into air higher, and higher, at a rapid pace, soon leaving all behind me. Looking down I could see the cluster of buildings that made up my astral village, and they were quickly disappearing below me. They got to the size of a drawing-pin head before I began to think that this was a mistake. What was the point of being up here? I travelled on and on, all I could see were green fields, so I decided it was time to change tack.

I concentrated on travelling to my real village of Braunston, so that I could continue with some proper research, that has interest. I thought about the place, imagined that I could fly there, and lo and behold, and within a split second, I had returned to my bed. What a mistake to consciously bring a projection to an end....I should have known better than that.

Whilst a projection is in progress, I have often noticed a perceptible background hiss that, I assume, is detected by my astral ears. As the cable transmits the senses from, and to, each body, it is also quite likely to be emanating from my physical head. If you completely cover your ears with your hands, you will get a good idea of the sound that I am talking about. Perhaps it is the sound of our inner workings, blood pulsating, etc.

I have just mentioned the transmission of the senses through the cable, and I have experienced all of them, both ends, except taste. I have no recollection of having tasted anything whilst fully conscious and projected. In my dreams, for sure, but never when I have been in an astral environment.

MONDAY 5TH MAY 1997

I had an unusually long sleep this morning, managing to reach 5.30am before awaking to start my preparations. It is important to crowd out everything else other than out-of-body projection, so that nothing else can pollute your thoughts. I returned to bed around 7.05am, and proceeded to relax. In my imagination, I pretended to be lying with my back against the inside wall of a big slippery ball, and as I rocked, I found that I could slide around and around the inside, to my hearts content. All this slithering, however, began to make me feel rather travel sick, so I had to stop. As a youngster I suffered terribly with travel sickness, and I really thought that those feelings had long gone, but apparently not.

I then tried to take my mind off the queasy feeling by concentrating my vision on a spot on the ceiling, and imagining that the vibrations were happening at that spot. I then, mentally, drew the vibrations down into the inside of my head. I have to say, I think it was a useless exercise, I think that it is far better instilling the vibrations in the usual way, but you must get into the habit of trying different

223

things out. That is, another reason that I have progressed to the extent I have.

The instigation of the tingle factor is merely the 'starter' that gets the real *mega* rush active. This major rush then excludes your input and takes over control of what happens next. You are only allowed to regain control once you have put a minimum distance between you, the spirit-body, and your physical shell. You could go all your life by gaining awareness solely through the lucid dream experience, and if you did, you would think that all this tingle stuff was a load of bunkum. We all live on the same world but how individual it can be to us all.

It is not simply a case of having your body very tired and your mind alert, not at all. Yes, your body must be properly tired enough to sleep, but *mentally* is where the secret lies. The knack is to relax the mind but be certain that you can still, idly, concentrate on relaxation and projection. It is like allowing yourself to go into a controlled daydream, an altered state of consciousness, just hanging on to perceived bodily sensations without using direct conscious thought.

You see, consciousness is lost before consciousness is regained and, therefore, we must make the gap in the middle as short as possible, for more surety of success. The *later* we can hold on to consciousness, as sleep comes on, the more likely we are to catch consciousness again as our body projects. So part of the trick is to be not *too* mentally aware, part of the trick is to also relax the mind but only enough to keep awareness apparent. If the tingle factor doesn't induce the massive rush I will, purposely, turn on my side and go to sleep, giving my *subconscious mind* a chance to do its stuff now that it has been primed.

This was, indeed, what happened to me this morning. I had gone to sleep, following all my preparations, and it was left up to my subconscious mind to decide whether I should project or not. I awoke, just enough to realise that I had been asleep, so I induced the tingling vibrations and relaxed inside. I felt the rush and exited my physical body with ease. No sooner had I got out, I was back in again! I did this three times, and actually found that, on this particular occasion, I could do it at will.

After returning from the third trip, I must have lost consciousness, because I regained my consciousness whilst I was part way through an unconscious projection. *I became aware that I was standing on a grassy area, in the centre of a large, and beautiful, city. The weather was warm, there was a blue sky above, and I felt so good that I reached up, into the air, and flew with complete confidence. I found that, once again, I was capable of anything, I tried soaring upwards and letting the impetus carry me to the point of stalling, before swooping down again, only just clearing the ground. The exhilaration I felt cannot be conveyed by the written word, the sheer carefree enjoyment cannot be surpassed by anything on this earth. Individual parts, maybe, but as a complete experience, never! My oobex research went out of the window, for I was a boy at play, and I indulged myself.*

At one stage I landed on the top of a park wall, and proceeded to hop, from there, to a garden wall and on to more garden walls, and up onto roof tops, back down to a verandah, back to a wall. I could flit from fancy to fancy, literally, as free as a bird. During one of my aerobatic displays I was flying low along the surface of a road, and I heard someone shouting, not at me, but just shouting to their friend. I noticed that they were calling in French. Was I in astral France? Were they visitors to my astral England? Or does it really matter?

I, finally, perched on a little wrought iron balustrade overlooking a window where I could see a f emale, sitting at a desk, doing some work. I watched her for a while and found myself back in bed. You bask in the glory of the projection whilst you analyse what has just happened, and the sleep you enjoy following a projection, is often, as it was this morning, full of vivid dreams.

TUESDAY 13TH MAY 1997

This morning I went through the usual procedures, waking up, going back to bed again, all the normal things that you have to do. On returning to bed and relaxing, I found that no matter how many exercises I did, I could not reach the depth that I needed to, not quite deep enough to induce a possible projection. This does happen on occasions, and can be due to the many influences that emanate from your personal lifestyle, the food you eat, the drink you drink, how happy you are, how well you are, how tired you are, the state of mind that you're in. I could name hundreds of causes that have the potential to throw you off course, so don't worry too much, it's called life.... Accepting that a projection *wasn't* going to happen, I turned over onto my left side and went to sleep.

At some stage I awoke, and knew by experience, not to move or break the subtle trance state that I found myself in. The flick of an eyelid, a rogue thought, anything can break this precious balance. If you can maintain this state, you are maintaining the state of a diver on the point of overbalancing into a dive. A mistake, is where you have become *too* aware of the position you are in. It sounds difficult, I know, but with practise, you should be able to remain sleepy, but aware of what is happening. Simply be cognitive of the situation, lower the strength of the heartbeat, relax your head and shoulders on the first outbreath, relax the chest and abdomen with the second outbreath, and relax your pelvis downwards with the third outbreath.

Think height, induce the tingle vibrations and wait for action. It is one thing reading this, but it is totally another thing to have this in your head to use in this kind of situation. That is why it takes practise, and is the reason for holding practical courses, here at 'Ivydene', to help those that have a real hankering to achieve this phenomenal ability. When that action happens it will be out of your control, and you will find yourself existing in a spirit plane. Well that is what happens ninety-nine per cent of the time.

This morning, a peculiar thing happened, which is why I am including this episode from my records. *My spirit-body left my physical body only to the extent of moving down to the bottom of the bed, and twisting to a position at right angles to my material body. To complicate matters, I could feel the new position of my spirit-body, but the sensory feelings in my physical head remained. I had the extremely uncomfortable experience of being in my spirit-body, in one position, and yet fully aware that my head was feeling unchanged on the pillow! The rest of my physical body I could not feel at all. I found this situation very difficult to come to terms with, and one that I would not care to repeat. I have not experienced this unfortunate experience before, and I hope that I never will again.*

It is apparent to me that this separation was not fully executed, and I was too close to my physical body for the process to be successfully completed. I opened up my physical eyes while the remainder of my senses told me that I was lying sideways, down at the bottom of the bed. I moved my head, and I was all back together again, pondering over this strange projection. Or should I say, partial projection.

MONDAY 2ND JUNE 1997

I dreamed this morning that I was having an astral projection. Because I have had so many projections, and devoted a great deal of time and effort into producing them, I suppose that I should have been prepared for this eventuality. I dreamed that I became aware whilst already projected, and I checked the spirit cable to convince myself it was real, just as I would in reality. I dreamed of the sensations that I feel during an oobex, and all of it was correct in every detail. During the time of the dream it felt real but when I awoke the level of consciousness was completely wrong. I realised, with certainty, that it was just a dream. The consciousness within the dream was not conscious enough, it is only once you have *awakened* that the real difference can be appreciated.

With a proper out-of-body experience, you will be aware that you are in exactly the same state of consciousness, at the same level, the same everything as you normally are during the day. Following every projection, my eyes open with the same consciousness that has been with me throughout, not broken or altered in any way. It is vital that you use this as your guide. The awareness that you have whilst reading this book is exactly the same awareness that you have when projected.

TUESDAY 3RD JUNE 1997

This is another projection that is worth recording because of the fact that very little preparation was needed for its production. My partner had to get up early to go to work, so I read a book that had absolutely nothing to do with spirit projection, I was reading simply to pass the time. I got to a part in this book that was very sad, and I felt those feelings of sadness within me, as we all do, in this situation.

When we feel this emotion, it is felt within our spirit selves, the real us, inside.

That is why, when we feel sadness, that 'spine tingling' sensation is felt and our hairs stand up, a common reaction to many emotions. Without realising it, I was priming my spirit-body, and exercising it, prior to going back to sleep. I had no, and still have no, idea how long this tingling sensation had been going on for, perhaps a good half an hour. This morning, I was so tired I needed to catch up on my sleep, and I did not do any preparation at all.

I became aware that I was dreaming, so I manually induced these same feelings within me, and I was hit immediately with an immense rush that overtook me. The best kind to possibly hope for. *I found myself in my astral bedroom again and when this happens I tend to get away as quickly as possible, to put some distance between me, my spirit, and me, my physical. It is not important with astral projection, but with etheric projection you will become sucked back in if you get too close to home.*

Because it was so obviously astral, I resisted this temptation, turned around, and looked at the place where I had just come from. Had this been an etheric projection I would have seen my physical 'ghost' lying in bed apparently asleep. But this was an astral projection, so I saw nothing. The bed wasn't exactly the same, this one was neat and tidy, as opposed to the indescribable heap of bedclothes that masquerades as the real thing.

I made my way downstairs, but I remained in an inquisitive mood, so instead of leaving by the front door, as is my usual way, I left by my back door instead. I walked down a nice wide well-kept lawn with no flower borders, but well looked after and neat. Several shrubs and trees broke the monotony of the grass. I got so far down before turning round to see where I had come from. A theme it seems. I was looking at the back of a white semi-detached house of reasonable size, but nothing spectacular. The light outside was at that peculiar stage of being neither light nor dark, the kind of light that is found very early in the morning, and I noticed that next door there was movement in an upstairs window. There was also the dim yellow glow of a lamp.

I willed myself to fly up to the window to see who was about. Passing through glass is a treat, because of it being so thin and transparent, it makes it different to a wall. As you press your face up to it, it stretches a little, so just before you break through it, it moulds itself to the shape of your face, so you can even have a proper look inside a room without, actually, entering it. Anyway, I did push my way through this window to find a young woman wearing a night-dress, sitting on the side of her bed. Astral people are lovely people, friendly, homely and always accept seeing you, never surprised when you drop in. The exception to that rule was the girl in the bar that I had trouble with once before, do you remember? Even then, all that was for a reason. The astral plane, to me, is like being a member of a family of like-minded people. Not always agreeing, but then again, I often find myself disagreeing with myself, and putting another side forward for thought. I think that we all do this, if we are honest, I would hate to be inflexible. Perhaps an argumentative, dogmatic, person has an astral attitude that reflects their situation, another reason why it is necessary to understand the big picture, and sort out your life here on earth, prior to dying. Why continue living with grief, even after you have died. A happy release, oh no, not always!

Getting back to this young lady. She was very pleasantly mannered, and we spoke in length about life in general. Nothing deep, just in a chit-chatty sort of way. I

remember asking if her parents were downstairs, and she
replied that they were in their bedroom. We talked about
the fact that she didn't live here on her own, and she asked
me where I had come from, all that type of thing. I stayed
there talking for a long time, too long, which is typical of
me, and I was also becoming too interested, because I lost
my new-found friend and remember no more.

I would like to mention the act of flying. This word
'fly' is only used to describe the action of movement, and
travel, through air. There is no arm waving, no need for
wings, or anything like that. One simply *thinks* of moving
through the atmosphere, and it happens. Of course, if you
wish to wave your arms around you can. When you read the
word 'fly' you can, if you wish, substitute 'aerial motion'.

MONDAY 23RD JUNE 1997

I got up at 4.30am, this morning, and returned to
bed at 5.35am. I followed my normal procedures and,
eventually, found myself becoming aware that I was
dreaming. In my dream, I was flying towards a brick wall
that had a covering of trellis, with a climbing rose growing
over it. The sort of thing you might see up the side of a
house, or garage. At the same time that I was becoming
aware of my flying sensation, I was also becoming aware
that I was lying in bed at home. At this conjuncture, I
realised that a projection was on the cards, so I lowered my
heartbeat, composed myself, and relaxed inside.

Without any effort at all, the 'rush' was swift and
sure, I came out of my body, cleanly, to find myself in my
astral bedroom. This was, again, very similar to my earth
bedroom, as it sometimes is, so I took little notice, and
made my way downstairs, leaving my home by passing
through the back door. I wandered down to my lower
garden, having leaped the gate in-between, to arrive at the

stone wall that separates my garden from that of my neighbour. I 'elevated' myself over the stone wall to have a look around their house. Now, I was fully aware that this was my astral neighbours house, and not my real neighbours house, so I could go on with my investigations, wearing the cloak of a clear conscience.

Inside the house I found a young family in the full chaos of fulfilling a breakfast commitment. The parents looked to me to be in their early forties, with two children, all involved in this hectic melee. The mother was pretty and dressed in jeans, very slim, and wearing a blue tee-shirt, I didn't notice what the husband was wearing! One of the children looked just into teenage, and the other looked just below. This is purely a rough impression, for there was much going on and I wasn't inclined to stay. I left this happy, pleasant family scene, and pushed my way through a door that was a little way down the hallway. I had entered a bathroom that featured a young lady in her late teens having private times. She was sat on the toilet, deep in conversation on a telephone, completely naked bar a tiny light coloured top. I withdrew immediately, to find myself back in bed. My emotions had been aroused by the surprise of the situation, and the content. I was, well and truly, jolted back to my physical body, damn and blast it!

This conveniently leads me on to the subject of sex. Physical sex and spirit projection do not go well together. One or the other is fine, but not both, for the simple reason that you need to be emotionally calm for projecting, even thinking about sex isn't good. In the dream world, a complete sexual act *is* possible, and probably the best, because the spirit-body is bound to the physical body, as in waking consciousness and, therefore, is very real. Sex on the etheric, or astral, plane is different though and, obviously, does not involve having any input from the physical body, which remains, at home, in bed. I must say that the physical feeling of an orgasm is a direct feeling of the spirit within, and is very similar to the feeling when consciously experiencing the 'rush' when exiting the physical body in spirit form.

So we are then left with a spirit-body *and* all the power of our emotions. Etheric sex, even if it was possible, would require the other person to also be projected, and it is difficult enough to get one person projected, let alone two! So, I suggest, we can safely leave the etheric alone.

The main obstacle with astral sex, is that as soon as you get *seriously* aroused, the increase in your emotional condition will end your projection. Our astral bodies feel solid enough, as do the people that populate the astral environment, so the actual act could be achieved if emotions were not involved, which is, of course, impossible. So, am I writing off astral sex completely? Oh no!

We are still left with the ability to enjoy somebody else's intimate company up to a certain level. When projected, we tend to leave the baser animal instincts behind us. The animal in us really does relate to our physical body alone, and although your consciousness is the same, you lose the stress and worry of that physical side of life. A projected spirit is a calm, happy thing that has a countenance rarely felt whilst being physical. If your only reason for achieving an out-of-body experience is so that you can spy on your neighbour, forget it. Once projected, you realise how very petty, and small minded that thought was.

Let us assume that on your astral walkabout you have met someone you like. Because you have left most of the physical urge to have sex, behind you, barring the memory of it, you are free to feel love for this person. To a certain extent, you feel love for all the inhabitants of your astral world, but I am talking about that *special* love feeling.

There is no physical threat, so you cannot get into trouble, there are no pressures or expectations, just pure *love*. If your astral partner is also your physical partner then all the better! That shows that you are truly happy at home, but life is rarely like that.

As we have our astral bedroom, and our astral house, so we can have our astral partner. This is a boon for all those earthly relationships that are unhappy. Like life, we can also be astrally single, and have casual relationships. This is kept within your own head, if you are comfortable with it and it does not go against your own conscience then it cannot, and will not, harm anybody. In fact, quite the opposite. If your sexual preferences are not what is broadly accepted as 'normal' then where better to relieve your frustration, or fantasy, than astrally where no-one will be physically hurt. Rather that than emotionally wreck a physical life on earth.....

The feeling that you have for your lover is difficult to describe, as there is no direct equivalent to relate to. But if you can remember back to when you were first discovering your own feelings of love, the innocent feeling of intense love for someone very special. When just a look meant the world, and filled you with inner warmth. Also somewhat akin to the intimate feelings you enjoy, leading up to the act of intercourse.

This intense feeling of closeness and intimacy, can last for a good length of time, and is a very lovely, fulfilling, experience. If you are tempted to go further with your lovemaking then beware, because you will be risking all. A certain amount of body exploration is possible, but it has to be controlled. There is nothing worse than one moment enjoying the heights of passion, and within a split second find yourself back in bed all revved up and nowhere to go!

MONDAY 21ST JULY 1997

I had an out-of-body experience this morning, that had an added interest. I did my usual thing and returned to bed to relax. Linda, my partner, was there and unfortunately I disturbed her sleep, so we talked for a little while before she dropped off once again. I continued with my relaxation before, I too, succumbed to sleep. I became aware that I was disturbing my own sleep, and probably that of my partners, by the range of noises that I was making. I was huffing, puffing, holding my breath for long periods of time and then, suddenly, exhaling.

If you are awake when this is all going on, it must sound horrendous. I found it horrendous *myself*, but it did have the beneficial effect of preventing me from getting into too deep a sleep. Because of this, I was able to become aware, consciously, and yet retain the profoundly relaxed state, brought on by sleep. I knew the situation was ripe for a projection, but I had been here *too* many times, and *failed* too many times, for complacency.

I relaxed, further, my heart rate, I relaxed inside by sighing long on my outbreath, and I held my breath for perhaps six seconds, no more. This sometimes gives the final push required, to induce action. I projected almost immediately and was so surprised by it, that I returned just as quickly as I left! I lay there wondering how it all happened so quickly, and gave myself a moment to get over the surprise. *I relaxed again, and immediately projected again, to find myself standing in my bedroom. To my utter shock and delight, I found Linda standing beside me. She was wearing jeans and a light coloured top. I conveyed to her how marvellous this was, because she could at last, completely understand what this thing is that I do.*

I took her by the hand, and led her down the stairs, pulling her through the fabric of the front door, before she had a chance to question my actions. *The High Street, immediately outside our house, was recognisable, so we wandered along the road towards the centre of the village. We did not get far, however, before it became unrecognisable. We stopped for a moment to decide what we were going to do.*

'Come on you can fly!' I said. She only stared at me in disbelief, which is a perfectly understandable stance to take. Before she would allow herself to believe this, she insisted on jumping up in the air first. Little jumps initially, but getting harder, and higher, as she gained confidence. She remarked that it felt a little as it must feel to walk on the surface of the moon. As she came down from a high jump she fell over.

'Look, it doesn't matter, because it doesn't hurt, does it?' I said. And she agreed.

I took her hand and pulled her up into the air. Very gently, we flew along the road, keeping low to become used to it, and taking things easy, to see how things progressed.

'What shall we do now?' Linda called over to me.

We landed outside a large, white, Georgian house and I suggested that we went inside and had a nosy around. She again looked at me incredulously, and with a great deal of trepidation, followed me up the garden path. We clasped hands, and pushed our way in. It was a beautiful home, tastefully decorated, and immaculately furnished. We made our way up the broad stairs to the landing. In one of the rooms we found a sleeping child. She was no more than three years old and looked very peaceful and serene in her bed. We removed ourselves and mentioned to each other how lovely she looked, and we commented on the fact that we did not want any! I immediately found myself back in bed, with Linda fast asleep beside me.

Later, when we both woke up, I casually inquired as to how well Linda had slept that night. She told me that she had slept very well, thank you. I pushed it a little further by asking her if she remembered having any dreams. Her exact response was, 'Boy, did I! after you had come back to bed!' So, I asked her what they were about but, unfortunately, she could not remember, but said they *were very vivid.*

She had no knowledge of having any dream participation whatsoever and, indeed, that was probably the case. Although there is a faint chance that her dreams were masking the real actions taken by her unconscious etheric body, and that *my* astral body was masking the *real* actions of my *etheric* body, and in actuality, we had been together.

These are the kind of long shots that have to be explored, researched, and analysed, just *in case* it is true. Stranger things, I have found. The easy answer is that I was having a conscious astral projection, and Linda was having an unconscious astral projection. Linda usually has dreams that are very vivid nearly every time that I have a projection, so I am sure that my nocturnal meandering does affect her spirit system to an extent. I will continue to check this out.

At one point, in the projection, I had a fleeting look at my own hands. Only because it is another piece of information that needs to be recorded in the spirit of research. Or in the research of spirit! Anyway, I could not believe what I saw, my hands were dark, with long narrow fingers, almost alien looking, whatever that means? I have read that the brighter, whiter, clearer you are, the more spiritually advanced you are. In my case, I must be a very lowly spirit indeed, or else that is a load of rubbish! I think so.

I am also open to the possibility that my astral composition can change its makeup, or perhaps I caught it unawares in its natural form, before it had a chance to don its earthly cloak? I have checked the spirit cord, on many occasions, using my hands, and never have I noticed anything untoward with them. This book answers many questions, and poses many more....

THURSDAY 7TH AUGUST 1997

I won't bore you with the preliminaries anymore, unless there is something significantly different to warrant attention. I want you to imagine that someone is on the point of death, however they have got there is immaterial, but they know that the time has come. All of a sudden, the pain, and anguish, have disappeared and been replaced by a calm composure. They realise that death is a blessed relief to be embraced and resign themselves to whatever is in front of them. One final glimpse of their sad situation, and they give their last breath with a deep, inner, sigh of final resignation......

This is exactly what I want you to do, after you have become aware that you are waking up, following your relaxation procedures. When you are lying there, lowering the strength of your heartbeat, getting vibrations, and inducing the head thumps, remember what it must feel like to give your last, grateful, breath with that 'sigh of resignation'. Do it with a sense of contentment and gratitude.

This is the best way of describing to you this feeling. Of course, you are *not* about to die, your body will not let that happen to you, as long as you are reasonably fit and healthy! There is no more chance of you dying through astral projecting, then there is through dreaming, and if you are about to go anyway, then dying in your sleep has to be the preferred way to go. This 'final sigh' can, and does, make all the difference between a successful oobex, and failure. It *is* that important.

This morning I did all the above, and projected immediately the 'sigh' was instigated. I then proceeded to return, and leave, my physical body three times, simply because I was *able* to. *I found myself, in spirit form, standing in my bedroom, so I left my house by the rear door, and made my way down to the back lane, before turning right, and going for a stroll around the village. I noticed a house that had some lights on, so I went to investigate. I pushed my face into the glass of the window and felt it stretch around my features, there was no-one downstairs, so I pushed further and entered the building. The whole family appeared to be upstairs and, as I stood on the bottom step of the stairs, I could hear them having some kind of serious discussion. After walking in on that girl in the bathroom I am somewhat worried about this privacy issue, daft as that may seem, anyway it didn't feel quite right on this occasion to intrude, so I left them to it and returned to Ivydene.*

On my return journey, I was fighting the dual consciousness, and gained my reprieve. I decided to see if I could get any more information on the cable, and while I was at it, look again at the composition of my hands. I stretched them out in front of me, and had a good close look.

They were a normal pair of hands, not recognisable as mine, but a normal pair of hands. So what must the rest of me look like? These hands were paler, a little smaller and, most definitely, human *in appearance. This astral body seems to be able to alter its appearance to a degree, and if I get a chance to see myself in a real, or astral, mirror, I will tell you what I look like!*

On to the continuing mystery of the cable. There is one main strand (route or root) that leaves my head, just above the place where my backbone enters my skull. This strand is round, I have discovered that not all of them are. Some of the other strands are slightly flatter, and wider, the shape of an oval, but with flattened sides. I am certain that this, combined, cable is a strong thing, but because of its status as a lifeline, I have always been extremely careful with it. This morning, though, I went a stage further.

I pressed my fingers into the actual fabric of the main strand, where it was thickest and attached to my head. It felt as though it was full of ligaments, and tendons, running the length of the cable. As I pressed, they 'gave way' to go either side of my fingers under the pressure. It had a very firm and solid feel to it, and it exhibited a strong pulse. All in all, I counted five separate strands, but in all honesty, some were emerging underneath other's, and it is difficult to know which is which. That is why I say that I counted five strands, but there may be more. I would not be surprised if there wasn't a couple more not accessible to me, inside this root cage.

Finally, I felt the cable with the touch sensations within my hand. I did *not* feel my hand touching the cable through the touch sensations within the cable. If you grasp your own arm, the dominant feeling comes from your hand, and secondary from your arm. The only way to test this would be to get someone else to touch my cable, I think that may be a long way down the line! When I pressed my fingers into the fabric of that strand, I felt no pain. Perhaps that is an indication.

MONDAY 11TH AUGUST 1997

I gained my projection, this morning, through dream awareness. Everything about my home was correct in its detail, and it wasn't until I stepped through the front door, that I realised, for sure, that it was astral. It was the fact that the house opposite was no longer there, that confirmed it to me. In its place was an 'olde worlde' courtyard of modern homes, the like we see so much of nowadays. With a professional interest, I went over to have a look at them, the styles and decor.

The first house, I entered, was so untidy! A young mother was getting a little girl dressed and ready, so I went upstairs to see what was up there, and to get out of her way. In one of the bedrooms I found a younger girl fast asleep. As this house was adjoined to another next door, I pressed my head through this bedroom wall to have a look. It was completely empty, not a stick of furniture was there to be seen. I came back downstairs, through the chaos, and left this poor mother to it without, apparently, being noticed. Once outside, I raised my arms and took flight, over the house tops and into the countryside.

It was a lovely morning, but then again I have never known the weather to be bad in the astral environment. I landed by the side of a pretty little single track country lane, and thought to myself that it was time for a bit of research. I sat down on a bank overlooking a beautiful cornfield, and looked at what I was wearing. All a bit boring really, as I could see trainers, jeans, and a sweatshirt, usual apparel. My hands, also, were as my own should be. I then checked the cable at the back of my head. It fitted flush to my skull, without any apparent root structure, at all. The thickness, right at the head end, was about 2cms (three quarters of an inch) but had decreased, by around a quarter, an arms length away.

I willed myself to fly back to Braunston, in an effort to try and find a way to transfer to the etheric plane. I, certainly, found my home without any trouble, even though the front door had been replaced with another. Only a subtle change was to be seen from the outside, but as I pushed through I could see that the whole house had altered in its layout, although it still felt like home. It was now that I felt the dual consciousness and I desperately tried to hold on to this scene. I turned to the front door, and looked through the little window that it has in it, to see that the house opposite had returned, in all its glory. I opened my eyes in bed.

Regarding the astral cable. The individual strands twist together to make one super-cable. Whenever I have explored this phenomenon, it has generally been whilst my spirit-body has been in the *locality* of my physical body. On these occasions I have usually felt a root system. It appears from the experiment that I had this morning, that distance makes the cable twist and in so doing tightens down on itself. This has the effect of pulling, this combined super-cable, into the head, so that the root system is no longer exposed, and appears to no longer exist to the touch. Under tension, it sits flush to the skull, but as the spirit-body returns to the physical, it relaxes and unwinds slightly, to expose the roots again. See Figure 4, page 135.

WEDNESDAY 20TH AUGUST 1997

This morning a short, but interesting, projection. I became aware that I was waking up, and before that happened too much, I lessened my heart rate and sighed my inner sigh. The rush was massive. *Once again, I found myself on the end of that 'high pressure hose'. The only sense I perceived, was the sense of sight. Flying is too soft a word, for I was shooting around the interior of my bedroom like a mad bat. One second I was staring at a flake of paint, on the wooden ceiling, a second later I was so close to the floor as to see the minute threads of the carpet. All of this was in sharp focus, not as it would be if you were swung around physically by your feet. I was thrown along the wall, catapulted up to the ceiling again,*

*in and out of the furniture, along the floor, every way
possible. It was absolute controlled chaos. Controlled,
because my superconscious mind kept me within the strict
confines of the physical barriers of my bedroom, and
chaos, because I had no control over the random
manoeuvres that my real self was subject to.*

*After a period of time, which seemed like ages but,
in truth, was probably only a minute, or so, the throwing
motion lessened and, like a drunken fool, I staggered to my
feet. I was still in my bedroom, but instead of getting away
as quickly as possible, as I usually would, I stayed, and
turned to look at the bed. Again, my physical self was
missing, but I could see my partner, lying over on the other
side of the bed, very clearly, so I assumed that this was an
astral projection.*

*As I was watching I saw her move in bed, and this
seemed very real, and very normal, to me. I decided to try
an experiment. I placed both my hands, palms down, onto
the bed and pushed them under the cover towards my
partner, and across where 'I' should have been sleeping in
my physical body.*

*I touched 'something', and found myself lying in
bed staring up at the ceiling!* There was *absolutely* no time
lapse between me 'touching' and me returning. So what
really did happen here? Yes, I am open to the probability
that a wayward arm, or a leg, belonging to Linda, was
stretched out, unseen and under the covers. Had I touched
something like that, it may well have had the same effect of
returning me to my body and, I agree, this could *easily* have
been the case here.

What interests me, however, is the *possibility* that I
had touched my own physical body that was lying there,
unseen by my astral vision. This would account for the
instantaneous return. This would have benefited from a

243

slow motion replay, for the speed was too great for comprehension.

During the writing of this book, I have had the rare pleasure of answering some of my own questions, and in that respect I have found, and extracted, the following from the notes. These I recorded on Sunday 4th January 1998 and relate directly to the above episode.

After a peculiar series of events, I found myself projected into my astral bedroom standing beside my astral bed. My astral bed is always a brass bed, quite unlike the wooden Edwardian bedstead that I have slept in for many years. I could see the shape of my partner, clearly sleeping over on the other side of the bed, and she was facing away from me. I went over to my side of the bed and placed my hands, palms down, on the mattress just as I had done before. I pushed my hands across the flat surface through the area that my physical body should be occupying, to see if it was really there. I can report that there was nothing in that space!

I continued to push my hands over to where Linda lay, and as I got to the point just prior to contact, my hands were smacked away by something. It took me completely by surprise! It was the type of warning smack that a loved one would give as a playful caution not to go too far, that sort of thing. Definitely not meant with anger or cruelty.

The shock element brought me back to my physical body immediately, but it is interesting for me to know that my partner was protecting herself whilst asleep. I wonder if we all have this facility? As it was a smack that I could feel, it would appear to have come from her *astral* body as it was *my* astral body that felt it.

Chapter Eleven
Health and related issues

With a book like this, it is obviously full of very personal experience's, and although they are I hope, enlightening, it has to be recognised that it is also very limited in certain areas. On the subject of health matters, I can only convey to you how spirit projection has worked in relation to my own health problems. Apart from the very occasional attacks of 'flu and the common cold, I suffer with two long term problems. One is a lower back problem that stems from a disc having disintegrated, leaving me with two vertebrae crunching around on each other. The other problem is severe writers' cramp gained through all my years of detailed illustration. The latter is especially distressing to me, as it renders my right hand practically useless. I am only telling you this so that you can get some idea of what my personal research is based on.

Part of the reason for running courses and setting up a research foundation here at Ivydene, is to find projector's who have other health problems so that we can evaluate their experience's. This is an area that has *immense* possibilities, as you will see, and an area that has, as far as I can ascertain, commanded little attention in the past. It is important that this be addressed, as a complete section of understanding has hitherto been missed.

It is not necessary to practice, and experience, out-of-body travel, to believe in it. There are many things in life that we have to take at face value. I can watch a programme, on the television, perhaps reporting on the conditions that poor people suffer in other areas of the globe, and I can get a good idea of what that life is like. I certainly believe what I see, understand what I hear, and feel sorry, and saddened, for these people. In my own opinion, this falls short of conveying the *real* environment, the *real* plight of these people. There is a big difference between 'believing' and 'experiencing'. I am not actually present to smell the pungent air, to drink the filthy water, to feel the hot ground baking the soles of my feet. I am not being bitten by flies, fighting disease, and having to look at the pleading faces of helpless children. My next programme has started, and I am enjoying having somebody to make me laugh, whilst I languish in my easy chair, in my easy life.

To believe that out-of-body travel exists, and to *experience* that out-of-body travel, is two different things. Obviously, not everybody will be committed to the same degree, but at least they can experience *enough* of the process to personally believe in its truth. Perhaps enough to recognise one of the gateways, but not to pass through. Those that can put the time, and dedication into it, should do so for the benefit of the other's who cannot. Out-of-body existence is there to be experienced by *anybody* who wishes to do so, you do not specifically need strength, intelligence or special powers.

Access to the etheric plane is extremely difficult for most of us, and I have already said that I believe this is for a very good reason. To exist, on the earth plane, and to flit 'ghostlike' around your friends, enemies, neighbours, bank vaults, Royal Palaces, etc., would cause too much trouble, if it could be done at will. The appeal it would have for the criminally motivated, the industrial spy, the voyeur, or the just plain nosy, is obvious. The temptation is great enough to sway the most steadfast of characters, and can also make them a target for other's to use and abuse. I have looked at the negative aspects of etheric access. There are, of course, positive reasons why it would be a good thing to be able to project to this environment, the major ones being health, and help, in all its forms, this applies also to the astral plane.

Access to the astral plane allows all of the above, but without any of the dangers or violations of privacy. Becoming accustomed to astral life, with experience, affords you the particular mental attributes to be able to handle the difficult, and complex, issues surrounding etheric existence. To go straight from this earthly world to the etheric plane is asking for trouble, for yourself. It is like being given the controls of an aeroplane, and not having had any education or instruction to handle it. Eventually, you will do yourself damage. Astral projection is that education system, and it is vital to attend!

Sticking strictly to the health implications, astral projection allows you the opportunity to be able to help yourself, depending on the problem. Etheric projection, properly controlled, allows you the unique opportunity to help other's.

Confined to bed.

A general term that covers a whole host of circumstances, usually health related. There is very little that you can do in bed, except read and sleep, what you can't do is *physically* exercise. These are the perfect conditions, in which to try astral projection. The more severe, and long term the problem is, the more astral projection can help you.

Suppose you are suffering with the 'flu. You feel lousy, run down, generally miserable, and you don't sleep properly, because you are not getting any fresh air and exercise. Without knowing it, you are already loosening the bond that exists between the two bodies, because the weaker the physical body becomes, the less it holds on to its spiritual counterpart. This is, eventually how death occurs, and why, usually, death is painless when it comes following on from illness. Pain is physical, and is not transferred along the spirit cable when death is about to happen, or when a projection is under way. Unfortunately, the stress, and the memory of pain, can sometimes remain with the spirit following death.

Some anaesthetics have the effect of loosening the bond between the two bodies, so much so, that it has become quite a common experience to hear of people having an out-of-body experience at these times. An oobex is much easier to achieve, when physically weak, than when physically fit, and active.

If you practise the relaxation measures that I have laid down in this book, you will find that, even without projecting, you can achieve the state of painlessness. This also has the knock-on effect of reducing drug intake. Not only does it eliminate pain, it also eliminates bodily discomfort. So you can see what this means to our poor 'flu sufferer. To lose the discomfort, means that they can get to sleep, to astrally project, means that you can leave the great lump of skin and bone to get on with it, while you go out to play! The mental lift that is gained from the 'holiday' is quite amazing. You can breathe clearly, see clearly, and do all the fantastic things that your imagination will allow, and because you started from such a low point it will make it all the more incredible.

Now, what if we apply the same format to other problems that confine people to bed? What about the person who has suffered a serious accident, and broken their back so severely that they are going to be paralysed from the neck down for life? Think of the benefit that out-of-body projection would bring to that person and the *value* that person would put on being able to be free from time to time to do all the things, and more, that they used to do. Again, imagine the mental strength that they would draw from the experience. It is the physical body that has been damaged, *not* the spiritual one.

These scenarios show the two ends of severity, and how oobex can help all confinees, whatever the problem may be, from pain control, to mental freedom. I have to say that the physical body tends to repair itself a lot quicker, if the conscious mind is happier and holds less stress. Astral projection is a great stress reliever, and I know.

Sleeping disorders.

Just two words that cover so much! I suppose that the majority of this book covers, what some people would call, sleeping disorders. You now know that this term is erroneous, and gained through an understandable ignorance of the true facts.

Night terrors are quite common, especially with children, the reason being that children aren't generally carrying the amount of conscious baggage that adults carry, and therefore find the fearsome gateways to the astral environment a natural occurrence. These 'gateway' fears are responsible for thousands of children having to sleep with the light on and being afraid of the dark. If we are honest, being afraid of the dark, even in the secure confines of your own home, often stays with people all throughout their lives.

These fears seem very real, they are meant to, otherwise they would not work, and they are so realistic that people believe the very devil is after them. It is possible that this is where the image, of an existing 'devil' originated from. We know that this is not true. These are not bad or evil images, in spite of their appearance. They are 'purely', honestly, and *only*, frightening. Many things in our day to day lives have the potential to frighten us, without being bad, or evil. This is simply another example, and so we have to lose the prejudice that has built up around these images. By understanding how the system works, we can educate people so that they not only lose these fears, but *embrace* them into their lives for their eternal benefit.

Sleepwalking, is again quite common in children, for the same reasons as I have given above. When it happens to adults it can be both inconvenient, embarrassing, and downright dangerous. I wouldn't suggest teaching a three year old how to have out-of-body experience's anymore than I would let them swim in an unsupervised pool. Some things are potentially dangerous to young minds that would be quite safe for adults. If a *parent* understands what is happening, they can help the child in many subtle ways. If an adult sleepwalks then they, most surely, are in a position to help themselves, with the benefit of oobex understanding.

Sleepwalking, or somnambulism, is the physical manifestation of out-of-body travel. When our spirit-body leaves our physical in either the astral, or etheric form, it is usually an unconscious act. The knack is to convert this into a conscious act. With somnambulism, instead of the spirit-body leaving the physical body behind, it takes it with it. Now all sorts of problems can be encountered by the sleepwalker, unbeknown to anyone else.

1) They may be operating in a dream environment, so that their physical sleepwalking sensations are converted into a dream reality.
2) They could be operating, unconsciously, on the astral plane.
3) They could be operating, consciously, on the astral plane.
4) They could be operating, unconsciously, on the etheric plane.

5) They could be operating, consciously, on the etheric plane.

6) Who knows how many 'further' planes there are! And there are further planes, as you will have already found out, and as you read further. Thankfully, most are out of reach to all but the intensely dedicated.

All we can be sure of, as onlookers, is that they *are* sleepwalking. These people have inside them the subconscious will to project their spirit-body, and it is the actual fear that they are going to sleepwalk that sets up their subconscious mind to make it happen. The more they worry, the more they create a subconscious *need,* and *expectation* to sleepwalk. Sufferers of this condition have to understand the problem before they can begin to help themselves. These people will also be having actual out-of-body experience's on a *subconscious* level, and *never* know. Indeed, if they weren't seen, many sleepwalkers would not realise that they had been sleepwalking at all..... exactly the same as in spirit projection.

Choices have to be made. Do you learn about oobex and use your naturally found ability to enjoy the fantastic world of spirit travel? Turn something ugly into an angel? Or do you learn enough about spirit projection to learn how *not* to do the things that will induce the phenomenon? The latter is a little more difficult to do. Either way, with the correct help, you will be able to completely 'cure' yourself of this problem.

I would also like a study actioned that investigates how, and if, sleep quality and duration is mitigated by the quality and quantity of our eating habits. It is just possible that there is a direct link or pay-off between the energy sources.

Physically handicapped.

Much research is needed into this aspect of the health arena. Some people are challenged in this way from birth, and I would expect to find that their spirit form mirrors the physical counterpart, when projected. But, and it is a big 'but', they will still have all the additional freedom, enjoyed by other's during an out-of-body projection, in spite of their disability.

Maybe for the first time in their lives, they will be able to enjoy full mobility, and total freedom, in all its forms. With practise, astral projection *can* be a regular event, and because of their unique situation, it is nearer to *their* grasp than mine.

It would also seem likely that, should their disability have happened *since* birth, they would have a perfect spirit-body in which to enjoy the benefits that *can* be had with serious practise and, if necessary, instruction, here at Ivydene.

Partially sighted and blind.

As far as I am aware there has been no research carried out that relates to spirit projection of the blind or partially sighted person. There has, however, been research into the content of their dreams and how the dreams differ to those of sighted people.

As far as the perception of 'sight' within a dream is concerned, very much depends on the age that the blindness began. People that are congenitally blind, i.e. blind from birth or very soon after, with very few exceptions do not have a visual element within their dreams. The predominant sensory mode is auditory. There is a critical age of between five and seven years. Those blinded prior to the age of five do not have visual dreams, but those blinded after the age of seven tend to be able to retain enough memory of vision to maintain the visual element. Over a period of a lifetime these visual memories tend to fade or deteriorate as the time progresses. Obviously when we, sighted people, dream it incorporates our visual memory from many sources, our physical eyes being closed.

I would dearly love to do some oobex work with a suitable blind person to further, and extend, this dream research into my realm of spirit projection. Indeed, being blind should not prove to be a hindrance in this at all, quite the reverse. I have read that hypnopompic phenomena is more common among the blind than the sighted. I'm not *too* sure about that, except a blind person does have compensatory senses that are sharper than those of a seeing person. So maybe they can more readily recognise, and therefore be more able to take notice of, these sleep sensations that prove so elusive to us.

Now we must look at what a blind person can expect when successfully projected. A very difficult thing to do! The spirit cable carries a sensory element for sight, so if this is defective within the physical structure of the brain it will probably be defective within the spirit-body. So physically blind could also mean spiritually blind. As you are by now aware, there are spirit environments that are attainable that do not require a cable attachment to the physical body, so would the same apply? If a person has gone blind *since* birth it may be the case that vision will not be impaired during a projection, in the same way that a physically severed arm will still exist in spirit form.

In a report written by H. Robert Blank MD. he mentions a remarkable, but unexplainable, feature contained in many of the dreams of the blind. That feature is the frequency with which the flying dream occurs. He states that this sensation of floating through the air is very common.

One gentleman was actually experiencing this phenomenon in around seventy per cent of his dreams.

Clearly this gentleman is in the enviable position of being able to project his spirit-body on a regular basis, should he wish to do so. When I project, I close my eyes and it is my other senses that enable me to detach my consciousness from my physical being. These 'other senses' are sharper, and more easily controlled by the blind, because they are in constant use during waking times.

Another gentleman, an ex-soldier, reported that he dreamed of being in a battle situation and suddenly realising that in actuality he was blind and should not have been involved as a 'seeing' soldier. This is a good example of his superconscious mind giving him a sign by alerting his conscious mind to the fact that he was dreaming. This was his opportunity to turn his vivid dream into a lucid dream, and thence into a projection if wished.

Sufferers of severe illness and the terminally ill.

It goes without saying that very severe, and painful, suffering would negate most attempts at out-of-body travel. It would be too difficult to get through the relaxation procedures. Drugs may help, but which ones would be safe? If they only affected the physical body, it might be possible, and certainly worth testing. If they altered, in any way, the conscious thinking mind, then they could very well be extremely dangerous. We already have plenty of evidence relating to mind altering drugs, and they should play no part here. The very essence of oobex relies on you being conscious in your own normal, day to day, consciousness. *That* is a healthy mind.

The terminally ill, again, covers a huge spectrum of circumstances. Please don't think that I am being negative in trying to find conditions that don't suit out-of-body experience, what I am doing is finding opportunities where people are ill, but also in complete control of their senses, and can be helped. If someone is dying, whether they know it or not, understanding the process (here I go again!) gives them a peace of mind that cannot be gained from elsewhere. Yes, they can be given love and support, but oobex can give them confidence, and knowledge of where they are going to go to, *before* they die. That confidence will often take most of the stress out of the situation.

It is comforting, also, for their loved ones that are left behind, knowing that death is not final, and that these poor people will actually be going to a far better existence. Somewhere where they can be pain free, and happy, in a place that is familiar to them, not foreign, but somewhere they have *themselves* created during their lifetime. The *real* home from home and no worries whatsoever. This *is* all possible through education and experience, and within the grasp of most people.

Sexual deviance.

An illness? yes, in some cases and not in others. But where does it change from innocent to problematical? Please bear in mind that the following story is a general example, and must be viewed as such, with all its inherent limitations. There is nothing wrong with healthy sex, and if it helps a couple in their relationship to use adult magazines, or to watch videos, then we are not to judge. If it works, then fine and dandy. The crucial word here is 'relationship'. Like a steam engine letting off steam, sexual pressure has to have a release valve somewhere, especially for those people under a certain age, and this is governed for the most part by nature.

Women have problems directly related to sex, but they are generally kept in-house and are usually not a problem to general society. Let us be honest and say that the majority of sexual problems that affect society, emanate from younger men. These are often men who either don't have a constant and loving partner, or who are not sexually satisfied at home by their spouses. These males fantasise about other situations with other people, and the more the fantasy becomes important to them, the more it embeds itself into their psyche, leaving reality to wither away. These people can become loose cannons that are unpredictable, even to themselves. Not necessarily bad people at all, but through circumstances, find themselves out of the *main stream* of what is expected.

Quite by chance, they find that they get pleasure from unexpected sources. From peeping at other people through windows, and the very act of spying on people without their knowledge, is a turn on. So it eventually doesn't matter if that person is male, female, young boy, or a young girl, the *act* is still a turn on. This man is worried about himself, he questions himself, he tells himself to pull himself together..... until the next time. He will then justify his actions by telling himself that no-one is getting hurt, no physical harm is being done to them, so what harm is being done by looking.

Slowly, but surely, this man is heading down a path that has not been his conscious choice. There is many a man who has led a happy life with a wonderful partner who could, in other circumstances, have found himself in this position. Conversely, there has been many a so called pervert, who would have made a wonderful husband, if only he had been lucky to find the right person to spend his life with earlier on in his development. There is a female perspective on this but, as usual, it is the male antics that kick up the most dust.

So when this person goes on to realise that he can get pleasure elsewhere, and resigns himself to the fact that he isn't going to find that special person, because you *can* be hurt too many times.... Other factors come in to play. Pornographic videos can become commonplace, general respect for women can be lost. Prostitutes can be sought as a temporary stop gap and the perception of reality, within society, can alter and eventually become totally wacky.

We have the emergence of stalkers, benign or dangerous, and sexual abusers, even rapists. They have the ability to take their sexual frustration out on young boys and young girls, because they are stronger physically, plus they have the strength of their mental conviction. These two components allow them more of a chance to be successful in their crime. A grown woman is often capable of putting up a hell of a fight, while a young child makes easy pickings.

All this because these men have fallen out of the mainstream net, at the wrong time, and because of negative circumstances. The bottom line is that they crave love, and attention, they want to be wanted, and they have a sexual urge that needs to be fulfilled, the same as any man. There is no excuse being made here, they are doing wrong against nature, against God, and against universal law. The path that they have been drawn along, has been the path of subtle temptation, little by little, deeper and deeper, into obscenity.

These people aren't mad, they know that what they do is wrong. So where do they go for help? At whatever stage they are at, where can they go for guidance? I have a tremendous respect for the Samaritans, but people tend to think of them as a last resort before suicide, which is wrong, but nevertheless, a fact. These people *can* be helped, however far down the road they are, they *can* be brought back into society on a healthy level. They need to understand, and educate, *themselves* and seek proper advice from, amongst other's, the oobex foundation here, at Ivydene, if they are worried about themselves. Nothing can

257

possibly shock us anymore, and it *is* all research, knowledge that will, in the end, help other's. Good that comes from bad.

The beauty of oobex is that you can indulge yourself as deeply as you want to, without causing anybody *any* harm. You can find the love and attention that you crave without breaking the law. The irony is that once you achieve an out-of-body experience you will realise how petty the fantasies were, and how fantastic this new found environment is. Real goodness *can* emerge from these murky depths, and you *can* become a regular member of society, with an understanding conscience. If you are somebody that has done wrong, be assured that it isn't all bad. There *can* be a positive side to having done wrong, when you evaluate the effects of those mistakes during your present lifetime.

Abortion

Using the out-of-body experience will open up channels of understanding that enable us to look at various problems from an angle that is not purely physical. In the world today we have, amongst other's, two particularly emotive issues that seem to cut a dividing path through a plethora of opinions. Namely abortion and euthanasia, both having the common issue of life and death at the core.

If we begin with abortion, at some stage in the developing foetus the 'breath of life' is given to the baby, a new consciousness begins and the spirit exists. The process of the spirit transferring itself into the body of the child is a major mystery, however when we die we tend to continue to be interested in the affairs of our family and friends and because of this *link* it is more likely that we will reincarnate back into this *area* of life. Of course this does depend on many things, like how long we spend between earthly lives, and if we still have friends and relatives living on earth when

258

it is our time to return. Bearing in mind that a lot of our earthly acquaintances will also die, it is often the case that it is the *people*, not the *place*, that we reincarnate to, and that has been decided because of an attachment we have with *another* recently reincarnated soul. This often means that we will have dealings with the very same souls in more than one life, and it is common for the appearance of these attachments to leap-frog every other life, or so. The permutations are endless but if you intensely hate someone, in this life, and you never want to see them again, beware, for intense hate, like love, can bond you to this soul and there will be every chance that you will meet this person again. Next time it could be in less favourable circumstances, so be careful with whom you make your attachments in this life.

Even more of a mystery is where, or how, a brand new spirit is created to take its place in the body of the developing foetus, and I am not sure if this can ever be completely resolved. As I have said before, a physical body has a soul as surely as it has an arm or a leg, it cannot exist without one. When a baby is created, the spirit-body develops along with the rest of the baby until all elements are mature enough to sustain healthy life and birth can ensue. So rather than the 'breath of life' being given to a foetus, it has instead grown and developed along with the physical body. It is my belief that an existing soul can choose, or be chosen, to inhabit a virgin foetus for the necessary development it has to make. If that choice is *not* made, the virgin foetus will continue to exist and develop as a new spirit.

When a baby is aborted we have to look at two things. Firstly, how this affects the parent, or parents. I believe that you are the parent *before* the child is born.

Secondly, how this affects the unborn child. Let us look initially at the child itself.

If this is a new spirit then abortion will do little harm because we have a life that knows nothing, a body that is not fully developed and a spirit that has not existed before. This soul will start again at another time. Many children, unfortunately, die from accidents and spiritually *have* to start again in another body. Lives are not governed solely by 'fate', accidents come along and disrupt our natural passage through life, and our future is redesigned to cope with the changes. We always retain choice, which is only ever any good if we know what the future holds and, thankfully, we don't, so what will be will be! An aborted foetus is no different to a foetus that has died from other means. For a new spirit this is not a major catastrophe.

With a child that has had a previous existence, the situation is a little different. It has chosen to inhabit that particular foetus for a reason, it would not have done so if it was likely to be aborted. It is my contention that termination in these cases are very rare for that reason. However, abortion happens as a result of varying circumstances and accidents must occur on occasions, simply due to the numbers involved. It is the *reason* that the spirit chose to inhabit this *individual* foetus that is important because it would have a real effect on the future. It was meant to be in that body for a purpose. This could be for the personal spiritual advancement of the inhabiting soul singular, or for the spiritual advancement of thousands of existing souls.

Mistakes will happen and there will be many regrets. Taking all this into account it will be seen that the greatest likely effect that abortion has, will be on the parent, or parents. Many good lives have been ruined by guilt, many children have not been conceived because the mother is convinced that 'God' will seek retribution. If a mother has had an abortion and years later finds herself pregnant she may believe that her new child will be at risk because of her, so called, sins in the past, etc. Should that child happen to be defective in any slight way, no amount of reasoning will convince the mother otherwise.

It is very important that we get away from all this nonsense. It does not happen this way. Life *does not* work like that. Making children is not the sole reason for our existence, *that* is an animal act that has the effect of producing more bodies for more spirits. Important though that is, the main reason we are here is for our own benefit, our own spiritual advancement. We are actually producing too many babies for existing spirits to inhabit, that is why so many new spirits are being created. Unfortunately, every new spirit then has to keep returning for self improvement and we must slowly realise that we are creating a nightmarish situation reminiscent of the 'Sorcerers Apprentice'. The more new spiritual souls that we create, the bigger the waiting band of reincarnating spirits becomes.

The world population is one thing, but you must multiply that many times to get the true picture. From a spiritual perspective, we need to cut down on the number of children being born. Obviously people are living longer, which doesn't help the situation, but I will speak on that subject later.

I have put the case regarding the child as clearly as I can, I would now like to talk about the parents. Fathers often never know that they are the parent of an unborn child, and if that child is aborted, it will obviously never affect them. Those fathers that *do* know can react in many different ways. It is sometimes more difficult to deal with a situation that is out of your control, but nature made you a man and men cannot give birth. When you are not able to influence a situation it allows you the freedom to express whatever feelings you wish with all the safety of not having the responsibility, the commitment or sincerity, required to deal with it. A little like the shadow government who can say whatever it likes in the sure and certain knowledge that it is not them that has to run the country.

There will be times when the father and mother are part of a stable and loving relationship but decide that a baby is not right for them, at the moment. Where the two parents agree they will be able to give each other mutual support. Where there is disagreement, the mother must always decide. The man does not have equal rights over the production, or non-production, of the baby because he does not have rights over another body. This is not an equal issue, the same as if the man decides to have a vasectomy, the man will make the final choice, of course. If the couple cannot agree to something as fundamental as whether or not to bring a child into the world then, I suggest, they *shouldn't*.

The real damage is done to the conscience of the woman if she has had an abortion *believing* it to be wrong, and she must *never* do this. This sometimes only becomes apparent after the deed is done, so either way, you may lose. If she has a loving partner, then seeing her like this, and being part of the decision making process, will cause him mental turmoil also. The mental stress can break up a relationship leaving the woman with all the recriminations and forever thinking that she could have brought up that child on her own, etc. A woman should ideally understand how the big picture of life unfolds before making this kind of decision. From a child she has been taught that killing anything is wrong, she will have read religious text telling her that it is wrong, there will be anti-abortion lobbies on television. There are so many pressures that come to bear, but if she *believes* it is wrong, then it *is* wrong. This is your own personal spirit link communicating with you.

262

The big issue here is *conscience*. If you can have an abortion and retain a clear conscience, then it is correct for you to have that termination. If it is carried out at an early stage, absolutely no damage will be done to any spiritual existence. This must also be understood by the doctors and nurses who perform the process. Not understanding the system can lead to a bad conscience that will remain with you throughout your life and beyond. It stays with you like a poison eating away at the inside of your head. The tragedy is that there is no need to feel this way, and counselling should be sought from someone qualified that does understand the oobex system. Even better than that is to practice oobex yourself and gain your own knowledge. A bad conscience is hell on earth, and a clear conscience is heaven. This situation will affect your spiritual environment accordingly.

The real offence is to bring a child into the world when you cannot look after it properly, or if it will affect the progression of your own spiritual development. Once a child is born, the commitment of motherhood has been made and must be honoured to the best of your ability. It goes without saying that contraception is the most effective way of protecting the world from mindless over-population.

Many women must be torn terribly between deciding what to do. If you *do* want a baby and are in a position to give that child protection, sustenance and love, then do so. If not then *don't*, simply continue your life in the sure and certain knowledge that you have done the right thing. To bring a spirit entity into this world that could be much better looked after by someone else is a selfish act. Experience the truth of out-of-body spiritual existence and understand how life works, you don't have to take my word for it.

Finally, it is the *quality* of upbringing that is important to a developing child. It is also just as important to the spiritual development of the *parents*. There is a giving, taking, loving understanding between parents and children that cannot be described. In an ideal world each child would have a loving mother and father to care for it, but we do not live in an ideal world, beautiful though it is. Single parents and same sex parents are very capable of bringing up a child, because it is the *quality* of upbringing that is important. Small, and close, families are better in that respect. A gay couple for the right reasons and with time to spend, will do a better job of raising a child than a heterosexual couple that are stretched and stressed. For all those people that think the child will also grow up gay please understand that nothing could be further from the truth, for that child will grow up with greater understanding and compassion and will certainly *not* be gay unless it was born that way.

Euthanasia

Practising out-of-body existence will colour your opinion on most things, for it *does* affect everything in your life. For some of us the realisations come too late to influence some situations and all we can do is live the rest of our lives in the correct fashion and advise other's in the hope that they will avoid the same mistakes. Something we all may have to face, towards the end of our lives, is serious illness. Of course that can strike us at anytime during our lifetime if we are unlucky. We are faced by the same pro-life people that we encountered in the abortion issue. *Life is sacred*, but it is also to be enjoyed for a specific reason and if that quality of life becomes non-existent, and there is *absolutely* no prospect of it returning, then the patient should be allowed to die with dignity. It is against universal law to obstruct the natural progression of a soul in the process of its evolution.

These people who believe that life must be maintained at *all* costs must surely believe that death is final, but even so, isn't that still selfish? Our medical knowledge is so advanced that we *are* able to make calculated decisions and I would go so far as to say that it is *more than straight forward recovery* that has to be observed. The *quality* of that recovery has to be taken into account and the benchmark, to look for, is within yourself.

If, for a patient or relative, recovery means being bedridden, having someone feed you, wash you, take you to the toilet, change you, give you pain killing drugs, would *you* be happy to spend the rest of your life in that situation. Then the do-gooders say 'It's all right, they don't know what is going on.'

We treat our animals more humanely than we do our friends and family. If something is seriously wrong with an animal, a faithful friend that has been our constant companion for, say, fifteen years we get advice from the medical expert and take appropriate action. We would not see the animal in distress or allow them to suffer any further than is absolutely necessary in fairness and respect to the beautiful creature. So why don't we think the same way about our fellow humans?

We should have a properly laid out legal process that involves the patient themselves, where possible, relatives and doctors all taking a part in making a decision that has the same standing, in law, as an instant and natural death. This advice from the medical experts must err on the side of caution, but remember these people are committed to saving lives, not killing people, so their advice will always be in the best interest of the patient. The decisions that they put forward will be policed by their peers by having an independent second and third opinion. I keep banging on about this, but when the day comes that the medical staff, *by experience*, know that life exists after death, and the relatives know that life after death exists, we can all realise that the gift of release can be the greatest gift that we can give to a loved one. But only with the strictest controls in place.

General development

Medicine, like all technology, is progressing at a tremendous rate. Eventually we will be recognised as a machine is recognised. If a part breaks down, it will be replaced. We will be genetically adjusted to remove defects, and we will live longer, for all this is in search of longevity, but where does it stop? I hear that we all could live to one hundred and fifty years old, but once this has been achieved the scientists will endeavour to extend our lives to two hundred years, and so on.

We have a responsibility to look after the physical body to the best of our ability, so we must be working on the good developmental aspects of our *spirit*. That is the most important area of improvement that can be made and yet so very little is properly understood, and so little is done. Where is the spiritual research into mental problems? Is it the spiritual soul that is damaged, or is it the influence of a malformed or damaged brain? Just basic questions that cannot be answered. This area is vast and yet ignored.

It is known that the brain produces electrical activity, and these waves are measured by an instrument called an electroencephalogram, or EEG for short. It is also believed, in parts of the world, that where there is no recorded electrical activity, i.e. a flat EEG, the patient is considered brain dead. I must make it clear that, in the UK this is not relied on as absolute proof of death. Raymond Moody reports that many patients, showing flat EEGs, have recovered to report details of near death experience's, *proving* that this test is unreliable in that specific sense.

Having had personal experience of, maybe,four or five environments, other than the physical, I can well believe this to be true. The centre of consciousness, incorporating thought and memory, exists within the spirit-body, not in the brain of the poor patient on the slab. During an out-of-body excursion the brain can run so slowly as to be regarded almost as dormant. This is indeed the case also with the heart, and *probably* all organs, in hibernation mode.

There are mental 'seals' that are supposed to keep past conscious experience separate from present conscious experience. I have already explained that sometimes these 'seals' are not quite doing the job and past life can encroach into the present. I have spoken about our astral environment, and sometimes the 'seal' that separates our unconscious meandering on the astral plane *will also* let information through. I myself have moments when I remember situations and conversations that I have never consciously had! I must add that intentional, conscious, astral or etheric travel is firmly remembered in the conscious memory.

The period between birth and death we know is called a lifetime and consists of a number of daylight units that we call days. Because of this, we humans have invented a concept called time, and we see ourselves as having a certain amount of time to do the things we need to do within these limits.

What we should actually be doing is looking at ourselves from a *developmental* angle, a spiritual maturity. We are given a life period to do this, and for most of us it will be long enough to naturally achieve a reasonable standard. Like all things in life, there will be people who show great maturity of spirit at the age of twenty, and other's that never get near it. That is why we need more than one go at attaining a standard, therefore, the age of someone is not as important as their maturity. People with a similar maturity level can be any age. Education is the bedrock on which realisation stands, and I am not talking about the pseudo-educated that only possess good memory retention!

If we now look at life as a developmental process, rather than as a period of time, we can understand more easily how it works. Let us take the game of 'Snakes and Ladders' as an analogy. Many people seem to go through life landing on all the ladders, confidently becoming spiritually mature with little effort. They go through life with few problems and few disappointments. Then there will be spiritual souls that are sitting, ready and waiting, on 'Start' who immediately hit the snake on the following square and are out before they have even played the game. These will be the premature deaths, the aborted pregnancies, etc. It follows that these souls must wait for another game to come along and have another go.

The bulk of us manage to get through life somewhere in-between the two, hitting some snakes, grabbing a few ladders, and think of ourselves as lucky if we don't suffer too much personal tragedy, etc. Generally gaining our spiritual maturity through the education that a lifetime throws at us.

Spiritual development can go *backwards* as well as forwards. Any of us, at anytime, can hit a snake that will check our development, or even erode the present standard, depending on the severity of the check. Sometimes it can be something very small and seemingly innocent, like a criticism or an overheard remark, that can cause you to, for example, lose confidence. From that moment on, whatever progress is made in life, you will always land on this snake that will bring you back and stop your further advancement. The actual causes of these obstacles are usually not consciously known, and this is where a good therapist, counsellor, or doctor, trained in the oobex philosophy, can help. It can also be as obvious as the deeply felt loss of a loved one, leaving a sadness too heavy to bear.

All the answers are stored in the subconscious part of the mind, and are reasonably accessible to the majority of us. Consciously knowing why a problem exists goes a long way towards resolving anxiety and avoiding that particular snake in your life. I will talk a little about therapy later, because it isn't all the same, and it isn't always beneficial.

We have wars, and natural disasters that mentally, and physically, can scar your life in varying degrees, and cause all sorts of problems. It must be said, though, that many a person's spirit has triumphed in the face of disaster and actually benefited from the experience. A slip down the snake can land you on a ladder that takes you far higher than you would have originally gone, so a human spirit can often greatly benefit from helping other's that have experienced horrendous events.

Very few disasters are one hundred per cent bad, and it is my experience that some good is to be found in all of them if you take the trouble to look. What I am *not* saying is that the good things justify the bad, that is not true at all. These are large events that obviously affect us and, therefore, we must consciously understand the reason for the influence it has on our lives.

As we live our lives we affect other's, it is impossible not to, and it is important to realise the extent of the influence you have over that other person's development. It would be easy for me to say that all influence must be positive, it would be nice if it was but, of course, it isn't. This is especially so when we are young and in the process of development ourselves. We fall in and out of love, and the breaking up is never easy. We say things that are insensitive and hurtful, sometimes on purpose, sometimes by accident. This is part of the natural process of finding a mate for life and, when that person is found, you can look back and be thankful that those relationships did break up on the path to finding contentment. Once you find your stable mate, you can then be cognitive of the need for positive input for, not only the two of you, but also for the benefit of your surrounding family and friends.

Abuse

Unfortunately, there are situations that fall outside the normal, where one person can mentally harm another person so severely that irreparable damage is caused. Abuse can involve physical harm, we know, and that part is usually repairable. It is the damage suffered by our spiritual souls that hurts us, with any type of abuse, these effects can never be fully appreciated. Here I am including all types of abuse, including the type of abuse when respect is lost for a spouse within a family situation. The very fact that two people are trapped within each others' company can also generate mental or verbal abuse from one or both parties. The situation, and circumstances, can often be part of the problem and cause irrational behaviour from one, or both, normally well balanced people.

The abuser also suffers, everybody suffers. The abuser abuses *themselves* every time they abuse someone else. This doesn't make their position any better, it makes it twice as bad.

When a woman is sexually abused, which may involve rape, it is her soul that needs help. It is her very self that has been damaged, and violated, it is only her inner strength that will give her any help. Another person, driven by an out-of-control animal instinct, can inflict so much harm as to not only negate the good spiritual development of a woman, but in extreme cases, will even kill for the pleasure.

How much work has been done to ascertain the spiritual development of the abusers? None! Are they all first timers? We do not know. In fact we know so little about the most fundamental aspect of *being* a *human being*. This subject, sadly, also involves children who do not have the experience, the development, to come near to understanding this subject, and they shouldn't have to, similarly with spiritual animals.

Most abuse happens in a domestic situation and is usually repetitive. It is this long mental cruelty, often suffered in silence, that makes people feel empty, and soulless. It is the trapped despair that causes problems, and spiritual development instead becomes bitterness and hate, not only eroding any development in this life, but also developments gained previously. Spiritual development can actually begin to work backwards to become spiritual degradation, so it is most important that a stop is made on this as soon as possible. Abuse transcends all spheres of life, especially mental abuse, because this sits equally in the domain of both man, and woman.

Education must begin with the abuser, or rather, the potential abuser, and we are all potential abusers, in that we can spiritually hurt other's by our own ignorance. If we can nail down the fact that this is just one life of many, if *enough* people can prove it to themselves to get the scientists going, then we can teach this subject in schools and spiritually develop our children earlier, with control, instead of leaving it all to the mercy of a haphazard life. A spiritually developed child will not be an abuser, they will not be so inclined to drink, smoke, or take drugs. They will understand that they have a moral duty to keep this transient body healthy, and to respect other's because we all interact with each other mentally. For most of us living in the world at the moment, there will be another life to come, we are happy to take out insurance to protect us in this life, but what about the next? It is our investment in this life that is an insurance for the next. We exist here solely to *progress*, that must be realised and understood, for it takes little effort to be kinder, more selfless and thoughtful to other's.

Treatment

We have a range of emotions that come into play at varying times, with varying intensity, every moment that we are alive. I think you would be surprised if you began to count every time you felt a type of emotion during a day. Movies, for example, are designed to provoke as many emotions as possible within a short space of time, to 'touch' you. All true emotions are felt by, dealt with, and emanate from, the spirit that is the essential 'you'. Whenever I write the word 'spirit', it means 'you', simply that.

These emotions are a reaction to stimuli, and vary in intensity according to that stimuli. In a normal and well-balanced soul, these reactions work within acceptable limits to help you deal with each situation as it arises. With every emotion felt, it is our own spirit-body reacting.

To put it in its simplest terms, it happens that during our developmental process, often as children, we may experience something that sooner, or later, causes us to emotionally react in an excessive, or incorrect, manner. Our subconscious mind will try to protect us by mitigating this excessive emotion. This is achieved by the often ingenious use of the vast storehouse of mental, and physical, problems that are available. For example, if our subconscious mind believes, through its developing experience, that automobiles are dangerous, it could cause us to suffer agoraphobia to keep us indoors. We consciously may not realise that it is a fear of automobiles that is causing the problem. If we try to go out to work, in spite of the phobia, the stress that this causes can lead to additional problems like digestive upsets, headaches, ulcers, etc. The permutations are endless, as no two people can ever lead exactly the same life.

In reality, the problems can be *very* intricate and require deep understanding and sensitivity. If you are lucky they really can be surprisingly straightforward. This level of seriousness cannot be ascertained without, or prior to, treatment. Once it is understood when, and where, you first reacted excessively, we can find out *why* you did so. It is this 'why' that has caused an emotional imbalance in the first place and can be corrected. The cause could be as blatant as sexual abuse, or as innocent as a remark overheard via the radio.

Working with the subconscious mind is certainly a delicate operation, but a therapist experienced in oobex systems can usually uncover the cause of the problem, in the majority of cases. In so doing, this will allow normal spiritual development to resume, although this *can* be a complex operation and may involve not just this present life. Obviously, a real understanding of oobex philosophy is needed for you to continue the remainder of this lifetime understanding yourself, and being tolerant of others. To date, very few therapists will be practised in this philosophy and caution must be exercised when choosing the right one.

Oobex therapy involves only what you have read here, which is pure relaxation, but with the important addition of a practitioner expert in guiding you through the process only as far as necessary to help you with a particular problem. Once you know *why* the problem exists it can be dealt with accordingly. In some cases the problem can be taken away completely, in others, having the understanding, and complete knowledge, of *why* it is there is enough to effect a *gradual* recovery. There are, of course, some ailments that we are stuck with, and in these cases it is important to be cognitive of the problem and work your life accordingly. This may involve altering the way we perceive certain situations, pain controlling relaxation, avoiding certain foods, the list goes on. As I have already said, the treatment will differ according to the problem, and it is the *problem* that determines the type of treatment.

I mentioned hypnotherapy earlier, hypnosis is an altered state of awareness, that allows the conscious mind to relax and so allows an interaction with a part of the *subconscious* mind. Hypnotherapy, is the art of dealing with the mind, in a responsible manner, to resolve certain physical and mental problems that we have collected during our lives. Most of these problems have come about because of action taken by others, and how we have *mentally* perceived those actions. *But.....*hypnotherapists are a mixed bag, consisting of the highly qualified, at one end, through to the well meaning, but clueless, at the other, so be careful. There are also many different systems of treatment, and everyone thinks that theirs is the best, unfortunately, there is no official standard. My best advice, if you are thinking of going down this particular route, is to understand the oobex philosophy yourself first, you will soon recognise if the therapist is talking the same language as you are!

Health is a vast subject, and one that cannot escape the microscope of the spirit projector. I do need your input to build an Association of Projector's who will spread the word, spread the methodology, and most importantly, bring back detailed reports from the field of life. This is an immense undertaking and one that I am prepared to address, but only with your help. I am not special, I am one man, you are one reader, please help me.

Chapter Twelve
The animal connection

As human animals, we eat meat, just as other animals eat meat. I would not expect a cat to eat vegetables or to restrain itself from catching, and eating, wild prey. I hate watching a beautiful animal bringing down another beautiful animal, and devouring it. I don't like it, but it is a fact of life, a natural act necessary for the continuance of life. Once upon a time we would have done exactly the same, hunted, killed, and devoured, to feed our family through necessity.

Since those times we have become 'civilised' and 'educated', and this is no longer what we have to do. That basic function is still with us, like a shadow in the background, in the same way that all basic functions are still with us. If society broke down, we would degenerate into a fine old mess, and all these base instincts would reappear frighteningly quickly. During the last war, when meat was rationed, boys would go into the countryside and hunt rabbit, hare, and game, for the table, because we are naturally a part of the food chain. In many parts of the world this is still common practice.

Now civilisation is an extremely good thing, as it keeps us secure, it allows us to interact with others and gives us a quality of life for all the right reasons. Unfortunately, the whole world is not yet civilised, nor does it have the correct values, and this comes down to education and circumstances. If we, as humankind, can get the education right, then we have the grounding on which we can build our civilisation upon, and it is this education that differentiates between us and the cat, or should be! This all encompassing ability to think, and rationalise, is what makes us able to leave the blind instinct behind with the wild animal, and live in a civilised manner.

So, as a human animal, I eat meat, but I eat as least as possible, and where I have knowledge, I buy a product that can guarantee that the animal has been raised in a good and healthy way. If I was a hunter living thousands of years ago, the meat on my plate would be similar to this, healthy, but wild. My problem is with the way most animals, intended for consumption, are kept and treated. All life must be respected, especially when we are not cognitive of the feelings, and the spiritual make-up, of the animal, or bird. Research into this side of life is difficult enough with communicative human beings, so extending our reach to encompass the other animals is a near impossibility.... but not completely.

All human beings, irrelevant of their intelligence, have a spirit-body, and a spiritual side to their lives, this we have established. So are we arrogant enough to think that this doesn't apply to animals also? What evidence do we have to support the theory? Throughout history there have been 'ghostly' sighting's of 'headless horsemen', for example, so part of the sighting must have included a horse. Also many sightings of the witches 'familiar', her cat or bird. We could say that these were extensions of the human influence, and not animals in their own right at all. That may be correct, but how superior of us not to think that they could be phantoms in their own right and only linked to human phantoms as a matter of choice.... as in life! There have been countless examples of phantom dogs but very few, if any, phantom cows, or goats, or budgies, or goldfish. Why?

Animal phantoms exist for exactly the same reason that human phantoms exist, because they have made a tie, in their earthly lives, that was so strong that it cannot be broken without help. So, obviously, we are talking about animals that have a closeness to humankind enough to create a bond, i.e. cats, dogs and horses, to name but three. The bond of love, or usually blind commitment, for an animal, is so great that death does not sever the link completely and it is not allowed to continue on its path of development. You see, I am already saying that animals have exactly the same *kind* of spiritual system as we do, albeit *possibly* in a ruder form. But does this apply to all types of animals, or just some?

Let us look at dreaming, for if an animal dreams it does so for the same reason as we do. Therefore, they will have a spiritual system. So how do we know which animals dream and which do not? The answer is observation, and I need your help again! All animals sleep to rest, so that they are always prepared immediately to hunt, or escape. Any animal that is physically tired is easy prey to starvation or a predator. But that is not the sole reason.

I have a cat, and often when she sleeps she will give off classic signs that she is dreaming. I can observe rapid eye movements, noises from her throat, lips curling back, and her claws extending and retracting in their sheaths. Without a doubt she is hunting in a dream environment that is giving her some amount of reality. The same thing happens with my dog, she will even bark in her sleep, and the lower end of her legs will twitch as she is running in her dream. The real clincher for me, was an experience I had that happened a year or so prior to my keeping detailed records.

I haven't mentioned much about my etheric experience's in deference to my neighbours, and because they happen so rarely, but on one such occasion I had been out and about around the village and was making my way home. I must just mention that when projecting like this I like to know that my physical body is secure from interruption, so I am usually sleeping on my own, in a locked house with the bedroom door closed.

On this occasion I had got back to my house and pushed myself through the front door. As I got to the top of the stairs I noticed Roxy, my Irish Water Spaniel, asleep as usual on her bed. Without a second thought, I passed by her on route to my bedroom. As I did so, another 'Roxy' peeled off and came with me! She was about three-quarters her normal size, but other than that she appeared perfectly normal. Foolishly, I was worried about her being out-of-her body and being on her own, just at the time when I was coming *back* into mine. I pushed my way through the fabric of my bedroom door and she followed me, as though it was the most natural thing in the world to do. I knelt down and pushed her back through the door but she wasn't having any of it! It turned into a game and she was enjoying it, no sooner did I push her back than she reappeared!

This all lasted only a few moments and should it happen now, I would obtain a lot more information from the experience. Nevertheless, it did happen and I am totally convinced that some animals have the same spirit system as we do. There is a moral question here and that is, should we humans be feeding on animals that have a soul and spiritually exist? Are we not, through ignorance, running the risk of a type of cannibalism? We do not yet know, in the case of those species that do have a spiritual system, if it is a separate and sealed system, or if they are connected into ours. Some people will say that animals, particularly domestic, develop this ability because of their proximity to us humans, a kind of extension of ourselves, and that may be possible. Personally, I don't think so, it is a very superior position to take, but I am very open minded about it and that is why I need your help.

It is very easy to 'humanise' animals and we must be very careful not to do this. By 'humanise' I mean that it is easy to look at an animal and give it human characteristics by interpreting their mannerisms as though they were a fellow human being. We love our animals, or should do, so it is difficult to be impartial enough to record any observations that would be of any use. That is why we must begin, at least, with the sleeping animal. I need you to write to me and let me know whether your animal appears to experience dreams, and just as importantly, *whether it doesn't*. We have enough information regarding cats and dogs already, so it is everything else that I am interested in however large, however small. Observing the sleeping habits of wild animals, and birds, would be especially significant, as no human influences will have been felt.

I am not sure where this book will be read, or by whom, but if you work on a farm, or in a vets practice, in a zoo, or game park, you may be in a position to observe the sleeping animal, so please let me know what your observations are. This will especially apply to the uncommon animals, like badgers or otters, for example. It would be nice to have this information covering all major species. Does the subject sleep soundly and solidly all night, or do they show the signs of dreaming, as I have previously described. It may well be the case that all birds, and fish, do not dream. We may find that sleeping dolphins do dream, and sheep don't, for example. By analysing the results we may establish that we have two classifications of animal. Those with, and those without. The interesting part would be to see where the line falls and whether we have enough evidence to probe further. For all those people that believe that *all* animals have souls, fine! Let us put it to the test, and see.

So come on, all those of you that have any kind of access to any kind of animal at all, please drop me a line and let me have your observations. Perhaps it could be part of a class project, teaching children about greater awareness. This must be solely from the perspective of the animal though, for giving me information about animals that are part of your own dreams is not what I am looking for here!

My theory, put very simply, is to roughly create three basic classifications of possible intelligent life forms, birds, fish, and animals. I am not expecting a great deal of positive results from the first two categories, if any at all. I am expecting to find that the animal world is split into those that dream and those that don't. By consolidating the findings, it would then be necessary to test the results with controlled trials on certain species. Where it is confirmed that an animal has the dream experience, we can be sure that it does so for the same reasons we do. Therefore the animal has a spirit, and will also have a soul. If this is the case then we should give it the respect that we give the human animal. To breed that animal for slaughter, and consequently food, would be wrong, as wrong as cannibalism.

Of course all animals should be treated with respect whatever they are, and yes all animals, birds, fish, whatever, feel fear and pain. There is a food chain and we are part of it however detached we have become from the killing end of things. You see, depending on the results of the survey, it will be interesting to look at the animals that are found to have a soul and try to work out the differences with those that don't. Is it possible that nature has decreed that animals with a soul are less preyed on than others? Could it be generally the case that animals without a soul are preyed on a great deal and are naturally seen as food for the rest? If this is the case then we may have to radically rethink our eating practices and persuade others, also, of the truth.

If an animal possesses a soul then it is in the business of improving the quality of the spirit each time it is returned to experience a life on this earth. If we human beings raise that baby animal in artificial surroundings, force feed it for eighteen months and then kill it, what progress can that spirit make? We are going against nature and especially universal law, which is the greatest crime of all. Just like our own laws, ignorance is no defence, we must thoroughly investigate this issue for very many good reasons. Some of our human practices are not even for the eventual production of food. Some killing is perpetrated for the sake of a skin, a tooth, a hoof, a severed hand or powdered bones.

The human population is increasing too quickly for the good of our planet. The animal population is *decreasing* to the detriment of our planet. If there is be a future for humanity, a balance must be restored. We must improve the spiritual quality of living humans by controlling the population, and understanding the needs of our brothers, and sisters, that make up the rest of the animal kingdom. Why are we so determined to be blind to the problems that are happening now, and right in front of our eyes?

Chapter Thirteen
In conclusion

I have endeavoured to keep my investigations and explanations within the realms of astral and etheric projection. I have also tried to keep things as simple as possible, because life, essentially, *is* simple. It is us that make it complicated.

To many people, spirit projection involves a complicated system of levels, depending on your experience, the use of secret mantras, the necessity of masters, of adepts, etc. I know that there are some people who construct a circle that they then lie within, before attempting to project. Well, I have never knowingly seen my 'master' and I would have thought that by now I would have, or am I doing such a good job on my own? Perhaps he keeps missing me! I have also never needed the aid, or protection, of a circle, that strikes me as somewhat paranoid.

Having said that, I do believe that when we die we can continue to have an interest in an earthly life and my mind is completely open to all the possibilities. I will know for sure one day.

There are a few good books around that incorporate some of these esoteric values, that have been written by practical projector's, and I would recommend any publication by Douglas Baker. You will see that if you read all the books, that I have mentioned within these pages, there are recognisable traits that follow roughly similar paths.

I do have one major bone to pick with Douglas Baker, concerning his reservations about the existence of the spirit cable. In his book 'The Techniques of Astral Projection' he rightly airs the fear that most projector's have regarding the importance of the spirit cord and whether it even does or does not exist. Speaking with the experience of many thousands of projections, he states that he has never seen a cord, either linked to him or to any other person, and goes on to say that this doesn't mean that the cord does not exist. I am happy with all this so far. Unfortunately he then advises that should you ever see your spirit cable you should take a pair of scissors and sever it! I do think that this advice is wrong. Because you haven't actually experienced something yourself *doesn't mean that it isn't there.*

Many times I have carefully cradled the spirit cable in my hands, marvelling at the intricacy of the function it has, feeling my own heartbeat within its walls. This cable is the vital energy/sense link between the two bodies and *must* be respected for your own self-preservation. I do not believe that it is fragile enough to be snapped or ruptured, and I do not believe that astral scissors could cut this cable *anyway* so, thankfully, I hope that no real harm can happen as a result of this statement.

I must say that this strange statement continued to baffle, and worry me, for many years until I had a couple of experience's that made me alter my own understanding somewhat. I was experimenting with an old idea of mine that I was trying again, a type of mental set-up between relaxation and the sleep state. The following description comes directly from my records:

Last night we went to bed very early because we had recently had some very late nights, and early mornings, and it had all caught up with us. So we were in bed by 9.30pm and asleep by 10.00pm. I slept until 2.00am when I awoke and went downstairs to do some work on this book. I

283

worked for about an hour-and-a-half and then concentrated on spirit projection.

During this half-an-hour I worked on filling my mind with spirit projection, and just like the setting of the mental alarm clock, I instilled within myself the wish to become consciously aware, within my dream, 20 minutes after I have dropped off to sleep. One has to be careful here, because the success of this system all depends on reaching the required depth of physical relaxation first, and should really be done after the relaxation procedures have been completed. I am experienced enough to judge beforehand whether my relaxation is going to be complete, or not, so the risk is minimised. If the correct depth has not been attained, prior to the onset of sleep, then you will become physically awake and stand a good chance of this continuing for the remainder of the night.

Being deprived of sleep is the worst of all options, so this exercise should only be attempted when you have gained experience in all the other ways first. Please think nothing of spending a year or so, if necessary, mastering any phase of spirit projection. And if you should continue to use this system incorrectly, be warned that it is powerful enough to keep sleep at bay for several night's running. This serves no useful purpose whatsoever.

I returned to bed and carried out a full relaxation, ending with a reiteration of my wish to become consciously aware, within my dream, 20 minutes after the onset of sleep, not 20 minutes from that moment because it can take several minutes for sleep to come on.

I became aware in my dream that I was lying in bed but had forgotten to turn the light off, so I was rising from the bed to get to the switch. As this action took place I realised that I was having a lucid dream and quickly grasped the situation to take full advantage. The bedroom was not my physical bedroom because I was part of a dream. I then made my way outside and assessed the best way of becoming projected. I tried to instil the vibrations, without any joy, so I threw myself onto the ground to arouse the fear factor, but still nothing. The main problem for me was keeping my concentration, if my lucid dream became vivid, all inner control would have been lost. I made my way to a tall block of flats that had an outer balcony, and climbed flight after flight of steps until I reach the dizzy height of around ten floors. At this moment my logic and experience fight with my natural fear, but I know that I can jump safely without any harm coming to me. The fear involved with these jumps is more than enough to bring the vibrations rushing in!

I sat on the side of the balcony, swung my legs over the edge, and leapt into thin air. I dropped like a stone straight downwards. The ground came hurtling up towards me and I had to make a decision whether to smash into the pavers or to fly into a horizontal plane before it was too late. I decided to put the brakes on instead. I slowed my descent right down until I actually stopped in mid-air it, literally, felt about an inch or so above the brindle coloured pavers. The point is, that through all this excitement, I had still not been able to instigate the necessary vibrational 'rush' needed to project me into my astral body, and I was baffled. What did I have to do? I felt that I was treading new ground, not quite an astral projection, more real than a lucid dream. The intensity of the thought brought me back to my bed where I tried to analyse the situation. I could only come to the conclusion that the whole thing had been a lucid dream with a *particularly* realistic nature.

The following morning I decided to try it again and see if I could have more success. My build-up was exactly the same as it had been for the previous evening, to see if I could replicate the experience. The only change I made was in the very final stage where I was waiting for sleep to come. Instead of allowing my mind to dwell on having height, and floating, etc. I let it do its own thing but in a controlled manner, a little like a dog on the end of a lead. I would let it go about its business but before it could wander off forever, I would pull it back to me. As I became aware that my mind was wandering off into the realms of sleep, I would bring it back to full consciousness, maybe in all about five times. Again, to do this correctly, you must be sure that your relaxation is so deep that it does not keep you awake and stop the sleep process completely.

I gained consciousness within my dream, as before. This time I found myself in a street of shops and houses, very ordinary and unassuming environment, nothing strange whatsoever. I thought to myself that I would try and investigate this situation, do a little research, and find out more about this 'lucid dream' environment. I decided to try a favourite trick and conjure up someone famous, I chose Clint Eastwood. I tried and tried but nothing happened.... I began to feel suspicious. I ran my fingers over my body to see what I could find. My body was not astral, as I know it. It wasn't the solid squeezable, pinchable, smackable astral, where I can stamp my feet and do all the things I am used to doing. This new body, that I felt, was finer, more subtle. My first impression was that it was similar to jelly (gelatine), soft and almost imperceptible. I put my hand to the back of my head to find that the cable was not present, so I gently ran my hands over the rest of my body to find that I was not attached, anywhere, to anything that I could feel, or see. There was no hint or sign of a cord, no pressure on the back of my head, and no increased heartbeat at the back of my head.

Instead of being worried about this, I must admit that it felt right for this body to have no apparent attachment.

The thought then crossed my mind that had these two projections been the only type of out-of-body experience that I had ever had, I would have happily assumed that they were astral, and I would have agreed, one hundred per cent, with Douglas Baker that a cord does not exist. I was a little mystified but decided to have a look around my environment to see if there were any other changes.

I found that I could fly very easily at both the slow and the very fast speeds, just as I am used to doing in my astral body, but without the feeling of air rushing past my ears. I walked up to a building and simply walked through the wall. I didn't have to press myself up to, and against, it before I could pass through. Now this was becoming really interesting! I applied the same trick to the glass windows, but instead of the glass stretching around the contours of my face prior to allowing me through, it gave way immediately, as if my face was breaking through the surface of water. This new body of mine appeared to be much less dense than anything I had felt previously.

I was in a town that I felt I recognised, a busy and modern town, and it seemed to me that every corner I turned, I had turned before. Perhaps I had come here before when projected subconsciously, who knows? One can't help dodging the traffic, I know it isn't necessary, but I just can't bring myself to walk through speeding cars because it feels so real. Anyway, I wandered through the shops and slipped down the back alleys that I 'knew' as though I was revisiting a place that I hadn't been to for a few years and I wanted to see if there had been any changes. I was walking across a yard when suddenly I felt as though I was losing control, I stared into the corner of

287

this yard, and concentrated on the stone walls that were facing me. I thought to myself, I know this feeling, this is the same as the astral return. After a few moments, my control became strong again, and I continued my walkabout. Twice more this happened before I gave in and returned to bed.

Upon immediate reflection, I know that this experience was not what I call an astral projection because my conscious level wasn't exactly the same as waking consciousness. Not exactly, but very nearly. It was like the physical/astral consciousness but without the memory of all the intricate bits and pieces that we harbour in our daily lives. I suppose, just like the body itself, the consciousness was also finer, more subtle. It is also very likely that this type of body is the one used by many people, including Douglas Baker, and called by them, the astral body, and hence the absence of spirit cable awareness.

My own inclinations are that I projected in yet another mode, this was not the earth/etheric environment, and yet I can't confirm that the plane was astral, but it gave that impression to me. I will have to do more research to find out whether I can be seen by the inhabiting people, etc. Maybe this 'spirit only' type of body projection is to the astral environment, what the etheric is to the earthly environment.

It is becoming apparent to me that, just as we have different types of spirit-body, we also have a different spirit cable to match that particular body. Our *astral* body has an *astral* cable, and that differs to our *etheric* body which sports an *etheric* cable. It will be possible to know, early on in the projection, which body is in use by the root structure, and makeup, of the cable. That detail, unfortunately, is destined for a future publication.

I have been asked about the existence of the third eye. Again, I have no practical experience of it. I do know that concentrating on the spot between, and just above, the eyes, is good for keeping the conscious mind aware whilst the physical body relaxes into sleep. But then again, so is any other part of the body when used to focus concentration. I have said that the spirit cable joins the spirit-body through the back of the skull, I have omitted to say that it leaves the physical body through the central forehead. Is this where the idea of the existence of a third eye comes from?

This will all have wait to be addressed in the next book I'm afraid, along with all the other, hitherto, unanswered questions and uncharted territories.

Talking about unanswered questions, there is one final experience that I would like to share with you. Knowledge is based upon experience and truth. There is also conjecture based upon experience. For example, nobody for *absolute* certainty, knows what is in the centre of the moon, but based on experience, and logic, a guess can be made, but it is still conjecture. We don't know about the existence of the 'big-foot' or the 'lochness monster' but, just like UFOs, we admit a *possible* existence, based on the experience's of people like you or I. Enough sightings, from a range of sources, eventually make it a possibility to get serious about.

My writing is based upon my experience's and of course it contains a small amount of calculated conjecture. However there is conjecture that can sometimes stretch things a little as does this final exhibit.....

There are hunches in my head the truth of which will need to be verified (to myself initially), or not, accordingly. One of them is that we have multiple *conscious* minds that work separately from each other, and are used for the different spirit environments that we inhabit. These conscious minds sharing the same common subconscious.

When we project and access the astral environment or, in fact, any of the other environments, we find that they are as *real* as the earth environment that we enjoy whilst we are *here*, on earth. It is quite possible that we exist in these other environments simultaneously as we exist on earth. It could be that 'I' am somewhere else at this very moment, doing something completely different, in a land as real as this one, totally unaware of any of my other personalities. We may all be doing the same thing.

It may be an element found within certain types of schizophrenia, and *with* further research, perhaps an insight into the condition. There may be leaky points within the subconscious mind that fail to completely separate these existence's from each conscious mind, and we experience something that I call *crossover*.

There are times when I am lying in bed, or sitting quietly in a chair, not thinking about anything in particular, and I recall a complete situation, or conversation, that I have had. Because it is such a normal a thing, I don't give it a second thought. A moment later I realise that the memory was completely false. *At the time* it was absolutely real, and I knew that the situation had happened, a second later it was, not only foreign to me, but forgotten and never to be retrieved for the I, me, here.

So, couple all this with the following experience, and I find myself deeper in the realms of mystery, and this really could get me locked up!

TUESDAY 21st JULY 1998

This morning I did the full relaxation procedure and I had a few things on my mind. On a Tuesday morning the recycling people come round and pick up everyone's waste glass and they make quite a row. I try to incorporate this into my system *if* the timing works out right. It can work in your favour by keeping your conscious awareness a little longer, if you are lucky. My dog barked around 5.30 am and woke my partner who then went to the bathroom, and all during my relaxation process which extended it a little further.

I 'fell' out of my body just as soon as I realised the state that I was in, tumbling and tumbling, before speeding along in a straight line, all in dark oblivion. The wind rushing past the speeding spirit-body, whilst in complete darkness, is a marvellous feeling.

When my sight came to me I could see that I was zooming along the edge of a field just above the tree tops. I came to a stop on the edge of a bank and tried to move my hands in an effort to find my spirit-body. I thought, 'Where is my spirit-body? Where are my limbs?' As I thought this, my hands came round in front of me and I found the ability to walk. I looked down from the bank into what was once perhaps the route of an old railway line, or river, but there was no water down there. Looking across to the opposite bank, maybe 50 feet away, I noticed that the other bank was higher. I merely had to 'think' myself up into the air in order to fly across and see what was over the other side. I levitated up over the trees, a little like a helicopter would and I could see in the distance, the lights of a large town, or maybe city, spreading out across the horizon. I knew that I had gone a long way to have got to this point, and I had spent a long time travelling in the darkness before flying along the edge of the field, so I was wary of going too far and risking the loss of the projection.

Nearby were the beginnings of the outskirts, as usual a modern estate of houses, or two, before you reach the more established buildings. I moved over to this area with a determination not to lose my awareness. I just had a look round, generally noticing the paving stones, looking at the texture of the roads, and trying to soak up the total structure as a complete view rather than picking on one thing.

I came to a complex of offices, public buildings, and underpasses, etc. A well used area, some of the paving slabs were cracked, some of the underpasses were dark because the lights were broken and hadn't been replaced. The light was a half light, more like dusk than dawn, and there were people around, not many, but some. Already I had ventured further than I had originally intended but my consciousness was strong, so I was more than happy to continue.

I turned a corner and before me, in the distance, I could see several sets of open double doors with people milling in, and out. A little like the entrance to a cinema or an art gallery. I decided to see if I could go and see what was going on. It was mainly full of young people and, as I got nearer, I got the distinct impression that this was a music venue, a college or university.

Inside the doors, in the foyer, I noticed some large boards jam-packed with information, so I thought that it might be a good idea to try and read some of the notices displayed. The honest truth is that I could not read any of them. You have to be careful, as I have said, about focusing in on one thing too much or the projection will terminate before you know it. But the real reason I could not read any of the notices was because they appeared to be written in a foreign language.

Now I am sure that the projection was happening in my own dear old England, not abroad anywhere, and I am sure the written language was not of western origin. There were eastern, up-and-down, type symbols, something that looked very much like Japanese, or Chinese writing. There were also 'phone cards, on display, that did contain some of the English written language, the words were: Details of how to telephone......something. So there were little bits of English but the vast majority wasn't. This may be the only way that my subconscious mind can fill these boards to make them look real, but without telling me anything. It is also possible that this board was for the benefit of foreign students and, if I had been able to look further along, I may have found the British section.

I made my way out of this building, while I still could, and went along with the flow of people, getting further away, until I found myself in a street of mature terraced houses. I wandered down this sloping road, and to amuse myself, I followed a group of people into one of these homes. Inside, party music was being played and many people were enjoying the occasion. I made my way around without anyone taking much notice of me, and I was still feeling very much in control.

Everything seemed to be quite normal until a lady came up to me and said, 'I didn't expect to see you here.' I replied, 'Oh really?' being my usual non-committal self. She then said 'come on' and disappeared out through the front door. I followed her outside and we strolled together down the road, she was chatting to me, and I was listening. She was about 5ft 5ins tall, with medium length dark hair, not fabulously attractive but then again certainly not ugly. She was talking to me as though she knew me very well, and accepted my presence without thought, in a matter-of-fact, relaxed way. She was talking to me about things I knew nothing of. I was beginning to feel uncomfortable, as I thought she must have mistaken me for someone else.

A young girl around the age of eight ran up from behind and walked with us for a little while before looking up at us and skipping off away. So I said to this lady, 'Who was that?' she turned and simply stared at me! Almost a little annoyed, and I thought to myself that I mustn't pursue this line, so nothing more was said. I had a very strong feeling that I was supposed to know this lady, and this child.

We had, by now, turned a few corners and had entered what looked like a town centre type area. We arrived at a place that looked a little like a bus station, but I didn't see any buses. It could have been something like a cattle market on a day of no business, or a railway station. It was a place where many people meet and gather for a purpose.

She then said to me, 'Now you're not meeting me here, we don't have to wait too long.' Sounding like a fool, I replied, 'What time was I supposed to meet you here?' Again she stared at me a little strangely and said 'In five minutes time.' So I said 'Hang on a moment would you, I have got something to do.' She said 'Where are you going?' and I replied 'It doesn't matter, if you just stay there for a moment, there is something that I need to do.' She looked and said 'OK.'

Like you, by now, I have got the distinct impression that she was treating me as though I was her husband and perhaps the father of the little girl. She was also expecting 'me' to meet her here in a couple of minutes time. I realised that there was a danger of the possible, and unthinkable, situation of meeting somebody called 'myself', the other 'me' that was supposed to meet his wife here.

Half of me wanted to get away in order to stop that situation from happening. The other half wanted to stay to see what would happen. Feeling very apprehensive, I decided to position myself out of the way, but in a position to see who the other me was. Then the most amazing thing happened.... I actually saw myself come out of the crowd!

The hair style was the same, as was the face, the same build, etc. The other 'I' was looking a little bit serious, but I might look like that anyway! There were some differences in style, the other 'me' was wearing brown trousers, a beige shirt and perfectly round wire-rimmed spectacles, but apart from that, no difference. I looked the same age, literally a dead ringer for me, this 'earth' me. I looked at him.....and he looked back at me. As I walked past him, he slowly turned and stared and, as I moved away, I put my finger in the air purely as a sign of acknowledgement. Just an acknowledgement to say that we had seen each other. I stepped out into this courtyard area, looked up at the roofs of the buildings opposite and levitated myself away.

I flew over the rooftops of these old market type buildings, this episode had such a profound effect on me that there really wasn't anything left to do here. I could feel the bedclothes around me as I flew, and by concentrating on them I came back to my physical body.

My mind was so full of many things, many questions. More questions than answers for this one. A really very strange experience that is another that will never leave me. I am going to keep a watching brief on my experience's with parallel lives in parallel dimensions, but I can't help wondering about that chap, the other me, who may well be living his life, alive and well, existing on another plane. That other plane, I know, is as real and solid as our planet earth, and I wonder whether he is discussing with his wife, also I expect in a state of some confusion, who the heck I was. His subconscious mind, however, could be the same one that I am using at this exact moment....

Assuming that this book is successful we will, of course, be able to try to answer questions like this, and continue to ask others, but whether it is, or not, the important thing is the fact that it *has* been written.

I have taken the foundation stone already laid by other's and built onto it a structure that I hope can be understood by all. How long it will actually take for these realisations to take root within the general population I don't know, but I will be supporting these findings and future research to the best of my ability, at least until my own death. The experience's that I have had, were gained through my personal endeavours, without being influenced by other's that run on the rails of established education and limit the free exploration caused by the beliefs of others.

I am inherently a very private person, who has laid out an overview of the most precious and private aspects of my spiritual life for, I hope, the benefit of others. I trust that you will find it in your heart to treat my advice and conclusions with sensitivity, respect, and consideration.

So over to you my friends, enlightenment is there to be found within all of us, it is never too late to save ourselves from *ourselves*.

The end?
I don't think so.

For further details please write to me at -

The Oobex Research Foundation
114 High Street
Braunston
Northamptonshire NN11 7HS
England
e-mail address: **graham@oobex.freeserve.co.uk**
www.oobex.freeserve.co.uk

Interesting reading

'*The Projection of the Astral Body*', *by* Sylvan Muldoon & Hereward Carrington. Rider & Co. Ltd. 1929.

'*Astral Projection*', *by* Oliver Fox. University Books. 1962.

'*Life before Life*' *by* Raymond Moody Jr, & Paul Perry. Macmillan London Ltd. 1990. Plus all works by these authors.

'*An Experiment with Time*' *by* J W Dunne. A C Black Ltd. London 1929.

'*Life after Death*' *by* D Scott Rogo. The Aquarian Press. 1986. Plus all works by this author.

'*The Techniques of Astral Projection*' *by* Douglas Baker. D Baker. England. Plus all works by this author.